DO NOT UNSADDLE YOUR HORSE

Margaret Phillips

MATHABO PRESS

© 2002 Margaret Phillips
Do not unsaddle your horse

ISBN 0 9543182-0-X

Published by Mathabo Press
7 Abbey Brewery Court
Swan Street
West Malling
Kent
ME19 6PY

The right of Margaret Phillips to be identified as author of this work has been asserted by her in accordance with the Copyright, Designs and Patents Act 1988.

All rights reserved. No part of this publication may be produced in any form or by any means – graphic, electronic or mechanical including photocopying, recording, taping or information storage and retrieval systems – without the prior permission, in writing, of the publisher.

Design & production co-ordinated by:
The Better Book Company Ltd
Havant
Hampshire
PO9 2XH

Printed in England

Cover by Graham Holman Studio
to a design by Margaret Phillips

Acknowledgements

My grateful thanks are due to David Parkins for his patience and generosity in typing and re-typing the whole of the original manuscript, to Sue Viner for reading it and giving valuable comments, to Peter Davies for persuading me to purchase a computer so that I could edit the book myself and to the Granary Writers for their enthusiastic encouragement. Without the support of these friends I might have given up on my task.

Chapters

Introduction i

1. Early days 1
2. The place of His choice 13
3. All things through Christ 23
4. The fleece 32
5. Where do I fit in? 41
6. Shoes, limbs and Leprosy 53
7. Livingstone the artist and other new friends 65
8. You must bear with one another's faults 83
9. The days of Idi Amin 98
10. Signs, miracles and blessings 112
11. Time to move on 123
12. A new job and a house to call my own 133
13. Bots'abelo — place of refuge 143
14. The challenge of the mountains 159
15. Frustrations and clashes 177
16. Perpetrators, police and Patch 188
17. Successes and surprises; joys and sorrows 201
18. Just let me finish the job 217
19. Homeward bound 230
20. Culture shock 1 — hospitalisation 234
21. Culture shock 2 — new fields of work 242
22. Continued links and friendships 251

Introduction

THE LETTER

It was the winter of 1964–65. The weather had been so severe that when my friend Pam Maclennan invited me to come and join her family for a few weeks, I gladly accepted. She and her husband, Graeme, and their two small daughters lived in a spacious cottage, which was warm and comfortable – luxurious, after my small caravan in the village of Ryarsh in Kent. I had been struggling to survive because of the sub-zero temperatures, which often froze my calor gas causing total power failure.

One night I snuggled into the warm bed and thought hard. I had tried over the past year to put a deposit on several houses, but each time something had gone wrong. I had enough money, but it seemed as if I was not meant to settle down. 'Perhaps I should be moving again,' I thought wearily. I had moved on average every six months during my college days and for several years after that, but now I had spent three years in the caravan and it had become home. It was enjoyable in the summer, but in the winter it was really tough. Even so, it was hard to imagine that I should be moving away from the area. Quite apart from my job, I was very involved with the youngsters in our Campaigner youth groups in my spare time and I had made many friends.

'Anyway, I'd better make sure that the Lord doesn't want me somewhere else,' I thought. 'Let's eliminate the possibilities starting as far away as possible.'

So I sat up in bed and wrote to my old college friend, Jane, whom I knew was home on leave from Uganda, where she had been working in a leprosy hospital.

'Just checking,' I wrote. 'Occupational therapists aren't needed in developing countries, are they?'

A week or two passed and I presumed my letter had missed her, or that it was not sufficiently important for her to answer.

However, in due course her reply reached me from Uganda. The contents of her letter set my head reeling. It was so utterly unexpected and not what I wanted to hear at all:

'During the past weeks I have been involved in correspondence and talks with Dr Paul Brand and others concerning a new project that is going to be set up in Addis Ababa in the near future. After a lot of thought by myself as well as many on the home staff of C.M S. it seems right that I should move on from Kumi and do this new job in Addis.

The few helpers I have trained cannot carry on the work that I have started at Kumi successfully, and we are sure that there should be someone to replace me. I am writing to ask whether you could think about this opportunity, and consider whether God wants you to move on from where you are and perhaps go to Kumi.'

I wished the letter had not come. It made me feel unsettled and nervous; but how could I forget about a real need, especially when the request came from a friend to whom I owed so much? I mentioned the matter casually to some trusted friends who had spent many years in Nigeria. "Well," they said, "there's no reason why you shouldn't completely change your way of life."

Completely change my way of life! Would it really mean that? What was I to do? This is the story of how the Lord guided me – a story of twenty-one years in Africa working with leprosy sufferers, and of how Africa claimed a large part of my heart.

The book is dedicated to all the courageous leprosy sufferers I have known, without whom none of these pages would have been written.

Chapter 1
Early days

"Hey! Stop shaking the branches!"

My elder sister, Celia, was higher up in the laburnum tree threatening to dislodge me from the lower bough that I had reached with difficulty.

"Well get off then, I want to come down."

We tumbled to the ground. As five and seven year olds we had enjoyed the spacious garden of our home, which was close to the sea and ten miles from Dublin, all our short lives.

"Come on, let's put all the toys out on the garden steps!"

This occupied us for hours as dolls and teddies were lined up in the sun. Then off we would go to see what the gardener was up to, brushing our way past lavender and thyme with their familiar fragrance and the brilliant gold and orange nasturtium flowers. When we were tired we sat on the low wall by the front door gazing at the sea, watching the waves, which looked like hundreds of white horses when it was rough. Life was good but such idyllic days were not to last much longer.

Neither of my parents was Irish and my father, realising that war was imminent, decided that it would be best for us all to return to England. He was considerably older than my mother and he planned to retire early. He held a responsible job as chief accountant at Guinness's in Dublin, so this was to be a big change for him.

My mother tried to pass this information on to us as gently as possible:

"We may be moving back to England so there will be lots of new things to look forward to."

"Will we have a big house and will Nelly come with us?" we asked.

"I don't know – oh, no, Nelly won't come. We shall manage on our own."

This was to be a new way of life for my mother too. She had become used to maids and Nelly lived in. This allowed

Do not unsaddle your horse

time for her occasionally to paint beautiful watercolour pictures of views from the house.

"Where will we go to school?"

For us it was an adventure with many unanswered questions, but for the present the prospect of the boat crossing was exciting.

"It was rough last time but I'm a good sailor." My comment was prompted by the fact that I had not been sick on a previous trip when the sea had been decidedly choppy.

It was the summer of 1939 by the time we were settled in a house near Guildford in Surrey. Every day my sister and I would cycle the mile from our home to St. Catherine's school, gas masks over one shoulder and satchels over the other. As time went by, air raid sirens wailing their unwelcome news would often interrupt our lessons. Our teachers would calmly take control of the situation: "All go out quietly and sit against the walls in the corridor."

Sometimes it seemed a very long time sitting on the floor. The teachers moved up and down reassuring us and keeping us reasonably quiet. They themselves must have subdued any feelings of fear or responsibility very well because I do not remember feeling unduly anxious. We cheered when the all-clear siren eventually sounded its welcome message. After school I sometimes made a detour on my bike to see what damage the bombs had done. One afternoon, after one of these investigations, I arrived home with some breathless information, which clearly made my mother worried and angry.

"There's a house on the green that got a direct hit."

"Didn't I tell you, you must always come straight home? Which house is it?"

"That big one away from the road. It's still smouldering. The all-clear has gone so there's no danger now."

I tried hard at my schoolwork but arithmetic and algebra were always incredibly difficult to understand. I often begged my sister to help me but she was usually busy with her own studies.

"Oh, please help me with this homework."

"If you can't do it you should tell the teacher...."

"But I can't. I've asked her to explain again and I still didn't understand."

My mother would be drawn in next. She would try her best but it was like the blind leading the blind.

"Ask Daddy to help you, he'll be able to do it."

"No, no, I don't want him, he always does things differently to the way we've been taught."

Somehow I always completed the work and tumbled thankfully into bed hoping that my effort would not disgrace me too much.

Exams were even more of a problem. I could cram information for some subjects and memorise whole passages of Latin translations, but maths was another matter. Amazingly I did well in all my School Certificate papers. This must have been a relief to my father who had very high standards for his daughters.

The school tried to give its pupils some guidance about careers. A class would be seen by the headmistress, each girl having an individual interview in her office. I confided my thoughts about this to my mother who was sympathetic, knowing that it was too soon for me to make up my mind about my future. I was shy, immature and always one of the youngest in the class.

"I'd like to be an artist and live in a caravan."

"You can't tell her that," my mother declared, "What do you really want to do?"

"I don't know."

As the headmistress tried to encourage me and draw out my ideas I stared at the corner of the ceiling. Eventually I muttered a few careers that I knew would be acceptable to her.

"Perhaps teaching young children or occupational therapy. I'd like to do something worthwhile."

"Well, both of those are very worthwhile." The headmistress seemed pleased that she could jot down something positive in her notes. She smiled, indicating that the interview was over and to my relief I soon found myself outside the door.

Because I had not really decided what I wanted to do, I stayed on for two years in the small Sixth Form, taking four subjects in what was then Higher School Certificate. One bonus for remaining at school was that I was captain of the lacrosse team, a game that I loved. Another activity that boosted my confidence was Girl Guides.

My sister joined the local Company and attended a camp, which, because of wartime conditions, was held near our home. During those warm, lazy days I often sneaked down to the field and, lying behind a hedge, watched what was going on with binoculars. It seemed to be fun and well organised. I soon persuaded my mother to let me join too, although she was rather concerned about getting another uniform:

"The secondhand one Celia was given was quite good. Do you think they can find one for you too? We haven't got enough coupons to get anything new."

"Captain said there was a girl in the next village who has left." I said hopefully. "She thought I could ask if I could have her uniform."

Not surprisingly the girl was willing to part with it, for it was old and shabby; but I was happy. We altered it, washed and ironed it and pressed the brim of the felt hat over and over again till it was as stiff as possible. Captain was impressed with our efforts. She was a very good leader. Her husband had been killed in the war and she seemed to have devoted herself to the youngsters in the village instead of the family she might have produced herself. I have always valued the practical skills that I learned by camping and working for badges. My sister was also very keen and when the new Queen's Guide Award was introduced she was determined to win it. It was the highest award in Guiding.

"If you want anything badly enough, you can always get it," she declared.

I thought about her remark and agreed.

Eventually we both succeeded, receiving our badges from the Princess Royal at a big Guide Rally. I felt very proud. I loved these challenges and especially enjoyed the camps where we worked hard, cooking on open fires with huge quantities of food in big, black dixie pots. Often the porridge got burned and wasps plagued us by sitting on the slices of bread and marmalade, sometimes stinging the unwary girl in the mouth; but the delights of living so close to nature outweighed all of this. We often sang as our breakfast 'grace': 'God has created a new day, silver and green and gold,' and these seemed exactly the right words as we tried to absorb all the beauty around us. At dusk we gathered round the campfire with blankets and songbooks, to sing the old favourites before settling down on our groundsheets in big bell tents for the night.

Apart from Guides we had very few excitements. In our spare time Celia and I would dig the garden and cut the lawns. I worked quite happily under her directions.

"You dig the next trench and I'll get the manure."

"Okay, how deep do you want it?"

"One and a half spades. I'll be back in a minute. The beans will really like this soil if you do it properly!"

The fact that my father did not think he could afford the training needed for me to become an Occupational Therapist, made me finally decide that that was what I wanted to be. I visited a local hospital to see what the work might involve. The Head Occupational Therapist gave me some advice:

"When you have your interview, tell them you are interested in people."

"I'm not sure that I am…" I murmured.

"Well tell them that anyway, after all you will be dealing with people, not with papers or office equipment."

Her advice certainly seemed to carry some weight when I travelled to Oxford with my mother for the interview and I was accepted for a three-year diploma course starting in March 1951. Various grants helped to cover the cost.

Do not unsaddle your horse

Just before I was due to go to Oxford I developed whooping cough. I was worried and upset by this. My suitcase was already packed, including a new mauve dressing gown and a lovely plaid rug which we were asked to bring to supplement the bedding, which the college supplied. The whooping cough seemed to go on and on.

'How much longer must I wait?' No one could tell, but I knew I could not go to Oxford while I was coughing; it would keep people awake at night and that would be so embarrassing.

Eventually I reached Oxford two weeks late on a rainy Sunday, arriving at the railway station earlier than I had expected. I hung around for a while in the waiting room as I did not want to give a bad impression by reporting at the hostel sooner than I had said. Then, summoning up as much confidence as I could, I hired a taxi. I was nervous but quietly excited at what might lie ahead.

Almost as soon as I had unpacked my things and met the other five students with whom I was to share a room at the college hostel, I was swept into activity. Some of the girls were setting off for a Church service.

"Would you like to come with us? We go to St Ebbe's in the town. Lots of students go and it's really good."

I was glad to go with them. They were enthusiastic and I felt reassured, though slightly surprised, that I had linked up with this particular group. In time I too came to greatly appreciate St Ebbe's Church. It was there during my student days that I learned a great deal about practical Christianity.

I had been baptised as a baby and for a few years we had gone to Church as a family after we came to England. Then the practice seemed to fizzle out. Perhaps it was because we had to 'lay up' our car during the war. I was confirmed at school and we also had plenty of scripture lessons. But now, for the first time, I was confronted with the idea that I was not necessarily a Christian because of that.

My friends invited me to their Christian Fellowship meetings. I usually went along but I was slightly resentful of some of the girls who claimed to be 'Born Again'. Critical thoughts would cross my mind:

'I know my Bible better than they do! Some of them just seem to have their heads and shoulders in the clouds – they turn up late for lectures and sometimes they get just as frustrated as anyone else!'

But I had to admit that some of them were rather special people. Jane Neville was one of these. I watched her carefully. She got up early to read her Bible and pray, but it was the fact that she was of such an even, happy temperament, concerned for people and always the same, that made her different. She encouraged me and prayed for me I am sure. Without her witness I might never have become a Christian. She was later to play a very important part in my life.

I was struggling to understand what it really meant to be a Christian and I often saved up my questions for Jane.

"If you are all the time thinking of Jesus as being part of you, then you can't concentrate on what you are meant to be doing, at least I can't. How do you get round that?"

"You have to accept Him into your heart and then He's just there," Jane tried patiently to explain. "Its all by the grace of God when you really want Jesus as your Saviour – if you really want Him enough…"

College work was fairly demanding and to start with I had to work extra hard to catch up on what I had missed, so I could not give too much thought to these new ideas on Christianity. We had to become proficient in about fourteen different crafts. This was fun but for the final exams the samples had to be perfect and students often stayed up all night finishing their work to the correct standard. The college was housed in a collection of about twenty old Nissen huts left over from the war. Each one had a stove which was fuelled with anthracite in winter. Some huts were for lectures – (we studied anatomy and physiology and later orthopaedics, together with psychology and psychiatry.) Other huts were for specific crafts such as basketry, weaving or spinning and carpentry. In the summer it was quite pleasant working in these primitive conditions but it was not so enjoyable in winter. The fumes from the stoves made us sneeze and it was cold moving from one hut to another.

We wore bright green overalls that were supposed to cover every bit of clothing worn underneath. The principal was very strict about this. Sometimes a student would be very upset:

"She's confiscated my skirt! I can't cycle back to the hostel without it. What am I to do?"

Usually some kind friend would come to the rescue:

"You take my long raincoat and I'll wear your jacket. She usually gives things back the same day."

Very soon we began cycling each week to the local, very large, old mental hospital for lectures, so that we could see patients who were suffering from various psychiatric disorders. Later we spent some days in the wards. This was initially frightening. Many of the patients were disturbed and others were deeply depressed. Sometimes we found them crouching in the corners of dingy stone staircases – miserable bits of humanity who no one seemed able to help. Some of those suffering from schizophrenia believed that they were kings or queens. A middle aged, authoritative lady sidled up to me obviously thinking that I needed to understand her position:

"You met that lady downstairs in an office? Well, she thinks she's the matron of this hospital, but she's wrong, because I am."

I nodded wisely. Sometimes by the end of the day we would discuss what kind of mental illness we ourselves might develop if life became very tough. It was best to make some jokes, otherwise we would go to bed and have nightmares.

I often shared my thoughts with my fellow student, Karin:

"There are so many needy people in these big institutions. I really think they are the most worthwhile places to work if you have enough courage."

When we had to move out of the college hostel at the end of a year, Karin and I set about finding 'digs' where we could stay together. It was not easy because there were so many university students also looking for accommodation. Our first landlady cooked our breakfast and evening meal for us. Karin insisted that we always ate all the food set before us, often coaxing me to eat up the last piece of toast at breakfast.

"If we don't finish everything," she argued, "We won't be given as much next time and we may need it. If we eat a big breakfast we can save money on lunch."

Later we joined two other students and rented a flat. The electric wiring was decidedly precarious, and, scared that we would be blamed if it went wrong, we prayed earnestly that it would not cause problems until we left. We never stayed in any one location for long, because we were sent in small groups to various parts of the country for 'hospital practice'. I spent three months at Bristol, followed by Nottingham and then two London hospitals. In between some of these assignments we would return to Oxford for further tuition, linking up again with at least some of our friends, sharing experiences and usually taking over accommodation that had been vacated by students who were on the move. We became skilled at dealing with landladies, most of whom seemed to have double barrelled names.

At the end of our course each of us had to chose a "project" which involved research on some particular aspect of occupational therapy. We were all encouraged to tackle a different subject and by the time I saw the list, most of the topics I would have chosen had been claimed. In the end I selected what was then called 'Mental Deficiency', in other words, mental handicap. It was a subject we had barely touched on in our course, so it involved a great deal of reading and visits to several institutions. By the time I had finished I was genuinely interested in working in that field.

We eventually qualified – and a brand new set of occupational therapists thrown out into the work arena. There were many vacancies, which made choices difficult. We were told that our first job should be in a department where we would be supervised by a senior therapist. One of the hospitals for which I had made an application was therefore suitable. It had a beautifully equipped department and seemed to run very smoothly. Another place that interested me was quite the opposite. It was part of a huge establishment for mentally handicapped patients, with units in and around Bristol. There was a need to set up a new department of occupational therapy for 200 women patients who were housed in a large, old mansion, down a long driveway some miles from Bristol over the suspension bridge. The proposed department was to be in some renovated stables that already housed a sewing room.

I agonised over the choice. I was at home. My parents would not understand the issues. I phoned one of our tutors at the college and did not receive much guidance. Obviously the decision was mine and mine alone. I prayed anxiously, hoping for some inspiration.

'Lord, you know I really want to do the right thing and only you know what that is. Please show me what is right. Lord it's so important to me. Please help. I know I'm not really a proper Christian but I need to know your will and I've got to make a decision soon or they may give these jobs to someone else.'

No answer! I had to make up my own mind. In the end I opted for the tougher job, looking upon it as a challenge. After all, the Lord was quite able to make the people at the hospital change their minds about employing an inexperienced person if He did not want me to go there, even though I *was* the only applicant. But I was accepted, and soon I was out in the big, wide world, on my own, in my first job at Leigh Court.

I knew Bristol from the three months I had spent there as a student. To start with I lived in the big house where all the patients were housed. I found it very lonely. The nursing sisters, one or two of whom lived in, were elderly and uncommunicative. At meal times they sat at their own tables. They wore blue uniform dresses and starched white lacy caps tied under their chins, and they seemed to take life very seriously.

I felt they were probably suspicious of this newly qualified twenty-one year old occupational therapist who had arrived in their midst.

Very soon I started looking for digs in the Clifton area of Bristol. After visiting several possible bed-sitting rooms, I decided on one with a tiny kitchen for thirty-seven shillings and six pence a month. It was more than I really wanted to pay but the place was clean and the landlady was very keen to have me. Later I realised that she was interested in introducing me to her son who came home for weekends. To her dismay I only stayed for a few weeks as I found a better place for thirty shillings. It was more important for me to make my salary go a long way than to be bothered about boyfriends and also I had to concentrate on my job that was proving to be very tough.

The hospital administrators and the medical superintendent gave me considerable verbal support but the things I needed to get the department started were very slow in coming. I worked for hours in the evenings making plans and writing lists of equipment and materials. I was anxious to prove that I had not taken on more than I could manage and it was desperately important to me to succeed. Eventually I had enough supplies to take my first few patients. Many of them had been occupied in picking old pieces of worn out blanket to pieces. This was supposed to be used for stuffing but no one knew what it was that had to be stuffed and there were always huge sacks of the finished product which, I suspected, were probably discretely disposed of with other rubbish. Most of these women were quite capable of sewing and making rugs and they were delighted to be busy in my department with a variety of handicrafts.

In those days there was no hope for mentally handicapped people to live outside an institution, although most of those at Leigh Court could have done so with some support. So there was no need to teach them how to travel on a bus and go shopping, or how to plan meals and cook. Some of the women became very fond of me. They were starved of love. They started to call me 'Mum' and later I graduated to 'Gran'. It was funny because I was much younger than all of them . When they tried to hang onto my apron strings too much, it became a bit tiresome but on the whole I was encouraged and more and more patients became keen to join my group.

After about a year I was so busy that I needed an assistant but my request for this met with no response. I struggled on for some months and then decided to apply for other jobs in Bristol. Some of my Christian friends from student days were working nearby and I liked Bristol as there was plenty going on. I still did not feel I was really a committed Christian but I enjoyed attending some of the lively church services in the city. I also belonged to a very good tennis club.

I applied for a job in a general hospital and was quite surprised to be unsuccessful. Another applicant had more experience, I was told. It was then that two separate people showed me an advertisement about a job in Kent. It was similar to my present job but much bigger and it also involved starting a department from scratch. I dismissed the idea without giving it any thought. It was unacceptable geographically and anyway, I was just about to go on holiday with friends to Scotland.

As soon as I returned to Bristol I saw the very same advertisement again. Obviously no one had followed it up. I looked at the paper more carefully. Something urged me to apply and I was duly called for an interview. This went well and to my own surprise I accepted the job on the spot.

When I got back to Bristol I bought a map of Kent and spread it out on the floor of my bed-sitting room. The implications of what I had done suddenly frightened me: 'Just why have I been so hasty?' I chided myself. 'I don't know a soul in the whole of Kent! It's completely new ground!'

And yet in a quiet and very certain way I knew that my decision had been the right one.

Chapter 2
The place of His choice

It was the autumn of 1955 when I moved into a small room in the large, impersonal Nurses' Home of Leybourne Grange Hospital for people who were still called 'Mentally Deficient'. There were 1400 patients housed in red brick 'Villas' with about sixty to each. I was to start up the Occupational Therapy service, which once again was challenging and frustrating. Shortly after I arrived a physiotherapist and a speech therapist were employed to start up new departments, so we struggled along together.

'I'm lonely!' I thought to myself. 'Here I am, stuck right out in the country.'

Then I had an idea. I bought a brand new motorcycle. It was a Bantam 125cc and it was delivered to the Nurses' Home one Saturday. I had never ridden anything except a bicycle but I plucked up courage and asked a male student nurse who owned a much larger machine if he could teach me. Soon I was confident enough to start exploring the local villages and churches.

West Malling was the nearest small town and there was the tiny village of Leybourne, but the Church services were disappointing. Then one day as I was working in my department at the Hospital a tall man wearing a dog collar walked in. He introduced himself as Harry Parkins, the Hospital Chaplain.

"Where's your Church?" I asked him curiously.

"It's just through the wood at the back of the hospital," he informed me, waving his hand in a certain direction.

The next Sunday I made my way along a footpath through the wood to the ancient Church of St Martin's that serves the village of Ryarsh. I wondered if it would be different from the other Churches I had tried and to my surprise it was. It was 'evangelical' and the congregation gave me a warm welcome.

Harry Parkins preached a meaningful sermon and I came away feeling excited at the possibility of making some friends. Apparently there was a Bible Study at the Vicarage every Wednesday evening. I wanted to go to this, but the first time I only got as far as the front door. Shyness suddenly overtook me and I did not have the courage to ring the doorbell.

'Why are you so stupid?' I chided myself when I got back to the Nurses' Home. The following Sunday I made sure that that both Harry and Margaret Parkins knew I would be attending. The meetings proved to be very useful even though they mostly involved listening. There was little opportunity for discussion as Harry ably expounded the Bible passages but by now I was eager for this sort of teaching.

Shortly after arriving in Kent I had attended a weekend house party run by a Christian group at one of the London Hospitals. It was there that I finally accepted Jesus Christ as my Saviour. I returned to my very uninspiring room at the Nurses' Home full of excitement and anticipation. The Bible had become alive and relevant to daily life. I bounced up and down on the creaky iron framed bed in my happiness. I felt without a doubt that God had guided me to Kent and to Ryarsh in particular.

As I got to know the Church members I realised that some of them, like me, had clearly been led to Ryarsh. Harry Parkins was a man of prayer. He prayed earnestly that the people of God's choice would fill the empty houses in his parish. Philip and Mary Richmond had arrived a year or two before me and they became my very special friends. They had also recently become Christians and we had many common interests. I often visited them in their lovely old house on the hill above the village.

"You're like the sun in January!" Mary would say when I appeared at her door for the second or third time in a week.

I warmed to her kindness and when she and Philip asked if I would like to come and live with them as part of the family, I was overjoyed. I revelled in the beautiful surroundings, the well-cultivated garden and the animals – geese, a pony, two dogs and a cat.

Harry Parkins enlisted my help at his Sunday afternoon Bible Class that he held for teenagers, including his own three sons. It was held in his study and it was rather an austere time. I was scared of expounding the scriptures in front of the vicar and I prepared as carefully as possible. I must have gained more from the exercise than anyone else, but I often felt I had not done my talk well and recorded the fact in my diary. I gained confidence more easily when Margaret, Mary and I started a Bible Class for a group of the brighter women patients at Leybourne Grange. Their response to our simple Bible messages was very encouraging and they joined in lustily, and often not very tunefully, with the chorus singing. They loved any extra attention.

Most of my spare time was now filled with Church activities but both Harry and Mary were very keen to provide some Christian activities for the youngsters in the village. Following a very successful 'Caravan Mission to Village Children', which drew crowds of youngsters to a tent every evening for a whole week, it seemed clear that a start had to be made. Harry favoured the Campaigner Youth Movement, because it was strictly Christian and evangelical.

"I wish it could be Guides and Scouts," I admitted to Mary.

"He won't change his mind," Mary assured me. "He's wanted this for years. It should be good once we get the hang of it."

Campaigners was a uniformed movement and we planned to have four groups with boys and girls meeting separately. The leaders, or Chiefs as they were called, had to be committed Christians so Harry was fairly limited in his choice. Philip and I agreed to have the older boys and girls and Mary and Pam Maclennan the younger ones.

Pam Maclennan and her husband, Graeme, had recently moved into the village. They were not churchgoers when they arrived but Harry had felt very strongly that they should be brought into the fold. He visited Pam on Monday mornings when he knew she would be at home doing the washing. The Holy Spirit worked amazingly: Pam had been brought up in London and she was a sophisticated person, highly intelligent and practical as well as being familiar with high society. She was, perhaps an unlikely person to be won for Christ but she was drawn into the Church by Harry's persistence, and both she and Graeme became committed Christians. Pam was later to become my closest friend but for the present my life centred round the Richmonds. They were like an elder brother and sister to me.

We all worked very hard. Although Mary was at home most of the time, she also did voluntary social work. It was called 'Moral Welfare', and it was stressful because it involved young, unmarried mothers who were often in desperate situations. Philip was a Veterinary Officer with the Ministry of Agriculture and his was also a demanding job, especially when he was dealing with 'foot and mouth' outbreaks on farms. I was forging ahead with my Occupational Therapy department and slowly convincing the authorities that I needed more staff. I often noted in my diary that I was very tired. This was not surprising; I was secretary of the staff tennis club and often played on my free evenings. Now on top of all my other activities came the commitment to a youth movement that was new to all of us. It was a heavy undertaking but it seemed worthwhile. Life for me was good. I often wondered at God's grace in guiding me to Ryarsh, which, I was sure, was the place of His choice. I was glad that He could use me in so many different ways and give me such good friends.

I managed to visit home fairly regularly on my motorbike. My sister, now a qualified nurse and midwife, was sometimes home at the same time having a welcome rest. She was following up the possibility of working overseas and applying to what was then the Universities' Mission to Central Africa. I felt apprehensive of her plans but when she was accepted for training I backed her up with my full support.

"If it's God's will," I told her, "Then it will be all right."

I felt proud of her but my mother was very upset and angry that I was supporting Celia. My father said little but he certainly shared her disapproval. He was always anxious that we should be 'getting on' in our professions, which meant getting good salaries. Celia's work in Africa was not going to fill the coffers. Unperturbed, she set sail for what was then Northern Rhodesia (Zambia) in the summer of 1957, having completed some training at Birmingham.

Of course I did not lose touch with Jane. She came to visit me and I showed her my department and heard about hers.

"I'm probably leaving soon," she told me in a matter of fact way. "I may be going to work in a Leprosy Centre in Uganda."

I was not surprised; she was such a special person.

"I'll have to do some training at the Church Missionary Society's Training College and see how things work out. Maybe you can visit me there – that would be fun."

I readily agreed that I would do so but I was curious that Africa seemed to be claiming all the best people.

"First my sister and now you," I said thoughtfully.

"It looks as if *your* service for the Lord is right here," Jane said encouragingly. "Look at all your work with these patients and the way you are building up your department; and the Campaigners too, that's a tremendous commitment. We can't all be running off to far away places!"

Certainly I had no aspirations of following her; Campaigners was going well and was steadily drawing in children from the village. There was much to learn and we, as Chiefs, had to pass tests before we could wear the very formal uniform. It was not very practical for anything except drill.

"How can we play games in smart jackets and skirts?" we commiserated. "And those funny hats with the streamers behind and pom-poms on top! Black stockings and shoes too! It's all going to be very expensive."

"We'll get some old police uniforms," Mary decided.

Do not unsaddle your horse

She was always ready to save money and we had been told that they could be obtained at a very nominal price.

"The youngsters will have to pay for theirs but the dresses and shirts aren't so costly and the boys may already have shorts which they can use."

We used a building that had once been the village school for our meetings. The windows were very high, as was usual in old schools where the teachers did not want their pupils to be distracted. For our purpose it would have been useful if we had been able to see what was going on outside: occasionally windows were smashed by stones and we were never able to catch the culprits. Once when I was getting on my motorbike to go home, the engine failed to start. There was a turnip stuffed up the exhaust pipe. That sort of thing on a Friday night was almost the last straw but it reminded me of my Girl Guiding days when we had played a similar prank on our much loved Captain:

I must have been about fourteen years of age. Towards the end of our weekly meeting some of us had slipped outside the hall and tied a string with a collection of old tins to the back of Captain's car. We tucked everything under the vehicle so that she would not notice and we hung around when she was about to drive off so that we could enjoy her reaction. We expected this would be a cheerful and affectionate rebuff, but to our dismay she drove off clattering the trailing tins all through the village without even stopping to see what was causing the racket. We felt let down and very ashamed. She must have known who was responsible but she never mentioned what happened. By ignoring us she had punished us enough.

Campaigner camps were organised from the Headquarters and the first one I ventured on, with seven of my eleven to fifteen year old girls, was to Torquay. We left very early by train. I recorded in my diary that I was terrified. I was scared of losing them while we crossed London on the underground. One child at least had never been on a train before.

"But Mum says there's nothing to worry about," she explained to me, "because when you go through a tunnel, the lights go on."

The girls were very high-spirited. Sitting in a train at Waterloo one of them hurled some of her soft drink right across the carriage and through the open door. It was a direct hit at a railway official who was passing by. Fortunately he understood the innocent frivolity and my embarrassment and did not complain.

My work with the mentally handicapped patients became busier all the time. The trouble was that I never refused to take people who were said to be 'difficult'. They just provided a challenge. Sometimes tempers would flare, heralding an epileptic fit and a chair might be hurled across the room or a window suddenly attacked and smashed with resulting lacerations to the person's hand. It was not always possible to predict emergencies and I needed to watch for likely trouble spots in the room. As a result the quieter patients who needed encouragement were often neglected. Some could be left for hours happily hooking piece after piece of wool into floor rugs that were often of a high standard. Other patients were left to do repetitive work that I could obtain from local factories, such as folding greetings cards or cake boxes in a certain way. This could be somewhat disastrous:

"Just look at these boxes!" one of the staff declared when she was checking after a morning session. "Elsie must have cut her finger and there's a drop of blood in the same place on over a hundred boxes! And she was so proud of doing such a lot today."

"Throw them all away," I muttered wearily.

Sometimes there were too many frustrations and I realised that I was trying to do everything in my own strength. It was better when I made time to pray and read my Bible before setting out to work.

After about five years I considered the possibility of a change of job.

Do not unsaddle your horse

"I don't want to get into a rut," I told Mary, "How would it be if I learned to drive a car? Could you teach me?"

"It's very expensive to run a car," Mary said wisely. "What's your idea behind that?"

"I'd just like to do something different," I explained. "The Grange has been good and I really like the other people I work with, but if I could drive a car then I could apply for a job visiting handicapped people in their own homes."

Mary kindly set about teaching me on her very ancient vehicle. It was difficult to drive it because to change gears you had to double de-clutch. I thought I was very clever to manage this. Far too confidently I took the test – and failed. I was very annoyed and quickly arranged some proper driving lessons.

"You're hopeless!" the very blunt North Country instructor declared as I drove his smart, modern car down the road. "You think you know it all and you haven't even looked in the mirror. You see that roundabout there?" (It was a grassy mound with brightly coloured wallflowers in the middle.) "Someone once drove me straight over the middle of it – and you'll be doing the same if you don't watch out. Stop – stop the car! I need some cigarettes."

I drew into the kerb while he made his purchase in a nearby shop. He had succeeded in humiliating me so that I could now be taught. I have always been grateful to him. He not only ensured that I passed my test on the next attempt but he prepared me for the years ahead when I would be driving many different vehicles on all sorts of roads and tracks.

One day I came upon a piece of paper lying in the road outside my department. On it was printed a poem entitled 'The Indispensable Man.' It read as follows:

>Sometime when you're feeling important,
>Sometime when your ego's in bloom,
>Sometime when you take it for granted
>You're the best-qualified man in the room;
>Sometime when you feel that you're going

Would leave an unfillable hole,
Just follow this simple instruction,
And see how it humbles your soul.

Take a bucket and fill it with water,
Put your hands in it up to your wrists;
Pull them out – and the hole that remains
Is a measure of how you'll be missed;
You may splash all you please when you enter,
You may stir up the water galore;
But stop, and you'll find in a minute
That it looks just the same as before.

The moral of this is quite simple;
Do just the best you can,
Be proud of yourself, but remember –
There is no indispensable man!

Where did the paper come from? Was someone trying to send me a message? And if so, who? I never found out; but to me it was confirmation, perhaps from God, that after five and a half years in the job it was time to move on.

The caravan at Ryarsh with Becca

Chapter 3
All things through Christ

I bought a little Morris Minor 1000 car. It was a big wrench to move from Kent but I had secured a job in Buckinghamshire working with disabled people in their own homes and I was looking forward to the change. It was the summer of 1960. I was based at Aylesbury, my area spanning the north of the county. I enjoyed finding my way around the many attractive villages, but I missed my friends and on Saturdays I would set out very early in the morning for Kent. I aimed to get through the centre of London at dawn and arrive in Ryarsh for an early breakfast with Mary and Philip. As a result I never put down any deep roots in Buckinghamshire. During this time my father died. He had become very frail and although it was a shock, it was perhaps a timely death.

"She'll be coming back to us soon," I heard Mary say to Philip one day. "I can't see her settling up there."

Of course she was right. After about eighteen months I returned to Kent. I accepted a domicillary post similar to the one in Buckinghamshire but with less supervision. Once again I lived with the Richmonds. They had moved to a cottage in the centre of the village and I paid them £3 a month for full board on condition that when they had guests I vacated my room and slept in the conservatory. After a brief spell working in Bromley I was allocated a huge area in north Kent, based at Strood and visiting homes in Gillingham, Chatham, Rochester and Gravesend.

There had been an interregnum at Church. Harry Parkins had moved to another parish and Philip, as one of the Church-wardens, had been very busy keeping everything running smoothly. We prayed earnestly for the right person to be our new vicar and were thrilled when the Reverend Noel Bone agreed to come. He had been one of the most senior Chiefs at Campaigner Headquarters so we knew him.

Do not unsaddle your horse

"It'll be wonderful!" we enthused.

However, it was not long before his boyish exuberance caused irritation in the Richmond camp. Philip, who for a long time had talked of moving, of emigrating, or at least finding some venture in a new area, began to have seriously itching feet. He purchased some quarantine kennels in Folkestone, sold the cottage and moved on to new pursuits, with Mary, not very enthusiastically, supporting him.

Where was I to live now?

"I saw a caravan for sale," Philip announced one day. "It's about twenty miles along the road. How about having a look at it?"

I eagerly agreed. I hated the thought of yet another move but the idea of having my own home, however small, appealed to me. I smiled as I remembered how I had always wanted to live in a caravan.

"It's an awful lot of money," I murmured to Philip as we inspected the van. The owners wanted £245 and it seemed like a fortune.

"Yes, but it's not a bad price. It's in good condition. You wouldn't get anything cheaper."

And so the deal was done. The next problem was finding somewhere to park it – a place to live. Planning permission was not easy to obtain but after living in the van for a month under a tree in the vicarage garden, I was able to move it to a more permanent position in a secluded part of a large garden in the centre of the village. This was by kindness of the owners, Major John Shotter and his Swedish wife Gerd. I had the use of an outside toilet and a water tap fifty yards away and I was able to create my own little garden around my tiny home. There I remained for the next three and a half years.

The caravan was fourteen feet long and it had sleeping places for four people, although for anything but holidays this would have been far too cramped. I depended on calor gas for lighting, cooking and even ironing. Sitting on my bunk bed at one end of the van I could convince myself that it was really quite big – but more importantly it was my very own and I valued this new independence more than any small inconveniences which my new abode imposed on me.

Philip and Mary gave me a terrier-type mongrel puppy which had been born in their quarantine kennels.

"She will be good company for you," Mary said, although, like me, she was anxious that I might find it difficult to cope with her while I was working.

"No, I'll manage," I said determinedly. "She will have to come with me in the car every day. I'm going to call her Becca – it's an old name for the Matterhorn."

Mary smiled. She knew just how much I had enjoyed climbing holidays in the previous few years, and it was my great ambition to climb the Matterhorn.

I loved the little dog but at times her mischief was frustrating and embarrassing. One morning she disappeared when I was ready to set out for work. For several precious minutes I called her name and whistled for her to no avail. Then suddenly she came bounding through the hedge which separated us from a neighbouring garden, triumphantly trailing a string of a dozen raw sausages behind her. Hastily disposing of her treasure, and giving her a good spanking, I bundled her into the car hoping she realised she was in disgrace. I never discovered whose kitchen she had raided.

Some of the patients I visited were delighted when I took Becca to visit them, especially if they lived alone. This was before the days when 'Pat Dogs' became officially used as therapy for elderly or disabled people, so I kept fairly quiet about it and made sure the patients got the very best of the service I was expected to provide.

"Oh, she's just lovely," old Mrs Thomas declared. "Can she come up on my lap? Yes, you're beautiful…"

But Becca was a wriggler and as if embarrassed by all the compliments she struggled free. Before I could prevent it a large puddle appeared on the floor.

Mrs Thomas was severely crippled with rheumatoid arthritis but the loneliness she endured meant that my visits were very special, even if they involved mishaps.

"No, it doesn't matter at all, dear. There's a cloth in the kitchen. No, I love to see her and she's only a puppy after all…"

I was expected to provide some useful occupation for my patients all of whom had chronic conditions like multiple sclerosis and Parkinson's disease and were housebound as a result. Often they became a great burden for the rest of the family. Sometimes I could obtain light work from local factories, such as the assembly of small electrical parts and this provided the disabled person with a little pocket money. Otherwise I used a variety of handicrafts that, I hoped, would provide an enjoyable pastime. Other people in the team carried out most of the work of providing gadgets and alterations to their houses.

When I could manage a holiday I went to Switzerland with large parties organised by some Christian friends of Jane, the Martin Doyles. These people especially liked the mountain resort of Zermatt in Valais. As the mountain train wound its way up the valley they were continually moving to the window to catch the first glimpse of the majestic Matterhorn which towered above the village.

"Ah! There it is!" they would say reverently, but by the time the novices in the party had spotted it, it was again out of sight as the train turned yet another bend.

It was not long before I too became an admirer of this fantastic piece of rock. It had many different moods but often it would be obscured by cloud for days at a time as if it has completely disappeared. Then it would dramatically reappear, glistening brilliantly with its new coat of snow. On dull days it appeared as a flat, misty shape; then it would be 'smoking its pipe' with a trail of cloud wafting gently across it. The Matterhorn is not the highest mountain in the area but it appears to be because it is so very exposed. The mighty Matterhorn! It filled me with awe and excitement.

Even when I had visited Switzerland with my school many years before, I had enjoyed walking in the mountains and had been among those who had tackled the longest expeditions on offer. Now I had the chance of joining people in the Martin Doyles' party who had experience in rock climbing

My first climb, in the summer of 1958 was along the Furgg Ridge, which forms the border between Italy and Switzerland and has to its west the towering Matterhorn. Our little group left the Gandegg Hut at 4.15 in the morning and reached the first small peak at sunrise.

We were roped together in two groups of three, each with a guide. I had some good boots, purchased in Zermatt and I thoroughly enjoyed testing them out. The ridge demanded a certain amount of stamina and skill and as we helped each other along the Matterhorn loomed above us, ahead of us.

"It seems to get larger all the time," I murmured. "It's so huge and forbidding…"

"*You* could climb the Matterhorn," someone said.

Wow, climb the Matterhorn! I didn't reply; but I kept that remark constantly in my mind. What a challenge! Yes, one day I *would* climb the Matterhorn. Over the next few years this became my great ambition.

During that first trip to Zermatt I climbed several more mountains: The Rimpfischorn, the Briethorn and the Kleine Matterhorn, which was not serviced by cable car as it is today. The challenge of the mountains and the wonderful scenery, combined with spiritual teaching every evening, guaranteed to bring everyone home 'on a high'.

It was another four years before I had the chance of going again to Zermatt with the Martin Doyles. Half the time was spent at Saas Fee, in a different valley, where I was able to warm up by climbing the Allalinhorn. At Zermatt I enjoyed learning new techniques on four different routes on the Riffelhorn, a small but tricky mountain, and a memorable climb along the Leiterspeiz ridge. After such good preparation I confidently made plans with two other people to ascend the Matterhorn. I was keen to go as soon as possible but the others wanted to delay the climb a day or two. Then suddenly the weather changed. Cloud and rain set in. It was impossible to go. The illusive mountain had shattered my hopes.

"It's far too dangerous for any guide to agree to take people unless the weather is clear," experienced climbers on the party told me.

"Yes, I know. But it's so frustrating…" I was near to tears.

"You know, God always keeps the best till last," someone tried to comfort me.

Well, yes, of course it was possible to try again another year. Forcing away my disappointment I determined to start saving up right away.

The following year I heard of another Christian party that would be going on holiday to Zermatt under the leadership of the Reverend Dick Rees.

"I'll manage the Matterhorn this time," I declared confidently, but once again my hopes were shattered. The weather was not good enough during our entire stay. I had to content myself with climbing the very difficult thermometer route on the Riffelhorn and an ascent of the Alphubel and with drawing pictures of the Matterhorn. But Dick Rees obviously loved Zermatt and by popular request he agreed to organise another visit the very next year – 1964.

When we arrived the conditions for climbing were perfect. Without waiting for anyone else and not bothering to get acclimatised to the altitude, I hired a guide, quietly organised my provisions and set out for the hut at the base of the mountain.

My guide's name was Leo Summermatter. He was a tall and well-built man who had climbed the Matterhorn 253 times. He smiled modestly and said,

"When it was 250 times, we had a little party."

The hut was busy with many tough looking climbers and their guides confidently chatting to each other in a variety of languages. We had a simple meal of soup, bread, cheese and sweet tea. I didn't feel like eating much. I watched the sun go down behind the mountains with a glorious display of colour, waiting till the Monte Rosa was as pink as possible before taking its photo. Tomorrow was certainly going to be a fine day.

Nights in mountain huts are never very restful. Climbers sleep on long communal mattresses like sardines and without undressing very much. Rough blankets are supplied but if the hut is crowded there is almost enough warmth from your close neighbours on the mattress. Everyone rises well before dawn, for it is necessary to reach the summit before the snow gets soft in the heat of the sun. Leo and I set off, roped together and with a candle in a small lantern that enabled Leo to see the way. I simply had to follow in his steps.

The hut is situated at about 10,000 feet and the summit of the Matterhorn is over 14,000. As soon as we set out we were climbing, up and up, going at the usual rhythmic, steady pace, in time with each breath. I knew what to expect but I had not realised how much the altitude would affect me when I had not acclimatised myself by walking around Zermatt for a few days. After an hour I was exhausted and the guide began to get angry.

"You have to come," he warned, as I hung back at the steeper places.

Eventually we came to a standstill.

"You are not fit to do it," Leo announced. "You should not have come."

He could see that he was not going to get his full fee and the whole two days would be wasted.

I sat there on the mountain feeling weak and sick. Every step had been an enormous effort. But how could I miss this chance? In my dizzy state Paul's words from the book of Philippians flashed across my mind:

"I can do all things through Christ who strengthens me."

"We have to go on," I said. I've waited six years to do this. The weather was right so I didn't delay."

I was too weak and discouraged to say any more but somehow Leo decided to give me more help. He set a slower pace and encouraged me. Other climbers were passing us now and some of them, realising that Leo had a client who would probably not reach the summit, nodded sympathetically.

Leo ignored their concern. "Perhaps we will reach the Solway Hut," he said, "Then we will see…"

The Solway Hut was about one hour's climb from the summit. It was often used as a shelter for stranded climbers if the weather suddenly changed for the worse. We reached it after three hours of agonisingly slow slogging. I was fighting against nausea and breathing was an effort. Yet the Guide had plenty of strength and he was on my side. He had cold, sweet tea in his flask and that helped.

Above the Solway Hut there were fixed ropes on a particularly steep place. As we were late in reaching these, we had to contend with a group of elated climbers who were already descending the mountain. Passing other people on fixed ropes is not easy. I was relieved when they had gone.

"Only twenty minutes to the top," one of them shouted cheerfully as he clambered triumphantly below us.

And so it was! We reached the top of the Matterhorn in five hours instead of four, but we had made it, and the view was the reward. I tried to take it all in. Another couple took our photo with my camera. Leo gave me a kiss – ("Because it is a lady," he said.) I cut a hole in a lemon I had brought with me and pushed a sugar lump into the hole. I always enjoyed sucking the juice when I reached a summit but this time it didn't taste so good. Anyway it was dangerous to stay too long. Melting snow would soon loosen the rocks above our route. After half an hour we were on our way down.

The descent wasn't too difficult and when I finally got back to the hotel where our party was staying, I was happily exhausted but in reasonable shape. I was sharing a room with my friend, Marion. On my bed was a note from her:

"Congratulations!" it said, "I knew you would make it!"

I fell asleep on the bed. I *had* made it, but I very nearly had *not*! It was only by drawing on the Guide's strength and encouragement that I had managed. The climb had been a spiritual experience and it taught me a lesson that was going to be needed in the years ahead. I shared it with the group and wondered what God had in store for me. Perhaps there was some new challenge for me, too tough to tackle on my own, for which I would need the strength of Christ.

With my guide on the Matterhorn Summit

Chapter 4
The fleece

Back at the caravan life carried on as usual through the rest of 1964. Soon the golden autumn became dark and cold, making each day a challenge in courage and stamina. I was usually half awake when the local farmer arrived at the caravan door with my bottle of milk. He often tapped lightly on the window just above my head, sometimes with a brief comment about the weather:

"Too cold and wet today. You'd do well to stay in bed!"

"Not much hope of that!" I mumbled, "Oh, stop that Becca!"

The little dog, who was supposed to sleep on her own blanket in a box on the floor, had moved up from her forbidden place on my feet and started licking my face.

"No, stop it! Yes, I know we've got to get up. Oh, wow! Look at those icicles on the ceiling! Just tell me how I can heat the van without causing so much condensation! It must be freezing in here."

I checked the thermometer just above my head. It registered nine degrees Fahrenheit, but summoning up all my courage, I heaved off the nine carefully arranged blankets that were tucked tightly around me, crept to the outer door and opened it ajar. "Off you go, Becca."

Sometimes she needed a slight push, for the freezing air on her nose made her suddenly rather doubtful about venturing outside, although she knew the routine well. Soon she was back at the door whining to come in. I was boiling a kettle, relieved to find that the calor gas was still working; it froze more easily than water, so it had to be kept in an old tea chest, padded tightly with straw.

It started snowing as I was driving back from my mother's home after Christmas and during the next few weeks the roads became very treacherous as more and more snow fell. Each day when I returned with the car unscathed, I felt very thankful but then there was the struggle to have supper and get to bed before I was too cold to sleep.

My friend Pam, who was, like me, very much involved with Campaigners, realised my difficulties:

"Come and stay with us for a few weeks. It will be warmer soon and then you can go back."

I was reluctant at first. I felt I might be intruding on Pam's family but Graeme was also very welcoming and their elder daughter was away at school.

"You can have Sara's room," Pam said. "I don't like to think of you freezing in that caravan. You may be tough but it's not necessary to be a martyr. Your bedding must get damp and you could get pneumonia!"

I had to admit that, when it was not sunny on Saturdays, I could not hang the blankets outside to air and as a result I did not sleep comfortably. In the end I accepted her offer with considerable relief. It was the beginning of a very close friendship. Pam was not physically robust but she was becoming a strong Christian and she was wise and discerning. I loved being with her. She was concerned about me and sometimes tried to give advice:

"Why not try to buy a house? There must be cottages for sale in Ryarsh or one of the other villages."

I had tried to house hunt and each time I had found a suitable place something had gone wrong, even though I had enough money for a deposit. Why did that always happen? Did it mean that the Lord did not want me to stay put? I was so busy with Campaigners that I did not feel I should move away but just to be sure I decided to eliminate a few other possibilities. I started by writing to Jane, who, by this time was working in a leprosy hospital in Uganda.

Jane's reply was a great shock. She was supposed to be moving to Ethiopia and she and her colleagues were praying for a replacement for her. Did I think I might be the answer to their prayers? I was horrified! Every possible excuse crowded into my mind. If I were to go to Africa, who could take my place in Campaigners? My sister would think I was crazy or, even worse, that I was trying to prove that working in Africa was not so hopeless as she had said. My mother would be furious to have her other daughter waste valuable years in mission work.

It was about the last thing I wanted to do. I turned things over and over in my mind. 'What about my new car?' I had only had it a few weeks and it was my pride and joy. 'Would I be happy surviving on a low salary? And what about pensions?' The matter would not go away and there were few people with whom I could discuss it usefully.

'I've at least got to reply to Jane's letter. I'll tell her I'm not sure – I need to know more about the job. That will put the ball in her court for a few weeks and give me time to think.'

Back came a letter by return of post. Jane suggested I went to see a friend of hers who would be able to answer all my questions. So one Saturday, early in April 1965, Becca was left with a friend and I went to see Meredith Sinclair in her flat in south-west London.

Meredith, I discovered, was the Nursing Adviser of the Church Missionary Society. She had worked for a few years at Kumi Leprosy Centre in Uganda, where Jane was now, and she was certainly able to give me useful information, to such an extent that my head was soon spinning. The morning passed. We had a light lunch and then talked again. I made a few vague remarks:

"I don't know what to think. I wonder if I'm the right sort of person…"

Meredith's reply sounded strangely familiar and relevant:

"It's not the sort of thing you do in your own strength," she said.

I set out for home, still in a daze. Working on the principle of closed and open doors, I agreed to go for some interviews at the Church Missionary Society's headquarters in London, taking a day's leave for the purpose so that things could be kept secret.

The interviews were brief but they included a medical examination, during which it was discovered that I had a heart murmur. A letter was written to my G.P., who duly called me to his surgery. Ro Carr, my doctor, was a friend and a keen Christian. He thought it a splendid idea that I should work in Uganda and was quite indignant that they should have queried my health.

"What does it matter if you work here or in Timbuktu with a heart murmur!"

He wrote to the C.M.S. telling them that he did not consider my heart murmur to be of any significance. I saw his letter at the headquarters some months later. At the end he had written: "and don't you know she has just climbed the Matterhorn?"

Ro Carr's indignation did not carry much weight with the medical officer at C.M.S. He wanted the heart murmur checked properly. So I was referred to the Mildmay Mission Hospital in London for a full investigation. I realised that I might now be considered unfit for overseas service and that would be a way of escape. But I made a promise to myself and I suppose to God as well, that if I were pronounced physically fit after the hospital appointment, then I would offer to go to Uganda. I was glad that I would be able to make my decision so easily on those grounds.

My hospital appointment was at the end of June, a whole month after my interviews at C.M.S. I was feeling anxious and as I drove into the Dartford tunnel in the rush hour I found myself in a traffic jam. The fumes from all the vehicles seemed to enter the car and I felt faint and dizzy.

'I can't pass out here! Oh, dear, is it just because I'm panicking about the medical? I've got to get there... Oh, daylight in sight!'

...It was just in time. As I emerged from the tunnel I opened the window and sniffed some slightly fresher air, which revived me, and so I pressed on, following a carefully memorised route to the hospital.

After some days the results of the examination were reported to Ro Carr. He had been correct. The heart murmur was not significant and there was no reason for anyone to be concerned. So that was it! I had, as it were, put out a fleece before the Lord just as it was in the Old Testament story when Gideon had wanted a sign to assure him that God really was going to save Israel by his leadership (Judges ch 6 vv 36-40). God had made the Gideon's fleece wet with dew when the ground was dry, which meant that he was going to use Gideon; but Gideon also pressed God to give him a second sign so that he could be quite sure; so God made the fleece dry when the ground was wet as a sign of confirmation. With my one clear sign I felt I had enough guidance to proceed. I was accepted by C.M.S. and the people at the Leprosy Centre were informed that I would be coming in the autumn, in time for Jane to show me the ropes before she moved on to Addis Ababa.

As word got around that I was going to Africa people's comments were very mixed.

"What an adventure! I envy you – it's really exciting!"

"Aren't you scared of all those mosquitoes and getting malaria?"

"What on earth made you decide to do that?"

"The youngsters will miss you."

"Aren't you sorry to be leaving all your friends?"

The last remark was the one which was really painful; for the rest I could make light of my replies. Yes, I would miss my friends very much indeed, in fact my heart was very heavy as I realised what my move would mean. I still managed to see Mary and Philip regularly by driving to Folkestone for the weekend whenever I could. Mary was not keen on my plans and both she and Philip seemed unsettled themselves by my proposed move. They questioned me anxiously:

"What's the matter? You don't seem happy. Do you really want to go?"

"You could still change your mind."

"Oh, I'm all right. No, I *will* go. It must be right. Will you have Becca?"

"Yes, of course we will if you do go. But have you considered everything?"

"What about your mother? Does she know?"

"Yes, and she isn't happy. Nor is Celia. But I can't just forget about a need. If God wants me there then it will be okay."

I was often near to tears. I tried desperately to get my pension transferred from local government to the C.M.S. pension fund, without success. It seemed a terrible sacrifice to draw it all out, and perhaps it was not very sensible but I had now gone so far with my preparations that there could be no turning back.

Sometime during the summer, on a beautifully sunny Saturday morning, I received a letter from Jane saying that it was time I sent off my heavy luggage, which would need to be crated and go by sea. The Richmonds had already given me an old tin trunk, Pam had promised me another and a third was a gift from the friends who had worked in Nigeria. I went to collect these two trunks that very morning and started packing the things I had in the caravan. I planned to borrow a few cooking utensils and some crockery, so I was able to pack almost everything I had. By the end of the day the job was completed. I sat on the bed and surveyed my work thoughtfully:

'That's incredible! Everything I want to send has fitted into those three trunks exactly! I didn't need to pad with unnecessary things nor force things to go in when there was no space left. Yes, of course! That's God's second sign that it's right to go! How could I have doubted?'

Just then there was a cheery greeting: "Anyone at home?"

Round the corner of the hedge came the Vicar, Noel Bone.

"I was visiting someone nearby, so I thought I'd call in. You look busy!"

"Yes, I've just packed my things for Uganda."

"Great! Where do they have to go? I'm going to London on Monday. They would just about fit into my car, so I could take them if you like."

Do not unsaddle your horse

The next day I painted my name and new address on the trunks: 'KUMI LEPROSY CENTRE, P.O. KUMI, TESO, UGANDA.' When they were dry Noel came and whisked them away. Suddenly an overwhelming feeling of happiness and relief swept over me. I now knew for certain that it was right to go to Uganda and that God would supply everything I needed.

C.M.S. had agreed that I should go to Uganda on a single 'short service' tour of four years. This was the best arrangement, as I was needed urgently. Normally a missionary would be expected to do at least a year's training. I knew a little about this as I had visited Jane when she had been at the training college. At the time I had shuddered at the thought of ever being there myself – somehow it was too threatening, exposing people's weaknesses. I was glad that I was not going there but my lack of training meant that I was a very raw recruit. I made sure I knew where Uganda was on the map but my knowledge of the country was very limited and I had never studied anything about leprosy.

I gave up my job just two weeks before flying to Uganda. Philip towed the caravan out of its cosy position, leaving a surprisingly untidy gap. He and Mary used it for several years for holidays. My car was sold to someone in the next village and as it was only nine months old I felt he had acquired a considerable bargain. It was fortunate that there was so much to do; I did not have time to regret anything too sorely.

On my last Sunday evening at Ryarsh Church, Noel Bone, arranged a special valedictory service for me. I spoke briefly, telling the little I knew about my new work and testifying as to how the Lord had guided me so clearly and of the assurance He had given me that I was doing the right thing.

Noel preached about Paul and Barnabas, using the passage in Acts Ch 13 vv 1-3. The Holy Spirit had told some disciples to set aside Paul and Barnabas for a certain mission and so, 'After they had fasted and prayed, they placed their hands on them and sent them off'. Everyone gathered round and they did the same for me. It was an emotional climax and a memorable evening. I knew I would have good prayer support from the Church and this was tremendously important to me.

Pam looked after me for the next two nights. She was full of gentle but enthusiastic encouragement. It was she who drove me to Gatwick for my flight. It was Tuesday evening, November 16th 1965. I was off – into the unknown.

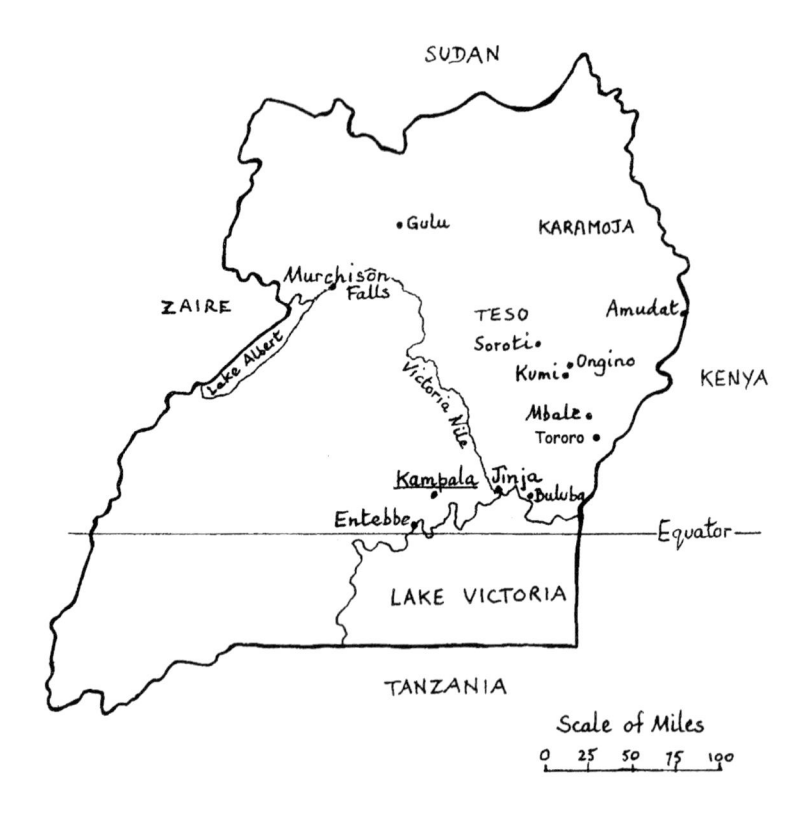

Map of Uganda

Chapter 5
Where do I fit in?

"Mon Dieu! We shall not arrive. *C'est terrible!"*

The timid little French lady sitting beside me on the plane started to panic. We had been airborne for only twenty minutes when the plane bumped several times and the Captain made an announcement:

"Ladies and gentlemen, we have a slight engine problem, so we are turning back to Gatwick for some checks. We are off-loading some of our fuel over the Channel so that we can land. I apologise for the inconvenience."

"We shall not arrive!" my companion repeated.

I smiled at her. "Oh, yes we will," I said confidently.

God had called me to Uganda and I was certain he was going to get me there in one piece.

"It'll be all right, you'll see."

And of course we did arrive safely. The Reverend Norman Campbell, who was the C.M.S. Representative for Uganda, had written me a welcoming letter in which he had told me to sit on the right hand side of the plane so that I could see the sunrise over Lake Victoria, as we circled around and came in to Entebbe airport from the south. We were far too late for the sunrise because of the delay but it *was* exciting to be coming in to land. I was met by Norman's wife, Irene, who had been patiently waiting to drive me the half hour ride to Kampala.

Irene spoke about the possibility of some political unrest that week and the reasons for this. It was not the sort of introduction I was looking for. I was feeling strange and wanting to take in what I could actually see, hear and smell. Later I jotted down my first impressions:

'*Looks* like Africa! Plants, etc. Banana trees, tall palms, red earth, gaudy flowering trees.... But – it all seems so strange: the smell, the atmosphere, the moist heat and shrill cry of birds, crickets, etc; the horrid, shabby shops all reddened with dust; the swarms of Africans living in scattered shacks and the contrast of these to the fine Kampala buildings; the realisation that I cannot communicate with these people or understand how they think and live...'

I needed time to take it all in but I was five or six hours late and Norman Campbell had made a very full orientation programme for me which, because of the delay, was due to start at once. He gave me a briefing almost as soon as I had arrived at his big mission house on Namirembe Hill. This included warnings about listening to what senior missionaries have to say, and the importance of having time for people and of simply sharing with them how Jesus helps you day by day rather than preaching at them.

"And remember," he said, "If people annoy you, *you* probably annoy *them* just as much."

This last remark obviously highlighted his own experience of living in a small expatriate community. I was later to learn what a sound comment it was.

I was allowed an hour to lie down before the evening meal. The Campbells had invited a Ugandan lady who had just returned from studying in the U.K. and now held an important post in the Ministry of Education. It was part of my orientation to meet her because she 'saw things from the European angle.' Most of the discussion was difficult for me to understand and I was too tired to make much effort. I was glad to get to bed.

During the following week I was taken to many different places in and around Kampala by various people, most of whom were C.M.S. missionaries. These people impressed me. They all had such worthwhile jobs and they were very dedicated. I felt very much the newcomer. First there was Namirembe Cathedral, the Uganda Bookshop and the smart little museum. Then back to Mengo Hospital for the official opening of a physiotherapy pool, donated by the Rotary Club. I heard about the many polio clinics that were being set up around the country by Mr Ron Huckstep, a consultant orthopaedic surgeon. He was doing great work in registering hundreds of polio victims, straightening up their contracted limbs and getting them to walk with simple callipers and wooden shoes.

"There's a long waiting list," one of the physios told me. "Even though many crippled polio patients prefer to keep their deformities."

"Why's that?" I asked curiously.

"Well, begging is more profitable if someone is seen to be very disabled. A beggar who can only crawl will do very well on a Friday when Moslems are supposed to give alms."

Ron Huckstep was clearly involving the physiotherapists in all his plans and it seemed that his enthusiasm was infectious.

I was taken to Makerere University, a large Catholic mission at Kisubi, which included a secondary school, and to several rehabilitation projects that provided training for disabled people in agriculture, tailoring, leatherwork and so on. Then on my first Sunday the enthronement of a new Bishop was taking place and it was suggested that I should go.

I felt rather self-conscious as I made my way up the hill to the Cathedral. I was a white person on my own in the midst of so many enthusiastic Ugandans all dressed in their beautiful, Sunday best clothes. People with tickets had to be in their places early. I had no ticket. I stood watching the important people arrive: Dr Milton Obote – the President of Uganda, numerous Bishops, the Achbishop... As the service started I edged up the steps of a side door. There were so many police around that I didn't like to push in. Two or three children wriggled inside and two women, begging to enter, were allowed to do so. Then a policeman turned to me:

"You go in if you can find somewhere," he said, "but there are no seats."

I smiled gratefully and squatted beside some Ugandan ladies, one of whom offered me two grubby handkerchiefs on which to sit.

Do not unsaddle your horse

There was a printed service sheet with the English version of the hymns beside the Luganda, so I was able to join in. The retiring Bishop was handing over to the new Bishop Nsubuga – 'his brother' – and his words were translated into English. It was quite emotional. Then came the Communion. 'How can they manage with so many people?' I wondered; but it all happened in an orderly way and there was a great feeling of awe and oneness. Shelters had been erected outside for food for the invited guests. I wandered up again in the afternoon and the festivities were continuing in an atmosphere of revival.

My orientation continued the next day with visits to various offices in Kampala with Irene, to apply for my driving permit among other things. We continued to Mulago Hospital to talk with the staff of the orthopaedic workshop and then drove back to Mengo hospital to see the physiotherapy department in action. Finally we went to a slum area of the city – a real shanty-town – with shacks, squalor and crime. Groups of men were sitting around beer pots drinking through long tubes.

"Most of these people are from up-country," Irene said. "They come to the city thinking the streets are paved with gold, but there's no work for them and they end up as thieves. They often drink right through the day and then there are arguments and fights at night. It's very sad."

I tried to take it all in, but how glad I was when Jane arrived. She was sympathetic when she saw the programme I had completed.

"They made you do all this! You must be exhausted. Kumi is very different to Kampala so a lot of this is irrelevant anyway."

"It was interesting though," I said, but from the way she spoke I realised that I would need even more orientation when I reached the Leprosy Centre. I hoped it would be of a more gentle nature.

We went shopping together for things I would need, including cutlery, cups, saucers and plates.

"It's important to have a design you really like," Jane said, "Even if it does cost a bit more."

I was reluctant to spend so much, but I obediently chose some attractive crockery. Later I realised that her advice had been good. It is important to have some items of daily use that you really enjoy when you are living in a very basic way.

We collected my driving permit and when Jane had finished all her other jobs and picked up two boys who had been admitted to Mulago Hospital for surgery, we set out for Kumi.

"I'll drive to Jinja and then you can do the next bit to Tororo," Jane said. "That part isn't so busy."

We passed a forest area with enormous trees, huge coffee and tea plantations and open savannah with boys herding small groups of cattle. The drive gave us the chance to talk while the two boys in the back seat were silent and wide-eyed at all they were seeing. We shopped for fruit at road-side stalls, buying quantities of tangerines, oranges (all green skinned), a big stalk of little fat bananas as well as a few pineapples. The journey took us due east, but at Tororo we turned north, passed Mbale and completed the last thirty miles to Kumi on a narrow but smooth tarmac road.

I was now seeing the district of Teso for the first time. It was evening and it looked golden as the sun stretched its beams across the flat savannah grassland. Little thatched homesteads snuggled in among the long grass. Boys ambled home with their cattle. We gave wide clearance to the few cyclists, for they behaved as if no other traffic used the road; it was certainly different to the busy streets of Kampala. We reached the small township of Kumi as the Indian shopkeepers were lighting up their *dukas* (shops) with candles and lamps. I was glad to have arrived.

* * * * *

The 200-mile journey had taken us four hours. Jane showed me to a Guest House, close to hers, where I was to stay. Almost at once I was rather sick, so she packed me into bed, arranged a mosquito net over me and left me to fall into a hot and fitful sleep.

The next day I felt poorly. I pottered about but spent most of the day sleeping. However, on the following day I had recovered sufficiently for Jane to show me around.

"The Centre is very spread out," she explained. "My house is two miles from the children's compound where we have 300 children with leprosy. Then five miles further on is the adult part of the Centre at a place called Ongino. That land was given because it was considered to be unhealthy. It's low lying and there are a lot of mosquitoes. A house is being built for you down there where most of the other expatriates live but it's not finished so you will be in the Guest House for some weeks yet."

So we set out for 'unhealthy Ongino'. It was Saturday. We went to see the hospital and some of the patients. There was a relaxed, happy atmosphere and the patients were laughing and chatting with Jane.

"What are they saying?" I asked her.

"They say that we look like sisters and they are very pleased to see you. You must greet them: *'Yoga'* is what you say. It means 'Hello', 'Good morning', 'Good evening', or anything like that, so it's easy."

I was surprised at what I was seeing. I had thought the patients would be locked up and crouching in corners of dark buildings but here they were enjoying a spacious compound. Yes, many were very crippled, but the place was attractive with whitewashed buildings and gay flowering trees.

We had coffee with Kay and Eric Johnson. Eric was a LEPRA worker (Leprosy Relief Association) and he and Kay were from Yorkshire. As Farm Manager, Eric had built up a special herd of cattle by crossing Red Polls with the local Zebu. He had cleared many acres of bush and erected miles of fencing to form paddocks. It was a tremendous contribution not only to the Centre but also to the whole district. It showed what could be achieved with sufficient effort even in such an unlikely place as Ongino. Eric had introduced bougainvillea trees to the area and the Centre boasted over a hundred varieties. He had planted large orchards with all kinds of citrus fruit trees, pawpaw, guava and pineapples and he had pioneered bee keeping. All this helped greatly in the fight against the stigma associated with leprosy.

Kay Johnson was a nurse but she was fully occupied with her three young children as she was teaching the two elder ones at home. They were all very much at home in Uganda, playing happily with the local children and enjoying the freedom of outdoor life. Bobby, the eldest, was an enthusiast for any sort of wild life.

"Would you like to see my stick insects?" he asked me.

Kay laughed. "I'm sure she wouldn't! But why not bring the monkey to show her. He's much more fun."

The monkey had been found injured somewhere and he was being looked after with the best possible care and attention. He was duly displayed and admired.

The expatriates totalled nine adults and Maurice and Janet Lea headed the team. Maurice had left a thriving general practice in Devon to become a C.M.S. missionary at the age of fifty. He had been Medical Superintendent at Kumi for twelve years, so he was somewhat of an authority on leprosy. Janet was a social worker, but she was involved in a host of different jobs, ably supporting Maurice and together they acted as mother and father for the younger expatriate staff. They were very loving and caring.

"Don't worry how long it takes you to get used to the place," Maurice said to me, and I knew he meant it.

It wasn't easy though. I wanted to make my contribution so badly and everything was new to me. I couldn't see where I fitted in.

"Will you be happy here?" one of the Leprosy Assistants asked me after I had given a talk at the Christian Fellowship meeting.

"Yes," I said firmly. I could still be sure of that. I knew God wanted me there and I just had to work through the strangeness and find my place. In a way it was an anticlimax. My preparations in England had gone so very well that at times I had almost wished for something to go wrong so that it would seem real, but now I was struggling and I didn't like it.

After a few weeks I became sick again. It was late on a Saturday night. I vomited so much that I became desperately weak. I decided that I must get to Jane's house before I was too feeble to walk there. Jane was wonderful. She turned out of her bed and made me comfortable in it. Then she called Dotty, her neighbour, who was the children's nurse and one of the LEPRA workers.

Dotty Jordan, a very blunt person who always said exactly what she thought, was from London. She had a great deal of experience of medical work in Africa and was somewhat older than Jane and me.

"We'll get you sorted," she declared good humouredly, "We can just make a night of it."

I was still being sick but she bustled around finding tablets and drinking water. It reassured me to realise that she and Jane would stay with me till I was able to settle down and sleep.

Over the next few days no one appeared to be concerned that I was so poorly, neither did they suggest that I had malaria because I was taking the wrong prophylactic tablets. Eventually I obtained a supply of Paludrine, and once I had recovered, that saw me through the whole of my time in Uganda without another attack.

The house that was being built for me at Ongino was nearly finished and just before Christmas I was able to move in. Jane had drawn the plans for it and I realised now that it would have been hers had she not been moving to Addis Ababa.

'So this is the house the Lord had for me while I was hunting for one in Ryarsh', I mused. 'How good the Lord is!'

I felt it was rather like getting married. Someone took me to Mbale to show me where I could buy some more household goods: a pressure cooker, an egg poacher, a kettle, an iron, curtain material and material for uniforms as well as some groceries. Janet came to chat with me, expressing her concern that I might find it difficult to manage on the allowance I was receiving, as it was so much less than my previous salary.

"No, I'll manage," I assured her. "I've always been careful with money and these expenses won't be repeated."

As with most new houses there were various things that did not work properly and these proved difficult for the builder to put right. It seemed as if some of the workmen had never seen a flush toilet before – (all the older staff houses had outside, 'deep-drop' latrines). They were delighted that it worked when one man stood on the seat pouring water into the tank above as if that was what had to be done every time it was used. Some of the light switches were a bit odd but I didn't want to make a fuss.

"You will need a houseboy," Jane told me.

I was reluctant to agree to this but Jane went on to explain that it was kind to give the local people work. She had employed a young man called Elimilech for seven years.

"I had to teach him everything – how to wash and iron, make the bed and cook, but he is really useful now. Perhaps he will agree to work for you when I leave. It's much further for him to cycle – eight miles each way, I suppose – but we can ask him."

Elimilech agreed. He was used to receiving regular payment and feared being redundant. Over the years he had used his meagre wage wisely. He had managed to pay the bride price for his wife and build a little homestead and he was very proud of these achievements as well as his small son, Oumujal. We visited him at his home one day and his wife served us with tea, bananas and roasted groundnuts in their spotless mud and grass roofed house.

For a few weeks I employed a young man called Gerefasio as houseboy. He had never worked in an expatriate's house before and he was very slow and careful. Someone had obviously warned him not to move things and one day I noticed

Do not unsaddle your horse

that he had polished the floor *round* a pair of sandals. I patiently spent time with him every day explaining what he had to do.

Janet arranged for a boy who was on holiday from secondary school to help me learn Ateso, the local language.

"You must use him as an informant," she said. "Don't expect him to teach you – let him answer your questions."

She produced an Ateso grammar book, a dictionary and some other simple books. I met Christopher in the cool of the church at 3.00 in the afternoon on most weekdays. It was really hot at that time of day and an effort even to walk there. I decided I must get a bicycle to save my energy and soon I was the owner of a sturdy 'sit up and beg' machine which proved very useful.

It was strange preparing for Christmas at the hottest time of the year. In addition to Jane's main duties she was organising nativity plays, the first of which was to be performed by the children before they all went home for the only holiday they were allowed to have during the year. The wide veranda of a large staff house on the children's compound acted as a stage and I helped Jane paint a backcloth which depicted an African bush scene which, we hoped, would make the story more relevant. I felt so grateful that the birth of Jesus took place in such humble surroundings and under conditions which these children could fully understand.

Excitement reigned as the children prepared their few belongings in tin cases or bundles and collected their bus warrants for going home. The medical staff were always worried about letting them go for fear that they would not return to continue their treatment.

"And just you remember to come back," Dotty Jordan warned a lanky teenager who lived a particularly long way from Kumi. "Term starts on January 25th and no later. If you don't come back for treatment you will finish up with hands like this –(she demonstrated a clawed hand), and a twisted face (another ugly demonstration), so just you remember…"

The little group of youngsters who had gathered for this impromptu lecture moved off with some stifled mirth. They were well used to Dotty's outbursts and did not take them too seriously; but hopefully the chance of free education would ensure their return, even if the need for swallowing tablets under supervision did not have the same lure. Schooling at any other school required fees which many families could not afford.

Jane was now free to turn her attention to the play for the adult patients which was performed annually by the staff. The patients came from a variety of tribal areas and at least three languages had to be incorporated for everyone to understand a little of the Christmas story. The performance took place outside after dark, with sufficient lighting for everyone to see what was happening and enough darkness for the actors to disappear when they needed to. The colourful costumes, carefully kept from year to year, the rhythmic singing and the serious attitude of the staff as they entered into their parts, all combined to make the evening very special. The patients' faces were just visible in the darkness. They were watching keenly, eyes agog. 'I wonder how many of them have never heard the story before,' I thought as I watched one patient leaping joyfully back to the ward on his crutches at the end. 'Has he really understood? I hope someone can explain the real meaning if he only saw it as a bit of fun.'

On Christmas morning crowds of people flocked to our church. Activities were organised for the patients after the service so that they did not get to the inevitable beer pots too early in the day and cause trouble by getting drunk and thereby disturbing the expatriates who had their own (very English) supper party in the evening.

"I think you've only just realised you're in Africa," Maurice said to me as we all munched our way through turkey and Christmas pudding. "Don't worry how long it takes for you to get to grips with the work."

Forty days had passed and I still had not really discovered what my contribution would be. Every morning I had been with Jane in the occupational therapy workshop and in the physiotherapy department, but her time was rapidly running out and soon I would be on my own. How was I going to manage?

Chapter 6
Shoes, limbs and Leprosy

I had never been very good at finding work to do when everyone around me seemed to be doing all that was needed. During my occupational therapy training I had received a very poor report of my three months' hospital practice at King's College Hospital in London. There were too many students for the size of the department, so I hung back and allowed my colleagues to deal with the patients most of the time. My report said that I was either lazy or I was not interested in the work. Fortunately my college did not take these remarks too seriously, as I had a generally good record. When there was no one else to do the work, then I was able to plan and apply myself to the task, getting fully involved and seeing progress.

So it was that when Jane left for Ethiopia, I *had* to take responsibility and begin to learn. In this chapter I deal with the nature of my work and explain about leprosy and its complications in some detail, including its long history that contributes so greatly to the widespread fear of the disease. I learned mostly by working with the patients and trying to understand their problems.

The workshop had two rooms, the larger of which was used for weaving. This was not a traditional craft but it was suitable as an occupation for even the most crippled patients. Colourful table-mats, cushion covers and small towels were produced and sold to visitors. The smaller room was for shoe and limb making. Several patients were employed there and they received a small wage for their work. Most of the shoes were made out of old motor car tyres, the soles being cut from the tread and the straps from the sides. The straps were stitched in place to form simple sandals. Artificial limbs were made out of wood and leather and were very heavy. This part of the workshop did not enthuse me. It was dirty and primitive but I knew it was an essential part of the hospital and needed to be developed.

My other duties included the supervision of the physiotherapy sessions that were held in another building, where one or two patients, trained by Jane, taught simple hand and foot exercises to the patients who needed them. Then there were health education groups to organise so that the patients could learn about their disease, how treatment would help them, how to recognise the early signs in other members of their families and how to prevent complications occurring, especially if they had suffered nerve damage and had loss of feeling in their hands and feet.

When I arrived at Kumi I had not received any instruction about leprosy, nor had I had time to do any personal study, so I was not only ignorant – I had some completely wrong basic ideas about the patients. I once asked Jane about some clinical details and referred to the patient concerned as a 'leper'. Jane, who was usually so placid and gentle, gave me a very angry response:

"You must *never* call patients lepers," she declared. "If you do, it implies that there is no cure for the disease and that they are labelled as having leprosy for life."

I soon got used to calling them leprosy patients and, like Jane, always cringed when uninitiated visitors used the word 'leper'.

Leprosy is a fascinating disease, despite the terrible deformities suffered by patients who do not receive treatment soon enough. It is one of the oldest diseases known, being present in India in 600 B.C. There are documents, which clearly describe the skin and nerve signs, and chaulmoogra oil was used as a treatment. The disease was spread to the west by armies of Alexander the Great around 327 B.C. It was called 'Elephantiasis', but it was clearly what we call 'leprosy' today. Somehow, after this, the term 'leprosy' became confused, because in the Old Testament the Hebrew word 'Tsara-ath' is used. This word is more or less untranslatable, but the root meaning is 'collapse', 'strike' or smitten by God'. Various stories in the Old Testament show that leprosy was considered to be a punishment from God for someone who had committed a serious sin.

Leprosy is dealt with in great detail in the book of Leviticus, Chapters 13 and 14. The diagnostic signs are given and hardly any of them are seen in the disease we call leprosy today. It seems that all the unsightly skin conditions, including mould and fungus, were grouped together as 'Tsara-ath'. The confusion continues to-day: I was to experience many occasions when someone suffering from a severe skin condition, which in no way resembled leprosy, would be sent to the leprosy workers, often by other health staff, who tended to be scared of that type of patient.

Whatever it was that was called leprosy in Bible times (and I shall continue to call it leprosy for lack of another word), it was obviously greatly feared. When Miriam was struck down with leprosy, as a punishment, Aaron said, as he begged God to forgive her, 'Let her not be as one who is dead.' (Numbers 12 v10). Leprosy could only be cured by God, so it was a priest who diagnosed it and he also had the job of ceremonially cleansing the person if healing took place.

In the New Testament leprosy is mentioned fifteen times and the Greek word *lepra* is used. This is another word that is difficult to translate but its root meaning is 'to husk, scale or remove the bark'. No diagnostic signs are given, so it is not clear whether what we call leprosy today was included. In the accounts of healing, leprosy and mental illnesses are the conditions that are singled out, probably because they were the most feared. The fact that Jesus actually touched someone with leprosy is very remarkable. He treated *everyone* as a human being no matter how repulsive their appearance.

In Mediaeval times the stigma towards leprosy worsened. The sufferers were often given over to the care of Monks. In England many old churches still have squint windows, through which the 'lepers' could see something of the service from a particular place assigned to them. In southern Europe there was a special 'Lepers' Mass'; the person was brought in 'as one dead' and the priest would read the rules he had to follow, including, 'I forbid thee to go abroad without thy leper uniform'.

It was not until 1847 that leprosy was clinically defined, (that is, leprosy as we know it today), and it was separated from all other skin conditions. Then in 1874, a Norwegian doctor, named Hansen, discovered the leprosy bacilli. At this stage the disease should probably have been renamed after him, but it wasn't. Countries in the Americas do try to call it Hansen's Disease, but most of the world stays with 'leprosy'. And so the battle with stigma goes on and on.

No real cure was found until 1941 when dapsone (a sulphone drug) was discovered in the U.S.A. This was a real break-through. The drug was cheap! Its use meant that leprosy sufferers need no longer be isolated in asylums but could be treated as outpatients.

The leprosy bacillus is probably spread by droplet infection although there may be other ways in which it is passed on. At one time it was thought that babies who were carried on the back of a mother who had the disease would catch it because their cheeks rubbed up and down on the mother's bare skin, but this was never proved. Whatever the mode of spread, about 80% of the population has an inborn immunity so that most people do not develop the disease even if they have been in close contact with an infectious sufferer.

When people *do* develop leprosy, the amount of resistance they have in their bodies determines the type of the disease. With no resistance the bacilli spread throughout the body, affecting the skin and, later on, those peripheral nerves that lie close to the surface of the body. When the patient has some resistance to the bacilli, the signs are more localised, resulting in a few skin patches but damaging the nerves much sooner because of the 'fight' which the body puts up against the bacilli.

The first type of leprosy is known as lepromatous and it is contagious and difficult to diagnose in the early stages. The second type, known as tuberculoid, is not contagious and much easier to recognise. In between these two types is borderline leprosy which is contagious and often the most difficult to treat because of the possibility of 'reactions' of the body to the bacilli, which, if not properly managed, lead to nerve damage. Treatment with dapsone was for a minimum of two years for tuberculoid leprosy but the lepromatous patients were supposed to take the drug daily for the rest of their lives.

When I arrived at Kumi in 1965, dapsone was the treatment for all the patients. Over the years it had been very effective, particularly as the majority of sufferers in Uganda had the tuberculoid type of the disease. It was much later that problems of resistance to the drug threatened to undermine its success.

Dr Wiggins, who was British and had been a director of Medical Services in the Uganda Government, established Kumi Leprosy Centre in 1927. Prior to his initiative, leprosy sufferers were supposed to live in 'camps'. The 'unhealthy' land at Ongino was provided when it was decided to separate the adults from the children. Other leprosy settlements in various parts of the world were set up around this time on sites that were also considered to be unsuitable for any other purpose. Carville, a big leprosy establishment in Louisiana, U.S.A. was built in a heavily polluted area that had the highest rate of cancer in the whole country. A centre in the west of Uganda was built on an island in Lake Bunyoni, a most beautiful place but quite impractical as far as administration was concerned.

The Misses M. Laing and A. Kent, C.M.S. missionaries, succeeded Dr Wiggins. Miss Laing was a large and powerful woman by all accounts. Mr Enabu, one of the older African staff members was himself a patient during those days.

"It was very difficult to get enough food for all the children," he told me. "So if there was a shortage she would go with a bodyguard of four strong men and some of us older ones and dig up people's *shambas* (gardens). And no one dared to argue with her!"

When these two ladies left in 1948 there were 300 children at Kumi and 800 adults at Ongino. Most of the staff at Ongino were patients and they were all accommodated together in wards, which were locked at night to prevent trouble. An English doctor, Harold Wheate, arrived later the same year and two Ugandan Medical Assistants joined the staff, Jesse Ndahura and Onesimus Busimo. To this day wards are named 'Laing', 'Kent' 'Ndahura' and 'Busimo' – a well-deserved honour, as conditions were very tough in those days.

* * * * *

As I struggled to get rid of my preconceived ideas, I began to see the patients as special individuals. I longed to know what made them tick – what they thought about the hospital – what they talked about all day. They seemed usually to be appreciative and to have a good sense of humour. The contrast between the appearance and attitude of a patient on admission and after a few weeks was often very remarkable. Many of them were very poor and they had often travelled a long way to reach us. Even the meagre food supplied at the hospital improved their appearance, which was surprising as our food budget was less than half that spent on local prisoners! Some of the patients occasionally complained about the monotony of beans and maize meal, but they were given meat or fish on special occasions and the women would often gather the leaves of wild plants to cook as vegetables.

The patients referred to me were always those who had loss of feeling in their hands or feet because they had started treatment too late, or had suffered reactions. The loss of feeling was due to damaged peripheral nerves and these not only give feeling but also control muscles. So many of my patients had clawed fingers or 'dropped foot' deformity – (the patient being unable to raise his foot at the ankle when walking).

Loss of feeling in a person's hands is a terrible handicap. All of our patients liked to cook, whether they were allowed to do so or not, and the local saucepans had no handles and were always gripped at the hot rim. Everyone used tin mugs for tea and these were handled without thought. Burns were very common. The challenge was to convince the patient of the cause.

One morning I found a patient with a blister the size of a tennis ball on her hand.

"How did this happen?" I asked her.

"It came by itself," the woman replied. "It wasn't there yesterday. The leprosy is eating my body".

Hands were also damaged when hoes and other tools were gripped too tightly because the person could not feel how much strength he needed to apply to prevent the implement from slipping from his grip. This was especially dangerous if the patient had clawed hands, when excessive pressure was taken on the fingertips. Some patients had no fingers at all. They had continually injured their hands and neglected the wounds because there was no pain. Their injuries had become infected causing bone absorption. Sometimes one or two shortened fingers remained and there were fingernails at the tips. This proved that the fingers did not 'drop off' – a view that was widely believed by local people.

I once heard Dr Paul Brand, the famous leprosy expert, tell a story about a group of Indians who were gathered around an open brazier in a city street, roasting maize cobs. One of the cobs fell into the fire and there was no way of rescuing it. Then someone spotted a leprosy sufferer with badly crippled hands standing nearby and she was called to assist. Without hesitation the woman put her hand into the fire and picked up the cob. Burns would have resulted – a horrible price to pay for a charred maize cob that she would certainly have been allowed to eat. What a terrible thing it is to be robbed of that precious gift of *PAIN!*

Most of our patients arrived barefooted, often with ulcers on the soles of their feet, – hence the need to provide shoes. Because they felt no pain these ulcers were often unnoticed or badly neglected. No one normally looks underneath his feet if he feels no pain. The damage was usually due to the wasting

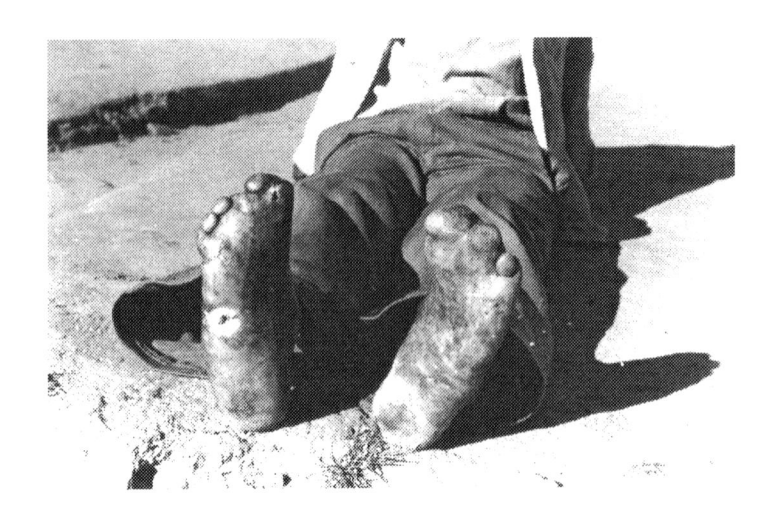

The ulcerated feet of a leprosy patient

of the soft tissue on the sole of the foot, so that there was nothing to cushion the bones against the hard ground when the patient took pressure in walking. It was easier to tell the patients that thorns and sharp stones caused the trouble but some of them seemed to think that the leprosy was responsible and that the damage would occur whether they followed our advice and wore sandals or not.

Foot ulcers had to be healed before the patient was allowed to walk freely. This meant using crutches or a wheelchair if one was available, and plenty of bed rest. We soon discovered that the ulcers would heal faster if the patient's leg and foot were put in plaster of Paris incorporating an iron walking bar. The patient then had the advantage of being mobile, but other patients often complained that the smell after some weeks was quite disgusting. They were right, but the treatment did work, helped by the maggots that took up residence inside the plaster.

Tyre shoes were not ideal, of course, even when they were lined with sorbo rubber, which we could obtain fairly cheaply from Bata Shoe factories in Kampala or Nairobi. The patients preferred *not* to have the lining, because tyre shoes which were made and sold in local markets had no lining and to avoid stigma it was better if their shoes looked like market shoes. We had to persevere relentlessly with our teaching, but I began to realise that some of the patients with loss of feeling in their hands and feet actually felt that these parts did not belong to them and they disowned them. Sometimes they wilfully tried to destroy themselves.

Even in the 60s it was possible to rejoin a hand that had been completely severed from the forearm in an accident victim. However, when such patients were carefully observed in the months following the surgery, it was found that many of them mentally rejected the part and some requested that it be removed because it no longer felt part of them – it felt as if it were stuck on because of the lack of feeling. This is what our leprosy patients must have experienced too.

Old motor car tyres were, actually, quite difficult to obtain in Uganda. I frequently visited the garages in Mbale, our nearest town, which was 30 miles away, to see if they had any to spare. Often I returned with tyres that were too heavy or which had wire mesh in the tread and these were no good for shoes. Soon the garages were expecting payment for the tyres. I remember an occasion during my first leave in England, when I was driving through the outskirts of a town and suddenly spotted an enormous heap of old tyres that were, presumably, going to be burned. I felt exasperated at the waste – but how could they be transported to Uganda?

When the foot ulcers were healed there was usually deep scar tissue and as this was often at places where the foot bends in walking the ulcer often developed again. Just before Jane left, a Lancashire clog maker, Dick Turner, came to show us how to make wooden shoes that would enable the patients to walk while the foot was held as if it were in a splint. He arrived at Entebbe airport carrying two clog-making knives, which measured about four feet in length, and experienced some difficulties in explaining their use to the customs officials. Under his directions two small, low benches were fixed to the floor of a spare storeroom and the knives were mounted on these. The clogs, made of musisi wood, were made to fit exactly the sole of each individual patient and as they walked they 'rocked over' because the sole was tapered towards the toes. These shoes proved useful until the scar tissue had lessened and the patient could use flexible shoes again.

Sometimes there were patients who had such severe ulcers on their feet that the only option was to amputate the leg below the knee. It was always a last resort and some patients took a long time to agree, always hoping that somehow the foot would improve. For others it was not a difficult decision. I remember one man who had been brought from a far away village, travelling on the back of a bicycle for several days. Under filthy bandages we found two inches of the tibia bone protruding from badly infected flesh. He had no foot and he looked desperately haggard and ill. He was glad to have his amputation as soon as antibiotics had cleared the worst of the infection. After a few months he was quite unrecognisable; he had put on weight, he was smiling and walking well with his artificial limb.

The most primitive artificial limb was a 'peg-leg' that was made from a piece of broom handle mounted on a sort of three sided box into which the patient knelt, with his (usually short) stump protruding behind. A small foot was added and leather straps held the knee in place over a padded surface. This contraption was unsightly but very practical. If it got broken he would usually be able to find some way of fixing it. Only when it was completely worn out would he need to return to Kumi.

As time went on an effort was made to produce limbs that were more cosmetically acceptable. These had leather sockets into which the stump fitted and some even had carved toes on the foot with painted toe nails! The patients who made these limbs showed initiative but they had never received any training and they were not of a high enough educational standard to be accepted for any relevant course.

I needed vision, bright ideas and some clear planning to develop the work, but at least I was discovering priorities, accepting the challenge and beginning to feel at home. I was also getting to know some very remarkable people.

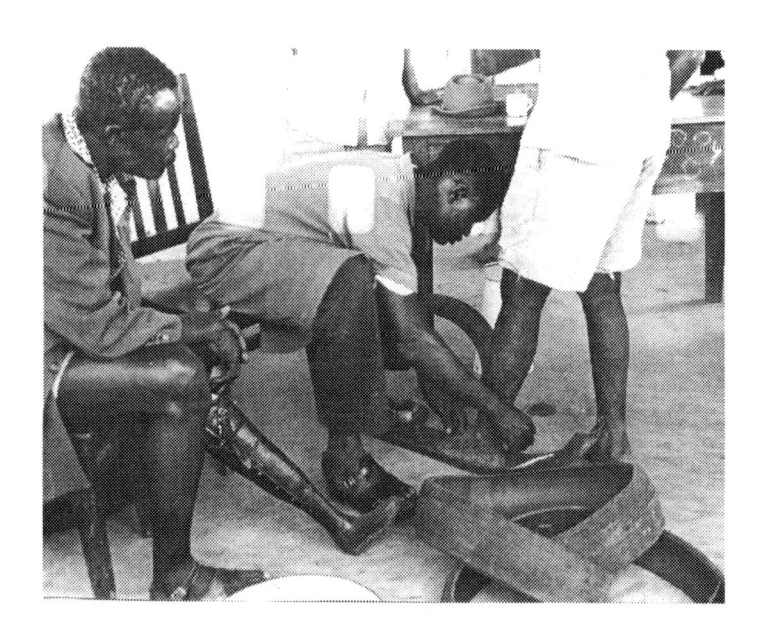

Above: Measuring a patient for motor car tyre sandals

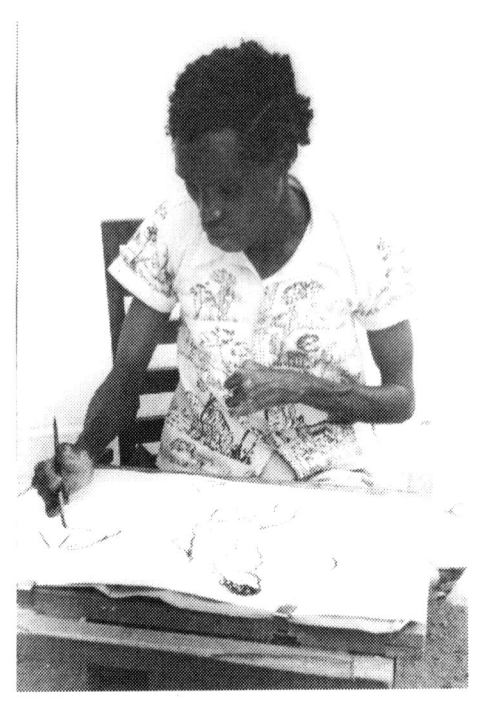

Above: Livingstone at work on a painting
Below: Livingstone with a finished painting

Chapter 7
Livingstone the artist and other new friends

He was tall and lean with sunken cheeks and a serious, sometimes almost fierce expression. He wore his hair longer than most Africans, spending time every day carefully combing out the tight curls in an effort to look his best. His face was intelligent, his eyes noticing everything around him but his hands were badly mutilated, just a few shortened and twisted fingers remaining and his feet were stumpy and ulcerated. This was Livingstone Chekweko, one of the most remarkable people I have ever met. He was probably about thirty years of age when I arrived at Kumi.

No one knew how Livingstone had contracted leprosy. His home was in the Sebei district, high on the slopes of Mount Elgon, where the prevalence of leprosy was much lower than in most parts of Uganda. As a result people did not understand what was causing the pale coloured patches on his skin or the severe pain in his hands and arms that stopped him from going to school. In any case money was short so he would probably only have managed a few years of education even if he had been fit. To amuse himself he collected succulent plants from the forest and made liquid from them so that he could paint what he saw around him with pieces of stick. The idea had come to him when someone showed him a photograph.

Months and years passed by and he suffered many reactions, the leprosy bacilli damaging his nerves and causing loss of feeling in his hands and feet. Mercifully, one day someone from Teso district called at the Chekweko home and recognised what was wrong. The visitor knew about Kumi Leprosy Centre and after several failed promises he eventually found a way for Livingstone to travel there. It was 1958, the same year that Jane arrived at Kumi, and it was she who helped him through months of weakness and depression by encouraging him to paint with proper materials. During this time he was suffering from TB as well as badly neglected leprosy and he was in a strange place where no one spoke his tribal language fluently. It was a tough struggle for him to rise above his problems. He told me that when he was put into bed in the ward he just wanted to escape. He thought his condition would deteriorate even more when so many very crippled patients surrounded him.

Jane had told me about Livingstone's background but it was only when I started working on my own that I began to discover his real character. He was often in the workshop helping the other patients with their weaving, or, when it was reasonably quiet, working on a picture. He delighted in the different colours and his paintings were full of life, often illustrating his home area with the many animals found there. Sometimes he would include people and illustrate some humorous event. Later he made pictures of the hospital staff, of expatriates taking photos, or people holding a huge python that had been killed on the farm.

Livingstone heard the Gospel message from some of the Church teachers. He enjoyed the evenings when they led prayers in the ward. To start with he could not understand enough Ateso to grasp everything that was said, so he used the time to pray, but some small booklets, in a language he could understand a little, helped him until he had learned enough English to be able to read the Bible. Gradually he became a sincere believer and was confirmed. With vivid imagination he began painting pictures of Bible stories: Noah's Ark, Jesus teaching from the boat and once, at someone's special request, Jesus healing the man with leprosy. He admired the faith of a very crippled lady, Joyce Ikulumet, who sang beautifully. When she was discharged he sometimes managed to send her small gifts.

I don't remember who had the idea, but it was decided in 1967 that Livingstone should collect a good number of his paintings and have a 'one man' exhibition of his work in

Kampala. Livingstone was very keen to do this. By now he was feeling stronger and the ulcers on his feet had almost healed. The leprosy had more or less 'burned itself out', so he was certainly not able to pass on the disease to anyone else.

There were 54 paintings for the exhibition. He had saved some money from the sale of other pictures with which he was able to have a smart pair of long trousers made. Using oil paints, he covered one of his shirts with pictures of animals and the workshop men made some special shoes using cork and rubber latex for the soles and leather for the straps. It was my privilege to drive him to Kampala where his exhibition had been set up at the Uganda Museum for a two week period.

Livingstone had never been to Kampala before, although he was so confident about the whole adventure that I could have imagined he had been there many times. On the 200 mile journey he showed a keen interest in everything along the way. At the Owen Falls Dam near Jinja we stopped for a break and to admire the great rush of water gushing from under the bridge. Livingstone studied this great engineering feat intently and with amazement and then enquired:

"How did they manage to hold back all that water in order to build the bridge?"

I had no idea. The waters of the Nile were enormously powerful and they were much higher on the other side of the bridge. Livingstone silently flipped a pen from his top pocket and made a sketch of the bridge and the water on the palm of his hand. Some weeks later he produced a painting of it.

I had arranged for Livingstone to stay at a Salvation Army hostel that was managed by a lovely Australian lady, Captain Stella. She welcomed Livingstone warmly and showed him where he was to sleep. I left him there with his few belongings that included an easel, table and folder which were all still sticky with newly painted varnish.

The curator of the museum had been extremely doubtful as to whether Livingstone should appear at the exhibition at all.

"People will feel too sorry for him," he said.

"But Livingstone is not a sad person," I had told him firmly, "And he will be desperately disappointed if he can't come."

The man was obviously scared of leprosy himself, so I was not very hopeful, but fortunately, when I talked with the officials at the Ministry of Culture later that afternoon, I found that they had made excellent preparations. Livingstone was to sit among his paintings and demonstrate the various ways he could work: with the brush in his crippled hand, or in his mouth, or fixed to a strap on his wrist. He was also expected to attend the official opening by the Minister of Culture and Community Development, the Hon C.B.Katiti.

There was yet another surprise. Arrangements had been made for Livingstone and me to appear on live television. I spent the night with Irene and Norman Campbell on Namirembe Hill and tried to prepare myself for the excitement that was in store.

Livingstone was amazed at the sights of Kampala with the impressive, tall buildings and busy streets, but he was not overawed. I parked near the office of the Director of Television and we made our way up a smart staircase. He sank comfortably into a large leather armchair and the briefing began. It was agreed that I would talk a little about leprosy, how it could be cured and what caused disabilities, and Livingstone would demonstrate his painting skills.

"And I would like to send greetings to my friends at Kumi, in Ateso," Livingstone said, "About ten minutes would do."

"You'll be lucky to get one minute," the Director laughed, but Livingstone was not to be discouraged so easily. Send his message he did, (he was very proud to have learned so many tribal languages from other patients) and he also rose to the occasion brilliantly, painting a zebra with the brush in his mouth, and quickly, so that the cameras could film the whole process. Afterwards we moved speedily to the museum for the official opening of the exhibition. Livingstone was completely at ease, chatting to people and answering their questions. I was amazed at his confidence and humility.

The Minister read the account of Livingstone's life and of how he had become a 'self-taught landscape and animal painter', from a pamphlet which had been produced by his ministry. It was quite lengthy and slightly over-dramatised but it pointed out that Livingstone was cured of leprosy but that: 'The disease has left his feet severely damaged so that if he left Kumi he could not manage to walk to the nearest treatment village for his regular check-up'. The account ended with praise: 'Each painting is a triumph over adversity and a victory patiently won by Livingstone Chekweko and Kumi Leprosy Centre in long years of struggle against a disease that, even today, afflicts 85,000 of Uganda's citizens'. Listed in the pamphlet were his pictures and their prices; we had worked together to give them all titles: 'Literacy Class', 'Ostrich Chase', Selling Pots', 'Animals by the river', 'Masai fight a Lion', 'The Good Samaritan', and so on.

On the way back to the Salvation Army hostel he agreed that it had been a good day.

"There's just one thing," he said. "I *would* like some bread. I don't like the posho (maize meal) they use at the hostel."

I wished he had said so earlier in the day. It was late and I did not know where to buy bread.

"I'll get you some tomorrow," I promised, and with that he was happy.

The next morning we returned to the museum and Livingstone sat and painted for most of the day. He was in his element. Quite a few of his pictures sold and visitors found it fascinating to see him at work. The fact that Livingstone had never understood about perspective made his pictures more meaningful. If something was important, then it was large and everything else was made to fit around it. When I managed to drag him away at the end of the day he must have been exhausted.

"What did you enjoy most?" I asked him when we got back to Kumi.

"Very wonderful safari," he replied, "But it was nice when we got back here and everyone came out to greet us."

Do not unsaddle your horse

At that time there was an old television set at the hospital, which sometimes worked, and many of the patients had seen us. It had boosted their morale and made them happy. As far as I was concerned it had been a triumph to have such a disabled leprosy sufferer among so many people in Kampala where the fear of the disease was much greater than it was in Teso. I hoped it had helped to change people's minds about leprosy.

Livingstone became more and more respected by both staff and patients. It was a common sight to see him walking around the compound with short, careful steps, or moving himself in one of the locally made wheelchairs with their big bicycle wheels, to save his feet from pressure. He would stop and talk to the other patients, particularly any who looked worried or anxious. He was a wonderful counsellor.

A blind and very depressed lady was admitted, with a severe type of leprosy and from a remote tribe, so that hardly anyone could communicate with her. Livingstone had become reasonably fluent in about seven different languages and he took her under his wing, listening to her and encouraging her to do clay modelling to keep her hands exercised. If ever I visited outpatient clinics the leprosy assistants' parting requests would often be:

"Greet the doctor – and Livingstone, when you get back."

"Sister, I'd like a word with you," Livingstone sometimes quietly murmured.

I would lead him into my office and close the door. It was usually to give me some useful piece of advice.

"Watch Owata," he said on one occasion.

(Owata was one of the shoe and limb makers and a clever workman.)

"Just watch him," Livingstone said. "Don't say anything till you have seen for yourself. He is taking leather and other materials for his own use."

He was always right! He was like a private detective. He was also very good at showing visitors around the hospital, which gave him the opportunity of practising his linguistic skills.

"I want you to teach me American," he said to me one day. "We get a lot of American visitors and I would like to be able to speak their language."

No doubt he would have managed an American accent had I felt able to mimic it myself.

Although the Church Missionary Society sponsored me, I was actually funded by The Leprosy Mission who also gave some financial support towards the running of the Centre. Soon after my arrival Eddie Askew, who was later to become General Director of the Mission, visited Kumi. He was exploring the possibility of making a film for use in fund raising and, impressed by Livingstone, he planned to base the film on his life's story. It was called 'How Great a Flame' and it highlighted Livingstone's faith that grew from a small spark. A local lad from Kumi was chosen to take the part of Livingstone as a boy and together they were taken to the home on the mountain where much of the filming took place.

The advice that Livingstone was able to give to the film crew was obviously very valuable. When eventually we received a copy of the finished product we all gathered after dark on the grassy area near the big concrete screen that was used quite often for showing films to the patients. Livingstone sat near me on a stool watching carefully. Afterwards I asked him for his comments. He seemed satisfied but he had picked up one small fault.

"The boy in the hut spoke the wrong language," he said. "The day they filmed that bit they left me behind, otherwise it wouldn't have happened."

It was a powerful film and it was put to good use in the U.K. over the next few years. How great a flame! Livingstone's faith continued to challenge us. His feet were always a problem and often he was forced to rest; but his intelligence, ingenuity, gifts and wise counselling made him very special. I valued his friendship enormously.

William Bingi of the Church Army

"Would you be able to give William some help?" Janet asked me one day. "We thought it would cheer him up to do a correspondence course in English and he agreed, but he's finding it hard going."

"I suppose I could try," I said, "I'll have a word with him."

William Bingi had just finished his training as a Church Army Captain in Nairobi when it was discovered that he had leprosy. He was Ugandan but from Busoga District, so he didn't speak Ateso, but the leprosy centre in his own area was Roman Catholic, and it was thought that he would feel more at home in our Church of Uganda (Protestant) establishment, where he could also do some evangelistic work. He came with his wife, Beatrice and two small children and they were given a little house near the Church.

William's English was already quite good but he struggled to understand the grammar. I got to know him well as I sat with him in his house in the evenings after work. He was depressed, so any encouragement we could give was valuable. His lepromatous leprosy often caused reactions and made him poorly and the disease seemed to go on and on with little improvement, so that he was losing hope of ever following his chosen career. He had a fine testimony and, when he was feeling a little more positive, he bravely shared it with us at the Christian Fellowship gathering one evening.

"I was a bad husband," he began. "And when I was converted I had to repent and put things right with Beatrice. People in the village noticed that I had changed: 'This William is not the same,' they were saying, and I told them that was true and that I now had Life."

When he went home from Nairobi and they knew he had leprosy, the people changed their remarks:

"William is dead now," was all they could say.

They feared leprosy very much and shunned him.

"I struggled with depression," he admitted. "I was tempted

to think that God had punished me and abandoned me and I begged Him to show me what I had done wrong."

His faith was smouldering but it was still just alive and he assured us that he knew God would eventually see him through his problems:

"Whatever happens, my future is with the Lord and I *have* real Life no matter how sick I am."

It was sad that William never tried to learn Ateso. It probably seemed an insignificant language compared to his, but as a result he always had to have someone to translate for him, sentence by sentence, when he preached in Church, and although he could evangelise among the patients who spoke Luganda, he could not communicate with the majority of them. I am sure he was hoping that he would not have to stay at Kumi long enough to necessitate the effort of learning another language.

It was always more traumatic for a well-educated person with a salaried job to be diagnosed with leprosy, than for someone who was just a simple farmer living in the bush. William had lost his job and with it much of his confidence and self-esteem. Without his strong faith he would have been utterly devastated. Beatrice bore him several more children and he was a loving husband and father. His leprosy improved only gradually, but his courage was considerable and we felt privileged to care for him.

Winfred and the Girl Guides

"Let's have a camp," Janet said.

Together we had re-started the Girl Guide Company that had lapsed for some time. Some girls had already been selected by the Matron who kept her eye open for those who behaved well and were conscientious about helping with jobs, like slashing grass in the big compound early in the morning. It was an honour to join. They liked the blue uniform and red tie and the chance to leave the compound for a few days camping was very exciting.

"If you're taking those girls off into the bush you'd better know how to treat snake bites," Dotty warned in her usual blunt fashion.

Grabbing a large mango that had fallen from the tree outside her dispensary she proceeded to teach me how to give an injection into it. By the end of the demonstration I didn't feel very confident about injecting any of the children but I hoped the snakes would keep away and gratefully accepted the large first aid box that Dotty had prepared, together with the leprosy tablets for the girls' regular treatment.

"The Guides are so shy," I remarked to Janet. "I wish I spoke better Ateso, it's hard for them to understand me."

"They understand you all right," Janet said. "They are taught in English in school. But girls are always shy. Many families don't even try to educate them, – they are underlings. Isn't it good that we can have Guides? It does help them to gain confidence!"

It was great to be working with Janet. She was always so enthusiastic and encouraging. We had some good tents and equipment which had been donated by Guide Companies in England over the years, so we checked everything, organised the food, bought new blankets and set off with our eleven excited children in two rather elderly Peugeot trucks. Glancing occasionally through the mirror I could see the girls laughing and singing as clouds of red dust from the murram road billowed around them. After two hours we arrived at Katakwi, our chosen place for the camp.

The camp site was beautifully shaded by tall trees. Blue kingfishers occasionally flashed by and baboons looked down on us from the rocks above. The girls worked very well. After a much needed night's rest I woke on the first morning to the sound of crackling sticks and a fire flickering in the pale morning light. The girls were already preparing tea. They needed no encouragement to start the day. Maize meal and beans formed the main part of their school diet. Now they were having *matoke* (green banana which is cooked and mashed), millet, ground nuts, meat and fish as well as bread and jam, sweet bananas and oranges. Meal times were mostly silent as we sat on the ground in a circle, everyone concentrating on enjoying the special food.

Water had to be carried from a borehole half a mile away.

"I'll take one of the trucks down there," I said to Janet, after the girls had been gone for some time with the water carriers. "It'll speed things up and if I drive carefully we shouldn't lose too much water. Otherwise the whole morning will be gone and it would be good to explore the rocks."

As I backed the vehicle close to the borehole I accidentally drove over the tin water container belonging to a local woman who was waiting her turn at the pump. This resulted in a profusion of angry Ateso, most of which was lost on me, although I clearly understood that she wanted five shillings so that she could replace her container. The Guides looked on silently while I struggled to apologise and explain that I would give her the money if she came with me to the camp.

Quietly one of the younger Guides came to my assistance.

"Captain," she said, "She is asking too much money. She can buy a new tin for two shillings."

I looked at her with amazement. I had not noticed her before and her courage and sense of justice were surprising. Moreover she was right. The woman was quite satisfied when I gave her two shillings. Now, as I began to watch this small girl, I realised that she was not only very intelligent but also a potential leader. Her name was Winfred.

Over the next few years we managed to camp annually. After Janet and Maurice had left Kumi and settled into new work in Northern Uganda, they invited us to camp in their garden at Gulu. Winfred was by that time one of the patrol leaders. Richard Holden, who was the administrator at Kumi, kindly helped by driving one of the vehicles.

From Gulu we managed another long drive to the Murchison Falls National Park. The Guides walked proudly through the reception area in Paara Lodge and stood on the veranda looking down on the river Nile. The lodge was full of overseas visitors and our girls in their bright blue uniforms attracted considerable attention. A Canadian lady remarked enthusiastically:

"I suppose those girls see elephants every day."

"Oh, no!" I said. "None of them have seen anything like this before. The whole experience is new to them. You don't find animals outside the national parks."

The girls were apprehensive as they boarded two boats with whispered excitement for a trip on the River Nile. Crocodiles with their mouths wide open, displaying their sharp teeth and apricot coloured mouths, lay innocently on the banks. Hippos lazily floated in the water, only their small ears appearing above the surface. Giraffe, elephants and water buck had come to the edge of the water to drink and many beautiful birds delighted us with their bright colours. A goliath heron appeared, nearly five feet high and very majestic, and fish eagles sitting in the trees made their presence known with wild cries.

Everyone sang happily on the way back to camp. Winfred voiced the general feeling:

"We had been taught about these places, – but we never *knew* ..." and then: "Oh, I am so happy!"

She was fortunate to have been able to attend the Gulu camp. At the end of the previous year she had received her 'discharge certificate', as she was cured of leprosy. She went home sadly. She had been head prefect and she was the only *girl* in the school to have been top in a class. She still had two more years to complete in primary school and she knew her family would be unable to pay the fees.

At the beginning of the new year she came back to Kumi with the vague hope of finding some help. The school Matron very soon noticed her in one of the dormitories.

"You were discharged, isn't that right?" she asked Winfred.

Winfred had to admit that was true.

"But there is no money for school fees. I just want to

finish my education. My brother has died and my uncle quarrelled with my mother and went away. There is no one to help."

The Matron knew what a good record Winfred had and she liked to have girls who were polite and helpful.

"Come!" she said, "We will see what Sister Jordan has to say."

They found Dotty in the dispensary and explained the problem.

"They always try this on!" Dotty declared, and then, looking more carefully at Winfred, she changed her tone.

"Oh, let her stay! She's a good girl and we can easily pretend she isn't cured yet."

Winfred realised how fortunate she was but she also knew that at the end of the year she would have the same problem about money. 'I *must* find some way of getting fees for her' I thought. 'Thank goodness there is time to plan something.'

The Commissioner for Guiding in Buckinghamshire took up the challenge. She enthused the Companies in her area to such an extent that Winfred was able to remain at school for the next five years. I had the responsibility of keeping an eye on her progress. Sometimes in the holidays she would come and stay with me, and at the end of her school days she spent several weeks working in my department, teaching health education to the patients.

"What do you want to do now?" I asked her. "You said you wanted to nurse but it's very difficult to get into any of the big training schools. What about teaching?"

Winfred was adamant. She wanted to nurse. I gave her as much help as I could and to her delight she was offered a place at Mulago, the big Government Hospital in Kampala. Then came the bombshell. She was pregnant.

She knew I would be furious and I suppose I was. She would not be able to take her place on the course and would just have to go home to her mother. The father of the child was a boy with whom she had been friendly at school and I knew his parents. His father was a Canon in the Church and lived not far from Kumi.

Do not unsaddle your horse

Winfred wrote me a letter pleading for forgiveness:

'I beg for pardon from God, you and the people who have taken me as their child … I beg you as a mother not to give up your task until I have achieved my goal.'

She explained that she was determined to qualify for 'public service'.

'Unless,' she said, 'God really does not want me to serve.'

Finally she said: 'I don't need to remind you of how much love and assistance you have given me. I don't want this wasted and even if I fail in life I will make sure that you don't feel you have lost me or you have wasted your love.'

How could I *not* forgive her? After baby Samuel was born she again managed to get a place at the Mulago School of Nursing. When I left the country in 1976 she was in her first year. In due course she qualified as a State Registered Nurse but the rest of her story must come later.

Winfred (centre) at girl guide camp

Winfred as a student nurse

Margaret Akello

Our school was noted for its high standard in sports. This was largely due to the excellent headmaster, John Eluru. He was a keen Christian and full of enthusiasm and encouragement. There was plenty of time to coach the children because they were always in the compound and he entered the best athletes for sports competitions, often with surprising results.

Joyce Icumar was a tall and very active teenager. She was also one of my Girl Guides so I knew her well. Below are some extracts from a letter that she wrote, at my request, to our Guide friends in England:

'I like very much sports at school because you go places. You know, I did wonders at long jump, high jump, 800m, 400m, 4 by 100m relay and I did my level best in high jump and from County to District level I was first.'

Then she was taken to Kampala to compete nationally:

'We did finals and I became third in the whole of Uganda with 4ft 11in! (1.50m).'

When the sports were finished the competitors were taken on a tour of Kampala:

'We entered the National Assembly where the Government side votes with the opposition side and where the Speaker sits. If the President is in they ring a bell for them to be ready.

Guides, work hard ... I think you will be surprised to get a letter from me – and it is full of mistakes. We learn by mistakes. Let God be with all the Guides in England.'

One day I found Joyce visiting the adult patients at Ongino. She was talking with one of the most crippled patients, a woman who was only able to crawl because her feet had become so deformed. Later I discovered that this was Joyce's mother. They were very similar in facial appearance and also in character, for the mother was a very determined person who bravely took herself home when we had supplied her with special boots. There they were, mother and daughter, the one so crippled and the other so athletic! Once again I marvelled that so many children were found and brought for treatment in good time, so that they never suffered deformities and were saved from all the stigma and difficulties experienced by people like Joyce's mother.

When Joyce was cured of leprosy and discharged I lost touch with her, but apparently she had managed to enrol at a senior school. Lack of money forced her to give up after two years but she then took a course in hotel management, securing a job for a short time. After that she joined the prison service as a wardress and was soon promoted to a senior rank. One day an advertisement for a post at Kumi Leprosy Centre caught her eye. It was for a rehabilitation officer in my department and she applied under the name of Margaret Akello.

Why did she change her name? Perhaps she thought I would never consider employing one of my former Girl Guides! Hers was one of the promising letters so she was called for interview and was offered the job.

Margaret was an ideal person for her new role. She had sympathy but also great firmness. She patiently organised health education for groups of patients and ran a literacy class for those who could be encouraged to join. It seemed that she herself had been saved from the ravages of leprosy so that she could serve in a special way. To this day she is still in the same post.

* * * * *

I was getting to know so many courageous people and they inspired me to work as well as I possibly could. Often patients whose lives had been disrupted by leprosy, managed to turn a pending disaster into something new and positive.

Timon Onying had badly crippled hands and he became a very reliable storekeeper and a supervisor for the bougainvillea nursery that Eric had encouraged me to start as a rehabilitation project. Timon learned the names of the many different bougainvillea trees and patients worked under his guidance planting cuttings and tending them until they were ready for sale. Hundreds were sold every year.

John Esunget, a young senior schoolboy with a big patch of leprosy on his face, eventually became records clerk – proud of his ability to find any patient's record however old it was. Michael Olupot, with lepromatous leprosy and only one eye, held a senior position on the farm. Several of the very capable Leprosy Assistants had been leprosy sufferers themselves. I felt I gained far more from these people than I was ever able to give.

Chapter 8

'You must bear with one another's faults'

"I really admire you going out there with all those snakes and spiders. And how do you cope with the heat? You must miss your friends so much and you can't even enjoy a bowl of cornflakes for breakfast! It must be very hard. And you are struggling all day to understand what people are saying...."

"Oh, you get used to all that," I responded to the admiring group at one of my supporting Churches at home.

"Do you want to know the hardest thing of all?"

"Well, yes!"

"It's getting along peacefully with the other expatriates," I confessed. "You see, when I was in England my close friends were never my work colleagues. There were plenty of other people to be with in the evenings and at weekends. But in Uganda if I want to meet other expatriates I have to drive fifteen miles to the nearest mission hospital and often there isn't a vehicle available. So you are thrown together with people who you may find very difficult, and there's no escape!"

It was true. I had always thought it would be wonderful to work with people who were all committed Christians, but Satan sees danger in such groups and spends his time causing misunderstandings, thus weakening the witness and wearing people down.

During my first year at Kumi the small expatriate community held together well with Janet and Maurice at the helm. They were older than the rest of us and they were exceptionally caring and loving. When they moved to Northern Uganda heavy responsibilities were placed on much younger people who were all excellent in their own way but had far less experience. We then had some problems.

Nigel Walker arrived at Kumi shortly before Janet and Maurice's departure to take the place of a retiring 'Business Manager'. He had offered to spend a year at Kumi prior to being ordained for the ministry, having just completed his training at Theological College. He settled in with enthusiasm, trained a young Ugandan to cook and clean his house and aimed to upgrade the Centre's bookkeeping to 'London Standard'. (We were never quite sure what that term meant!) In the cool of the early morning I often noticed him walking slowly round our compound among the bougainvillea bushes reading his Bible.

"He obviously bases his life on the scriptures," Janet remarked, "So really nothing bad can possibly happen, can it?"

At about the same time a new nursing sister arrived to work with the adult patients. Jo was also young and enthusiastic. Her father, John Taylor, had at one time been principal of a Theological College in Uganda and Jo had spent her childhood there, so she had a special love for the country and was full of confidence and bright ideas.

Maurice's replacement was a newly qualified doctor, Dundas Moore who was also from England and, like Nigel, was sponsored by C.M.S. for one year. There was a shortage of houses, so Sheila and Dundas had to live with Nigel until Janet and Maurice left. It was good that Dundas had a few weeks learning about leprosy from Maurice but sharing a house with Nigel, when he and Sheila had not only to get used to an African hospital but also to being newly married, was almost a disaster. They needed space so that they could adjust to a completely new way of life.

"We don't want all this performance on Sundays with roast beef and Yorkshire pudding for lunch," Sheila complained to me. "We just want to have a proper rest on our own."

After the Moores had moved into their own house things were easier but never very smooth. Being the only doctor, Dundas was responsible not only for the patients but also for the staff if they became ill. He was extremely busy. Malaria was very common and cerebral malaria in children was a killer. Leprosy reactions needed skilful treatment and he also had to turn his hand to midwifery, surgery and treatment of TB. Early one morning the Ugandan farm manager, who worked closely with Eric, had a heart attack and died. Dundas had been treating him over the previous few days. Messages of the death were sent to both Dundas and Jo.

Dundas had been working very late the previous night and he did not immediately rush to confirm the death. Jo, on the other hand, was quickly at the house of the dead man. Mr Emochu had been greatly respected and already the news was spreading far and wide. People were wailing and chaos seemed to reign everywhere. Trying her very best to help, Jo arranged for the body to be driven straight away to Mr Emochu's real home where the funeral would have to take place. By the time Dundas arrived on the scene the body had gone.

Dundas was furious. As a conscientious doctor, medical etiquette was very important to him. We all spent a miserable day in the hospital where everyone was gloomy and nobody wanted to work. At teatime Jo came to my house.

"I only did it to try to help," she explained. "Everything was getting out of hand, and Dundas was such a long time coming – I thought he wasn't going to bother. Have you talked to him? Is he still angry?"

"I haven't really seen him," I said. "But I don't suppose he'll forget about it in a hurry. It's not your fault – in fact it isn't anyone's fault – it's a misunderstanding…"

Just then Dundas appeared at the door. Indeed he was still angry. He sat down and explained just how he felt. We were all very upset.

'Why do things like this have to happen when everyone is trying so hard to work well and show Christian compassion?' I wondered; but there was no escape from the situation – we just had to work our way through it and try to communicate better with each other. Later I noted in my diary the relevance of Colossians ch3 v13 (Knox's translation):

'You must bear with one another's faults, be generous to each other, where someone has given grounds for complaint, the Lord's generosity to you must be the model of yours.'

Dundas and Eric shouldered all the Centre's administration when Nigel left in July 1967. There was no news of a replacement. Sheila, who did some very useful work in the physiotherapy department, was leaving soon as she was pregnant with their first child, Jonathan, (who was later to become my godson), and Dundas was to follow her few months later. We were going to be very short of staff.

In fact we were starting a period of nine months when we had no resident doctor. Eric coped nobly with all the administration and Jo and Dotty managed the medical work with occasional visits of doctors from other hospitals. Jo showed great initiative especially with the leprosy assistant students. These young men were selected by Medical Officers in the various districts of Uganda where more leprosy workers were needed. They came for two years and we usually had a total of twenty-four at any one time. Their work in the hospital had to be supervised and lectures had to be arranged. As they came from many tribal areas with different languages, they always had to speak English. We encouraged them to attend the Christian Fellowship meetings and many of them were happy to do so.

"What about having some debates?" Jo said.

"Okay," I said, "What topic do you suggest?"

"How about 'There is no God?' That should challenge them."

The meetings were held in the evenings under the trees in the hospital compound and when the patients saw so many students and staff gathering there, they joined the group, sitting just near enough to hear what was going on. Some of them understood a little English and they translated the gist of the argument to the others.

The debate was lively, even though it had been difficult to find anyone to propose the motion. The student who *did* agree to do so was actually the keenest Christian in the group. He used all the arguments he could think of:

"If there is a God – and he is supposed to be loving – then he would never allow the suffering we see around us," he declared, in an effort to be really convincing. "And you men, you have all studied science and the world is so complicated that it *must* have been formed by science not by a God making some sort of magic…"

As far as I can remember he didn't win, but as we were preparing to go home a certain very crippled patient who had probably understood very little, came along angrily to Jo and, in Ateso, reprimanded her very sternly:

"How dare you come to us here in Uganda with your bad ideas," he said. "Of course there is a God. Who do you think made the grass, the cattle and all the things we have around us?"

Still muttering angrily to himself, he stumped off into the dusk before anyone was able to explain to him that a debate is just a sort of game.

Roland Huskinson was our leprosy control field officer and like the rest of us, he was also involved in the training of the students. Husky, as we called him, had worked for L.E.P.R.A. for many years in Nigeria. He had met and married his wife, Edith, there and she joined him at Kumi from time to time when she felt able to leave their two teenage sons in England.

Husky was very talkative and he delighted in recounting stories from Nigeria – things that had happened 'over the other side'. He gave some lectures on clinical leprosy and when someone else took over from him and asked the students what they had already been taught, their united reply was:

"We have learned about Nigeria."

Husky had a heart of gold and a great sense of humour but he was rather deaf and if you wanted him to listen to what *you* wished to tell him, you had to be quite firm.

* * * * *

Do not unsaddle your horse

"I wonder what he will be like," I said, "So much is going to depend on him."

We had been told that a Dr Bert Landheer from Holland was coming to Kumi as Medical Superintendent. The Netherlands Leprosy Foundation as well as C.M.S. was sponsoring him.

Tall and lanky with reddish, auburn hair and smartly dressed, he appeared a little out of place. He must have struggled more than most of us to get accustomed to his new surroundings. He particularly hated the outside 'deep drop' latrine at his house and vowed that he would get a proper toilet inside even if he had to do the work himself. The fact that he never got his toilet was a reflection of how many other jobs he was to find of greater importance.

A few months after Bert's arrival I went home to England for my first leave. On my return six months later, I found him bursting with ideas and frustrated that he could not put them into practice quickly. He wanted better qualified African staff and training for other medical workers, especially medical students. Soon our only expatriate nurse who had come to work on a temporary basis, decided to leave and for nine months we had no replacement. I found this even more difficult than having no doctor. Bert could work through all the hours of the day and night if he felt he should and he expected other people to do the same. Although he was very ambitious, I considered his ideas to be reasonable and I wanted to support him all I could. We often worked late into the night with plans and letters that always seemed to be urgent. I was needed to ensure that the letters were clear and in perfect English. (Bert's English was very good but he was extremely particular.) We were thrown together and it wasn't easy. I admired him, so I found it difficult to refuse extra work. Sometimes we visited outpatient clinics together, once we went to Kampala on business. Our relationship was entirely based on work but people put their own interpretations on what they saw and at one time a rumour spread widely that we were engaged.

One evening we worked till midnight on a special request for funding from the West German Leprosy Relief Association. Their representative was at Buluba, the big Catholic Leprosy Hospital about 150 miles away. Bert took the final drafts to his house and typed out the detailed document through the early hours of the morning.

"You stay awake," he told me. "Then as soon as I have it ready, you drive with it to Buluba. The man is leaving for Germany later in the day and we have to get it to him before he goes."

At dawn I started the journey. Frequently I had to pull off the road and rest for a while as I kept falling asleep.

It was amazing that we were kept safe from any serious road accidents. I remember accompanying Bert on a week-long safari to Karamoja District – a primitive area in the northeast. In those days the Karamajong did not wear western type clothes: the men simply wore a dark cloth over one shoulder and ostrich feathers in their elaborate mud headdresses and they strode around with their cattle carrying a small stool and a long spear as they searched for patches of pasture in the semi-desert scrub. The women wore skirts made of skins and numerous strings of beads and metal rings round their necks, wrists and ankles.

The murram (dirt) roads were challenging, especially when it rained. The leprosy assistant who came with us had never been to the area before and was suitably impressed.

"When you drive through the rivers," he said to me, "We are all driving with you!"

Bert and I shared the driving. On the way home it was my turn. We had had a puncture and someone at a Catholic Mission where we had stayed the previous night had fixed the spare wheel on the vehicle for us. The truck was heavily loaded because we had several leprosy patients on board who had agreed to come to Kumi for treatment for their very severe foot ulcers. They were the most needy we had seen at the various clinics and they were gloomy and rather smelly. About

---

Do not unsaddle your horse

fifty miles from Kumi the truck gave a considerable shudder. I held the steering wheel as firmly as I could and came to a halt in a cloud of dust. Clambering out of the driving seat I was horrified to see, lying some distance behind us in the road, the wheel that had been changed earlier in the day. It was impossible to screw it on again because the thread on all the studs had been badly damaged. The wheel must have been loose for miles and I had not noticed it because of the rough road.

We were stuck! Soroti town was twenty miles away and Bert hitched a lift on a passing vehicle. It seemed an endless wait for the leprosy assistant, the miserable patients and me by the side of the dusty road, but just as it was getting dark, Bert returned in a truck with some Indians and we were soon towed skilfully to the town. I suppose those helpful mechanics must have found us a vehicle so that we could complete our journey that night; all I can remember is that we did reach home safely. The safari had been a success: we had seen many patients, encouraged and taught the leprosy assistants who were treating them and assessed the particular needs of the district. We had also had the joy of seeing a large flock of ostrich running alongside our vehicle when we were travelling at about thirty miles an hour. The huge birds overtook us effortlessly, crossed the road in front of our vehicle and finally disappeared between the thorn trees heading towards the distant blue mountains.

* * * * *

"The first lot of medical students arrive tomorrow," Bert announced one day.

"How will we manage?" I asked. His plans were at last taking shape, but were we taking on too much?

In his meticulous way he had employed a fairly experienced houseboy to prepare one of the empty houses at Kumi, acquired bed linen from somewhere, sent for food and organised transport to bring the students to Ongino each day.

"They'll be here for two weeks," he said. "I'll do most of the lecturing but I'll need everyone to help. The university has agreed to send four at a time. It's too good an opportunity to miss, so we must get on and do it."

The place was buzzing with activity. Various staff members had been sent on courses to upgrade their work, including the records clerk, a laboratory assistant and one or two nurses assistants. Then suddenly Bert's persistent requests for Dutch staff sponsored by the Netherlands Leprosy Foundation were successful and in the early 70s we welcomed three married couples with four small children. This provided us with two nurses, a physiotherapist and a builder.

The whole character of the work seemed to change overnight. Bert particularly enjoyed having Dick de Kruijf, an experienced nurse, with whom he could discuss his plans. I began to feel very left out. The Dutch people always spoke among themselves in their own language, although they knew how hard it was for me to be excluded. No doubt they had enough to get used to without having to speak English. Bert realised the difficulties and made a great effort to hold us all together by arranging social evenings every Saturday and by getting a tennis court made so that we could play together after work.

With all his new staff Bert's energy knew no bounds. Plans for buildings now went ahead: a new outpatient block, a theatre, a ward, a training centre and dining room for students and a proper kitchen and laundry for the hospital.

"You draw plans for a new workshop," Bert told me. "Try to look ahead and think what will be needed when we have more trained staff. And find out how much space is needed round machinery – there must be some safety rules about that."

I drew an ambitious plan. The building was 164 feet long. It was going to dwarf the present building that would remain adjacent to the new one. I included two large workshops, a machine room, two offices, a tearoom, toilets and an enormous storeroom. Past experience had taught me that there could never be too much storage space.

One evening while I was still working on the plan I had a bright idea. I mentioned it to Bert the next day.

"I've never heard of a shoe-fitting pit," I said, "But what do you think of the idea? It would be like a pit in a garage for inspecting cars. The patients would sit at the side and the technicians would go down into the pit and fit the shoes at a comfortable level – much easier than grovelling around on the floor."

Bert liked the idea. He knew it would be useful because we had just started using Plastazote for moulded shoes and the calor gas oven we had made for heating the material could be accommodated in the pit as well. I smiled as I remembered how I had learned about the use of Plastazote for orthopaedic footwear.

It was during my home leave that I had visited a hospital near London where a certain Mr Tuck worked. He had invented the material – a foamed polyethylene with low heat absorption called Plastazote. Pieces of this half-inch material were cut slightly larger than the patient's foot, heated and moulded straight onto the foot. A shoe could be made around the trimmed piece of Plastazote.

"Come and see some of our patients being fitted," Mr Tuck suggested after he had explained some of his techniques. "This morning we have two patients with Hansen's disease coming in – so you'll really feel at home."

Sure enough the patients had already arrived. They were quite badly disabled – two English leprosy patients, grumbling, in the same way as our Kumi patients:

"It's the shoes that are wrong! No, our feet are not the problem. The shoes give us ulcers. You're not getting it right. We need good shoes, we can't be sitting around all day, we need to walk…"

When the technicians, who were patiently trying to satisfy these patients, had completed their work they asked why I was interested in Plastazote.

"I work with leprosy patients in Uganda," I told them.
To my surprise they were horrified.
"What! Leprosy! What precautions do you take yourself?"
Hiding my amusement I gave them a few brief facts about leprosy without letting them know that Hansen's disease is the other name for leprosy.

* * * * *

One day a young man called John Michael Amusio turned up at my workshop asking for employment. This happened very frequently and we usually sent the enquirer away without a thought but Amusio had completed four years in secondary school and Bert thought he might be of a high enough standard to do some training. Mulago Hospital in Kampala was advertising a course in artificial limb-making, so we decided to sponsor him. He set off for six months with great confidence to join trainees from many other African countries and we hoped he would not be disillusioned when he had to work alongside technicians who already had good practical skills.

The course was organised by the World Rehabilitation Fund and the instructor was a very expert and energetic Spanish man named Juan Monros. Most of the patients that had been gathered in required below knee prostheses. The technique involved making a plaster cast of the patient's stump, modifying it so that pressure was taken on the correct places and then making the socket of the prosthesis around it using stockinet and epoxy resin. The socket was mounted on wooden blocks and a jointed foot was added. The patient was then encouraged to walk so that the alignment could be checked before the wood was shaped and the whole limb laminated again with more stockinet and resin.

We were thrilled when Amusio qualified. I attended the graduating ceremony in Kampala. The Secretary of the World Rehabilitation Fund had flown in from New York and the trainees were made to feel very important. I was not sure that this

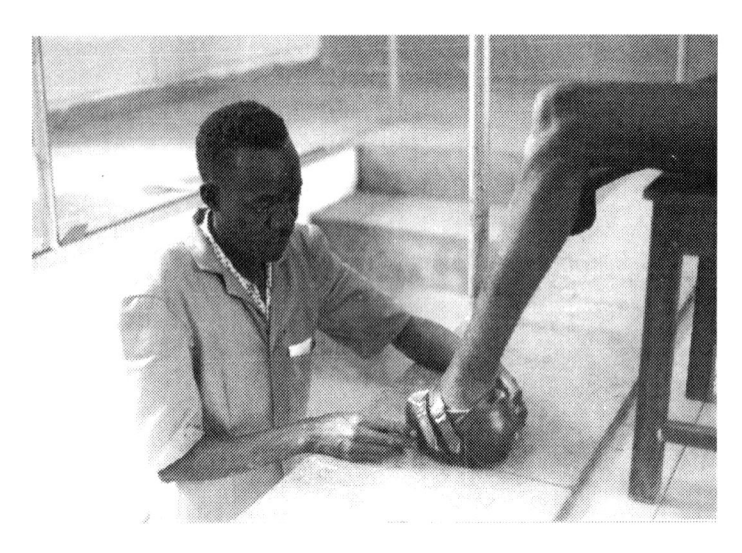

Above: Checking a plastozote shoe in the fitting pit
Below: Max working on an artificial limb

was a good idea. Amusio needed to prove his skills at Kumi before he deserved too much praise or even the rise in salary that he was sure to expect. He made a reasonable start when I had managed to obtain the necessary materials but Livingstone eyed him with some reservation:

"He is a big man now. But let him *show* us how good he is. Otherwise we will know that he has just wasted money down there in Kampala."

Unfortunately Livingstone's judgment was warranted. Before long Amusio was arriving late for work, very much the worse for drink. Then after some weeks he suddenly improved.

"I had some strong words with him," Livingstone said.

But even the strongest words did not have a lasting effect. It was very sad. We had not selected our candidate carefully enough. Later I got to know a Catholic Brother who ran a Rural Trade School in Soroti. He kindly recommended his very best students to me and eventually I employed four of his men, one of whom, Max Acamun, is in charge of the workshop today – an excellent and very well qualified technician.

* * * * *

The expatriate staff took it in turns to go on a weekly shopping expedition to Mbale, thirty miles to the south. Shopping lists had to be collected from everyone the night before as an early start was advisable. Sometimes people did not bring their lists and you had to go to their houses to collect them.

"Have you any newspaper?" I would often ask. "You know, they very often don't have any in the meat shop. It makes things a bit difficult if the meat gets wrapped in banana leaves."

"Do try and get some bread this week," someone might urge. "There was none last week and we aren't very good at making it."

Bert would usually have patients to be taken to the Government Hospital for X-rays as we had no facilities for this.

"There's Odeke to go – oh, and that woman – Amuge -

with the severe foot ulcer. She's refusing amputation and I need to see if the foot is really as hopeless as it looks – and two in the TB Ward for chest X-rays. Can you manage?"

This sort of request made me groan. The Government Hospital staff hated our patients. Two of these would need wheelchairs and even if these were available it was only sweepers who were allocated the job of helping to move the patients and they were hard to find. It all took considerable time and patience. Then there was the visit to the grocery shop, the bakery, the butcher and the market.

For all its confusion I enjoyed the market. The stallholders were cheery and cheeky, vying with each other to gain the attention of the Kumi shoppers because they knew we always bought large quantities of fruit and vegetables. There were piles of cabbages, egg plants, carrots and sweet potatoes; huge pineapples were heaped up on rickety wooden tables together with oranges, tangerines, bananas and passion fruit and large stems of matoke on the ground. I always had to make several trips to the truck with a heavy cardboard box for each family.

One bonus for doing the shopping was visiting my friend Edith Evans, a head teacher who lived in Mbale. She was usually home at lunch-time and was always wonderfully welcoming. Being employed by the Government, Edith had a lovely house and garden in a smart area.

"She's the only person I've met who has a proper house," Bert declared. "She has a carpet on the floor!"

I valued Edith's friendship. It was so good to spend the occasional weekend with her at her house and over the years we had several good holidays together. These breaks were very necessary as the pressure to forge ahead with so many new developments at Kumi was relentless.

"We'll make Lee Airport!"

Bert sounded jubilant. It was his latest bright idea.

"You see, if we have an air strip the Flying Doctors can come in from Nairobi and do some reconstructive surgery. We'll call it Lee Airport after Maurice Lee!"

Huge rocks had to be dug out and a suitable strip of land levelled but the job was completed in a few months. Of course the visiting surgeons would need a proper theatre but this was nearly completed. I well remember supervising the fixing of the huge, powerful lamp to the ceiling of the main theatre when Bert was away for a few days. It was one of the final jobs.

Whether all these new developments should have happened so fast is debatable. Bert had such clear vision as to what he considered necessary and he knew his plans could never be implemented during his time in Uganda unless he pushed ahead very fast. But could everyone else keep up with him, especially the African staff? Was he creating a very affluent hospital that was out of keeping with local standards? Was the place becoming a target for thieves? Would such a large leprosy centre be viable in the years ahead when the prevalence of leprosy might be much less? We did not like to think about these things too much. We knew that ever since the first missionaries had reached Uganda many mistakes had been made and we hoped we were not making a lot more.

I was frequently made aware of prayer support from many friends in England. Often when I wrote about a particular problem, things would become easier even before I received a reply. Somehow through all the struggles and mistakes there *were* many good developments and if life was tough I could always say to God:

"It was *your* idea to bring me here, not mine, so you must give me the strength to manage."

But soon there were to be some drastic changes that would affect the whole of Uganda. Everything at Kumi was going to become much more difficult.

Chapter 9
The days of Idi Amin

In January 1971 there was a coup. While President Milton Obote was out of the country, an army officer, General Idi Amin Dada took control. At Kumi we received the news twenty-four hours after the event. Apparently everyone in Kampala was happy; people were dancing in the streets. Bert was in Kampala at the time and on his return he had some rather more alarming stories to tell: many people known as Obote's supporters had been killed and others had disappeared. Obote was a Northerner, so people from that part of the country were at risk and many went into hiding. We relied on the World Service of the BBC for accurate news. Ugandan radio broadcast many untrue rumours, such as: 'The British have bombed Entebbe airport', and 'Kenya has invaded Uganda'.

"Who is Idi Amin?" I asked.

No one seemed to know much about him.

"He did his army training in your country," one of the Ugandan staff told me. "So maybe he will be very kind to British people."

"He's a Moslem," someone else volunteered. "He comes from one of the tribes up in the North-west – bordering on the Sudan."

Everything remained quiet in Teso apart from a few minor incidents. Elimilech told me one day that soldiers had been round the villages demanding that people hand in any shirts or other garments which bore the picture of Milton Obote. (Material with the President's picture on it had been very popular.)

"It was all right," Elimilech said. "They only wanted the clothes; they did not beat anyone."

On another occasion a small crowd of people who had been standing around in Kumi Township just as it was getting dark, were all rounded up and taken to the police station. They knew there was a 'curfew' but had not understood what it meant. Among their number was the Anglican Rural Dean, an elderly and highly respected man. When the soldiers realised who he was they released him at once, but the rest were held overnight.

Bert went on leave to Holland a few months after the coup. His vision for the work was vast and he planned to visit several European countries to encourage our donors to give generously. The population of the area we covered was nearly three million and we were treating 11,112 leprosy patients. It was estimated that there were another 31,657 untreated cases. Bert planned to argue that although our work needed to be based on outpatient clinics, we still needed better buildings at the Centre because of the need for training all grades of medical personnel.

As an independent establishment the Centre was funded from many different sources. The Ugandan Government and the Districts that we served gave grants; C.M.S., The Leprosy Mission, the British Leprosy Relief Association, the Netherlands Leprosy Foundation, Emmaus Suisse and the German Leprosy Relief Association all gave support. There was a Board of Governors that met regularly to plan and approve developments.

Jane was coming on a visit to Uganda and I was excited. Despite all the uncertainties we went on holiday to the south-west staying a few nights on the beautiful Bwama Island on Lake Bunyoni that had once been a leprosy hospital and in the Queen Elizabeth National Park, where we saw tree lions and other wonderful animals and birds. I wrote home happily to the Churches that supported me:

'This is a marvellous country with tremendous opportunities and there are many dedicated Ugandans in responsible positions. Pray that it may remain peaceful...'

One day a tall, well-built young man with a German accent arrived at Kumi.

"You did not receive ze letter?" he enquired when he was

greeted with some suspicion. "Herr Kober said he had written. You need a new farm manager – yes?"

We laughed.

"No we haven't had a letter, but you are welcome. How was your journey? Most people expect to be collected from Kampala…"

"Oh, dat vas very easy," he replied nonchalantly.

His name was Wolfgang Wotjinnek and later we discovered why he had travelled in such a carefree manner. He had escaped from East Germany some years before by scaling the Berlin Wall. He never told us the full story for fear of any repercussions. He was obviously a daring character but could he ever fill the gap that Eric would leave?

Eric found it very hard to be going home after sixteen years of dedicated work. Kumi had been his life and he had put all his thoughts and energy into building up the farm and the Centre as a whole. It was only for the sake of the children that he had finally agreed with Kay that the family must return to England. They hated sending the two older ones to a boarding school in Kenya, especially now when safety in travelling was less predictable. Idi Amin was making his presence felt with roadblocks manned by unruly soldiers who were often drunk. Sometimes the lake seven miles from Ongino was said to contain so many dead bodies that people stopped fishing. Amin's troops had been given the command to do anything necessary to 'maintain public order and security'.

I tried to think of all the questions I needed to ask Eric before he left. It was he who had encouraged me to start the nursery for growing bougainvillea trees from cuttings as part of the rehabilitation programme and we were selling hundreds of plants every year. I wanted to be sure I had the names of all the different varieties as well as the many different hibiscus shrubs and exotic fruit trees.

One of Eric's final jobs was to make a new four and a half mile by-pass road for the Centre so that we would not be troubled by through traffic. He was busy laying drainage pipes that went under the new road in an area that tended to flood until a few hours before the big farewell party which had been arranged for the family the night before they left. The gathering, held outside after dark, was attended by all the staff and as many of the farm workers and patients who could crowd in. There were some emotional speeches. Eric's contribution to the Centre was not going to be quickly forgotten.

Dotty retired in 1971, so there was another farewell party. She had worked for many years with the children in her own blunt but very reliable way. She enjoyed a glass of beer every evening and shared her lonely existence with a much loved and overweight Spaniel, Fais (Faith). I was sad to see Dotty go; she had a kind heart for all her bluff and I wondered how she would adapt to life in a flat in the centre of London. Fais was given to Benjamin, her houseboy, when she left and for several years she sent him money for dog food. Eventually, a long time after the dog had died, word reached Dotty that the money should be stopped.

The new staff members recruited from Holland and Germany were not necessarily Christians. Leprosy is a fascinating disease and people with the right qualifications, a sense of adventure and an urge to help the poor on humanitarian grounds were gratefully accepted by many of the leprosy organisations, which also paid good salaries to their workers. When conditions in Uganda became less stable some of our new staff may have regretted their decision to come, especially if they had young children.

Douglas and Jean Coffin arrived early in 1972 sponsored by the British Leprosy Relief Association. They had worked for twenty years in Malawi and were not very enthusiastic about their move. However, their experience was invaluable and Doug took over the training programme with great efficiency. The newly built training centre was complete and we had thirty-three students who were housed in much better conditions.

I was getting excited about my home leave that was planned for July 1972. On the recommendation of Juan Monros, the World Rehabilitation Fund had offered to pay for me to attend one of their conferences to be held in Sydney, Australia, and C.M.S. agreed to pay the airfare. Philip and Mary Richmond had emigrated to Melbourne some years before so I planned to visit them as well as seeing some of the work at Karigiri, a leprosy centre in South India. I was busy making preparations for my departure so that the work would carry on as smoothly as possible. I made sure that there were sufficient supplies of shoe and limb-making materials, cotton thread for weaving, rolls of the plastic tubing used for making bags for the plants in the nursery and paints and paper for Livingstone. A programme of health education was needed to ensure that regular sessions would continue, and all the staff had to be briefed on their various responsibilities. The new workshop building was progressing well with a good Indian contractor and I was sad to think that I would not be there for its completion.

Edith Evans saw me off on the train at Tororo. I was going to Nairobi for a couple of nights before flying to India. I remember thanking God that I had reached the day of my departure safely. I had often heard African Christians praying in that same way and I had never understood why they made such a big thing of it. Now I could say it myself because the previous three and a quarter years had been extremely tough. In every way it had been exhausting working for Bert and there had been the added uncertainty of life in Uganda under such an unpredictable President as Idi Amin who was so often making threats (mostly against the British) and hitting the headlines in the world media with his outrageous statements.

"Have a marvellous time," Edith told me, "And look out for the way the Holy Spirit is working in exciting ways. All sorts of signs and miracles are happening around the world..."

I knew what she meant. Edith herself had experienced a new baptism in the Spirit and some other friends had recently been blessed in special ways giving them renewed hope in the midst of many difficulties.

Fortunately I was spending two nights at St Julians (a Guest House run by a Christian community near Nairobi). I had spent a good night in a sleeping compartment on the train as it slowly chugged along its way, but I was exhausted and sick, so I spent the time in bed, cared for and no doubt prayed for by the small community, one of whom kindly took me to the airport at the appointed time.

As I emerged from the plane at Bombay it felt as if I was entering a bathroom where the hot tap had been left running for several hours. I never expected such humidity. I flew on to Madras and hired a taxi to take me to the railway station. Here I was besieged by 'porters' wanting to carry my luggage. One of them grabbed my two suitcases and rushed ahead of me so fast that I feared I would not be able to keep up with him in the crowds. I caught sight of him stopping momentarily to give one case to another man. Of course they both demanded payment when I caught up with them. It was all very confusing. Everyone seemed to be rushing, talking, begging for money.... It was a new and somewhat alarming culture for me, so unlike Africa.

I struggled into a crowded carriage and checked with its curious but friendly occupants that I was on the Bangalore line and that the train would take me to Katpadi. People nodded reassuringly but no one tried to speak any English. A small boy came along the corridor and did some tricks, squeezing himself through a small hoop and collecting a few coins for his performance. Through the window I watched the countryside – people toiling in rice fields and others moving slowly with bullock carts. Three hours later I reached my destination.

The week at Karigiri was useful and fascinating. The large leprosy hospital and training centre for leprosy workers was quite a show place. I picked up some ideas for health education as well as shoe and limb making although the shoes and limbs were of a much higher standard than our workers at Kumi were capable of making. I realised that this was partly because appearances mattered so much more in India but I was still anxious to upgrade our work.

Reconstructive surgery was performed regularly. Again it was much more necessary here than in Africa for no one with a clawed hand would ever be employed in India, nor anyone who had lost his eyebrows as a result of leprosy. In Africa appearances did not matter too much; the main need was for people to be able to work with their hands. Reconstructive surgery could straighten fingers but it would never give back the feeling that had been lost through damaged nerves. Indians, I could see, tended to follow the advice given them about caring for their anaesthetic hands and feet much more readily than Africans.

At the end of my stay in India I flew from Bombay to Perth in Western Australia. There couldn't have been a greater contrast. In Bombay people were living in cardboard boxes on rubbish dumps where children scavenged like chickens. Travelling in a taxi through the streets was embarrassing as half-starved women and children stood at the traffic lights waiting for the cars to stop so that they could knock on the windows and beg for coins. They peered in with desperate, dark eyes.

Mary Richmond's sister, Hannah, met me in Perth (she had been living there for some years) and during my overnight stop in the city she showed me around the shopping area and took me to a most beautiful park. It was late winter but the day was bright and spring-like and the air was fresh and invigorating. The luxury of everything was almost too much to cope with. My mind flashed back to the poverty of India and the pathetic life of so many of our patients at Kumi. Why was the world so unbalanced?

It was refreshing to be with Mary and Philip again although our different circumstances had made us grow apart in some ways. They had a bungalow at Werribee, near Melbourne, and another at Airey's Inlet on the coast to the south where there were marvellous walks through the bush. Kangaroos sometimes appeared close to the house in the early morning; we hunted for koalas and Mary pointed out many of the exciting birds by sight or song: small parrot-like red rosellas, blue wrens and the laughing kookaburras. I enjoyed the gentle greens of the bush with its many varieties of eucalyptus trees and flowering shrubs and all the different places I visited with my old friends but on the whole I found Australians very insular. Their continent is so large and they did not seem to have much interest in what happened outside it. They aimed for the 'good life', which meant having sufficient cars, camping and sports equipment so that they could enjoy every bit of spare time to the full. People did not know where Uganda was or what was happening there. In the back of my mind were always the questions:

'What's happening at Kumi now? What is Idi Amin up to?'

Almost as soon as I arrived in Australia news had come that Idi Amin was expelling all the Asians in the country who had British passports. (Earlier in the year he had expelled all the Israelis.) This did not seem too bad but a few weeks later I learned that he was expelling *all* Asians even those who had Ugandan passports and those who had no passports at all. There was a deadline of a few weeks for them all to be out of the country.

The implications of this expulsion were enormous. There were thousands of Asians in Uganda. Many of them were wealthy with bank accounts in the U.K. but others were poor and elderly. Idi Amin reckoned they were 'milking the economy' because they owned most of the shops and businesses. It was all part of the 'Economic War' that he was waging in the country. Our building contractor was an Asian – what would happen now to all the unfinished buildings at Kumi? All the little 'dukas' at Kumi were Asian owned and the post office was run by Asians. The garages where we got our vehicles repaired and the small supermarket in Mbale, in fact everything you could think of, depended on Asians. They owned the huge tea plantations, manned the hydroelectric works and ran the big Nytil factory that produced cloth widely used for school and hospital uniforms and other clothing.

In spite of these thoughts I managed to enjoy my holiday. A two day car journey took us to Sydney and during the week-long conference Philip and Mary hired a boat on the Murray River, cruising upstream and returning to collect me after a few days so that I could enjoy the river too.

"How did it go?" Mary asked.

She had helped me buy an outfit as I was to take part in a leprosy panel speaking on disability and I had no suitable clothes to wear.

"It was fine. I met Paul Brand and Grace Warren." (Both these doctors were leading experts in leprosy.) "And I had good discussions with some leprosy workers from Northern Australia and Papua New Guinea. They even wanted me to go and see the work there! But that's out of the question. I want to get on this boat now," I said impatiently. Some of the conference had been hard going, listening to rather involved papers that were not relevant to my work.

We idled upstream in the boat as far as we dared. Soon I had to fly to London, but I revelled in the beautiful scenery as the hours slipped by. Sometimes we rowed ashore in a little boat to buy food at small stores, exploring the mangrove swamps on our way back and occasionally we swam from the boat. The lower part of the river was tidal and Philip's calculations proved inaccurate when on the last afternoon we got stuck on a sandbank with the tide still on its way down.

"We can't possibly make it back to the starting place in time for your plane," he confessed, "I'm really sorry…"

"I *must* get that plane," I told him anxiously. "Can't I get ashore here and get to the airport by road?"

Fortunately this was possible. The last few hours were spent watching kookaburras close up on an island. Then there was a sad farewell as Philip rowed me to the bank and escorted me to a small railway station. The only problem was that my winter coat got left behind in the Richmond's car.

* * * * *

As on my previous home leave, I made my main base at Pam and Graeme's home at West Malling. Two miles away were some disused council office buildings and these were now housing a large number of Ugandan Asians. Local people were working hard to find homes for them and sort out their problems. Meanwhile there was more confusion in Uganda. A small army of Tanzanian soldiers had invaded Uganda in support of Obote. Nothing came of this but many expatriates started to leave Uganda because of the new insecurity. I was keen to get news from Kumi but letters were very few. They were getting lost or censored and one that I did receive from Bert was so heavily disguised by him that even *I* could not understand all that he was trying to say.

'It is difficult to write. So many thoughts in my head and so few words available to use. Gulzar (the building contractor) has left. All building work has stopped. Workshop still not ready. No hope of any building supervisor yet. If you can think of any please help, because I am desperate.'

In a secretive way he let me know that many people were being killed, that the country would take a long time to recover, that Dick and three of the Dutch wives and their children had gone to Holland and that I could write to Dick for news.

He added, 'I have gone back to my early school days when we used to sing (in Dutch) 'The God of Love my Shepherd is'. It helps, but you read Job 3:26.'

I looked up the reference in Job. It said:

'I am not at ease, nor am I quiet: I have no rest; but trouble comes.'

I wrote to Dick in Holland and received a reply by return of post. He and his wife Ella had been due for home leave but the Netherlands Embassy in Kampala had advised all women and children to leave Uganda, so that was why they had all left in a hurry. Dick said that they did not discuss anything with the African staff because they didn't know who to trust and there were reports of so many bad things happening. The African who they chose to drive them was one of the most reliable senior staff members though he was not a particularly good driver. Their journey to Kampala had been complicated by the fact that one of the wives had recently given birth to her first child. She had developed a breast infection which had been incised and she was so poorly on the journey that Dick was having to give her intravenous injections because she was sick if she tried to swallow antibiotics. However, because the soldiers at the many roadblocks could see that she was ill, they were saved the ordeal of opening all the suitcases on three occasions. Unfortunately not all the soldiers were so sympathetic and this caused lengthy delays. Dick wrote:

'At some checkpoints nearly everyone was drunk and really I was so afraid, but I did my best not to show it. The first question they asked was, 'Are you English? Do you disappear?' On the radio all these people are indoctrinated that the English helped the Tanzanians to invade Uganda, and of course everyone believes that when they hear it every hour. After we said we were Dutch they asked, 'Where are you going? Who is doing your job now? Are you coming back?' When we said 'Yes' they were a bit easier but on the whole it was quite unpleasant.'

Many expatriates left Uganda at this time but those who remained, quietly carrying on with their work, were greatly appreciated by their African colleagues. Things settled down somewhat after the initial panic. People knew that if they had to travel they would be confronted by many roadblocks and that when they went shopping they would have difficulty in getting basic foods like sugar, salt and bread.

The whole future looked uncertain for me but I was encouraged and blessed by the Ryarsh Church Fellowship. Malcolm Bury, who was vicar at the time, and his wife Charmian, as well as Pam, had all received special gifts of the Spirit similar to those that Edith had spoken about. Some of this rubbed off onto me. I set out on a very busy time of deputation, visiting the seven Churches to which I was officially linked through C.M.S. as well as many other contacts such as the Girl Guide companies that supported us at Kumi. During my six months' leave I slept in sixty different beds. At each of the Churches I was expected to stay for a weekend, during which I might be asked to speak as many as five times, including preaching and showing slides.

One of these Churches was St Giles in the Fields in central London where the parish consisted mostly of offices, the congregation travelling in from other parts of London. Gordon Taylor, the Rector, particularly wanted a link with someone who worked with leprosy sufferers because their beautiful Church stood on the site of an old leprosy hospital. During my previous leave the members of the Church Council had simply invited me to a smart restaurant near Trafalgar Square for a meal so that they could get to know me. This time I was not only invited for a meal but also to preach at Evensong. It was a very sophisticated Church and I was treated with great respect.

"When you preach," Gordon Taylor asked, "Will you speak from the chancel steps or from the pulpit?"

Without hesitation I opted for the pulpit. I did not have too much difficulty in making myself heard but I knew my message would be clearest if I had the higher position. Gordon Taylor nodded seriously and instructed his verger accordingly, so that the man knew where he had to lead me when the time came. After the service was over people seemed satisfied and Gordon Taylor nodded his approval.

"We have only once before had a lady speak at our services," he mused. "She was the wife of the Archbishop of Canterbury. She spoke from the chancel steps."

It was not difficult to speak about the work at Kumi or to link it with Bible passages. I had many transparencies and these helped to illustrate our need for funds and for prayer, thus helping C.M.S. to boost interest in the Churches. I was relieved that I was not expected to attend their training college during this leave. Maybe I was now acceptable.

It had not always been like that. At the end of my first tour Norman Campbell, as C.M.S. representative in Uganda, had tried to say that I needed training as a missionary. He was very uncomplimentary about me and very unfortunately his secretary put the letter he wrote to C.M.S. in the wrong envelope and it came to me instead of Meredith Sinclair in London. I was deeply upset and everyone concerned was very embarrassed. Meredith felt she knew me well enough not to take the contents of the letter too seriously and gently arranged for me to attend the C.M.S. training college at Chislehurst for just two weeks.

After this I had to visit three members of the candidates' committee in their own homes. This was slightly tiresome because I found myself having to explain the same things three times over. In each case the interviews included lunch and each time there were baked potatoes in their jackets. By the end of the third visit I felt sure that part of the test was to see if I would eat the potato skins. I made sure I ate every bit, even though on one occasion there still seemed to be some soil on the skin that had not been washed off.

I must have passed the test for my second tour had been as an 'associate' rather than a short term C.M.S. member and now that it seemed that I was going back for a third tour I was told that I could be a proper C.M.S. missionary. Certainly I had come in by the back door!

I returned to Uganda in January 1973. Two Dutchmen who had gone to Holland to join their wives for a short holiday had arrived back at Kumi just before me together with Dick. So once again the senior staff was complete, although Dick and the physiotherapist only stayed for three months before finally leaving.

I wrote home: 'Nothing surprises me very much; things are very different. Supplies of everything are difficult. We are struggling to finish buildings that were nearly completed when our Asian contractor left six months ago. There is fear and uncertainty that can result in apathy towards work. I wonder what threads to pick up and what to leave. I have been encouraged to find that the orthopaedic workshop staff carried on well with the work even though they have not yet moved into the new building.'

It was only after I had written this that I discovered that the workshop staff had been gathering together for prayers every morning before work. Laurence Angatai, the workshop supervisor, had been on a course at the training centre at Addis Ababa where this had been the practice, so he had introduced the idea at Kumi. Someone read a Bible passage and he expounded it and then led in prayer for the staff and the work. I am sure this made all the difference as they struggled along together in those anxious days. To me it was a sign that the Lord was with us and as conditions continued to get more difficult there were many such signs and blessings that made us feel that our work was not in vain.

Chapter 10
Signs, miracles and blessings

The 'Economic War' in Uganda slowly got worse over the next few years. Sometimes the electricity supply was cut off for days at a time. Our old emergency generator was temperamental and often failed to work despite Woolfgang's efforts to maintain it. No electricity meant no water.

People who broke the padlocks on the hospital rainwater tanks in order to get water for themselves would increasingly frustrate Bert:

"Who are these people? Are they staff or patients or villagers? Don't they realise how impossible it is to run a hospital with no water? They don't even turn the taps off properly when they have finished stealing. Anyone I catch will be taken to the police!"

I hated shortages of any kind so I could only sympathise with him:

"There probably won't be any more rain for weeks. Water from the swamp is all right for the cattle, but have we got enough petrol to keep using the tractor to bring it up?"

Water! It was such a basic item and so precious. Elimilech was rather more careless with it than I was and it worried me when I went home to find that he had used more than I expected – but then he had to do my washing. I tried to keep a bucket full in a large locked cupboard. It was horrible if there was not even enough to wash yourself after a hot, sweaty day in the hospital.

Other shortages were also worrying. Spare parts for vehicles were difficult to get even in Nairobi. Shopping expeditions were considered successful if you managed to bring back some flour and sugar but the shopkeepers might want to charge exorbitant prices for salt or soap. The expatriates all cooked with Calor gas and this was frequently 'out of stock'. We greatly valued the food which could be obtained locally, especially the fruit from the big orchard which Eric had planted some years before. I would often go there in the cool of the evening. There were huge grapefruit, different varieties of oranges, tangerines and lemons and, when they were ripe, guavas would heavily scent the air, the pale yellow fruits weighing their branches down to the ground.

Arriving home for lunch I often found Elimilech talking with someone who had come to the house with eggs. He would approach me for money.

"These five are good and he is asking for twenty five cents. The others were bad."

Elimilech tested the eggs by putting them in water; the bad ones would float. He knew I was always happy to buy any good ones.

People living nearby also supplied milk. Elimilech tried to make sure that any prospective 'milk-man' would be reliable. The milk was delivered in old bottles, corked with the core of maize cobs. It was always thoroughly boiled and when it was cool the thick cream on top could be eaten with stewed mangoes.

From my office window in the hospital I kept an eye open for the men who frequently cycled up from the lake with small fish strung on reeds dangling from their handle bars. Sometimes they had the slightly larger catfish, which had long whiskers and fewer bones. I preferred these. Not knowing the names for the different fish, I would often gesticulate, causing roars of laughter and promises that they would ask their friends to bring the ones with the long whiskers for me if I would buy a few of the ones they had with them.

Two or three evenings in the year flying ants would disturb us. They would arrive in huge droves after dark and enter our houses through the many gaps in the doors and windows, heading for the lights. The best thing to do was to turn off the lights in the house and leave one on in the veranda, otherwise the crazy mob would be zooming around everyone's faces and getting tangled up in people's hair.

It was when Winfred and another teenage friend of hers were staying with me during their school holidays that I learned the luxury of eating these ants. Joining in with all the local children they scrabbled around on the veranda collecting the ants as they started landing on the ground and shedding their wings. Carefully depositing them in my small saucepans they gleefully arrived in the kitchen, heated a frying pan and soon had them sizzling happily while they stirred gently for some minutes. There was plenty of fat in the little creatures so there was no need to add any more.

Winfred put just a few in a bowl for me to try: "You must taste them. They are so good!"

They were crunchy, salty and very tasty, and the girls assured me that they were also very nutritious. I believed them. I came to understand why Ugandan children get so excited when they see the dark clouds that herald the rainy season. The rain brings the ants. The children, in their eagerness to be first in getting some, find an anthill and cleverly make clay tubes which they attach to holes in the hill. They then beat with heavy sticks on the anthill to make the ants think that the rain has come. The ants are supposed to crawl up the tubes and into old cans which the children have rescued from rubbish pits.

As in most wars the majority of people pull together and become more supportive of each other. A small incident shortly after I returned from England highlighted this: I was in Mbale for the weekly shopping trip when a ragged individual on the pavement pointed at one of the wheels of my vehicle and indicated in Swahili that it was 'finished'. The tyre was almost flat and I started to get out the tools. Almost at once they were taken out of my hands and in no time at all another onlooker had changed the wheel. The puncture was mended within fifteen minutes at a nearby garage.

I remembered a similar incident that occurred in England the previous year. I was driving along the Kingston by-pass in a queue of slow moving traffic when someone looked out of his car window and said, "You've got a flat." I drew into a side road. The car was borrowed and the jack was broken. What was I to do! I knocked on several doors hoping to find out where the nearest garage was, but no one answered. I started walking up the road and eventually discovered a large garage, but it took a long time to persuade anyone to come to my rescue. They were all smartly dressed and busy with 'the books'. The tyre could not be mended that day, so I had to leave it. When I collected it the next day I was charged four times as much as I had just paid in Mbale.

During these difficult days in Uganda people not only became more supportive of each other but they also began to think more deeply about their faith in God. Bert gave a surprisingly positive message at one of our many farewell services for people who were leaving the country:

"Life is puzzling and we don't understand why things happen as they do. But as Christians we have great hope and in this world we have many chances of seeing God's love in action."

The Uganda Hospitals' Christian Fellowship group flourished; even the senior African staff came along to the meetings, which previously had only been attended by students, junior staff and expatriates. They sensed the need to draw on God given strength, fearful of what was happening to their country.

Increasingly we had to make trips to Nairobi for supplies. It was a 400-mile journey. On one occasion I was asked to go with a rather elderly vehicle because it needed new tyres. The evening before leaving I had a quick look at it. One tyre was so worn that it nearly had a hole in it. I shuddered at the thought of getting stuck on the road, for the other tyres including the spare were almost as bad. After a rather restless night I set out early with John, one of our drivers, who was in a carefree mood. He always wore a Moslem hat because he said he could get through the border more easily that way.

Soon after we had entered Kenya the vehicle wobbled ominously and John brought it to a halt. Sure enough it was a puncture. We carried on with the spare in place. 'Please don't let John drive too fast,' I prayed silently, 'And please Lord make those tyres hold out till we reach Eldoret'. The road was rough and pot-holed. Trucks and lorries ploughed past us every so often at great speed, sending up clouds of red dust. It seemed a long time before we approached the town with its welcome stretch of tarmac, but we had made it and soon we had brand new tyres on all our wheels.

I was always scared about the return journey. I made sure that I filled in the necessary forms before reaching the border otherwise people might notice that my hand was shaking. It was not illegal to bring goods into Uganda from Kenya but we were always laden with supplies: car spares, workshop materials and tools, sugar, soap, materials for uniforms and many other things. The officials could keep you waiting for hours complaining about what you were carrying or expecting bribes. Prayer seemed to help. On one occasion a young officer, peering into my vehicle, saw two stickers which I had attached to the dashboard. One said 'One Way' and had a hand pointing upwards. The other said 'God Loves You'. He became quite excited:

"Could you get some of those for me? I would like them so much for my friends."

"Of course. Give me your name and address. Here, you can write it on this piece of paper. Take my pen."

It was the easiest border crossing I had ever made! With a big smile on his face the young man was soon signalling for us to drive off.

Shopping in Kampala was especially frustrating. Sometimes there would be long lists of car spares which were desperately needed and the African shopowners, who had so recently replaced the Indians, often did not know what they had in stock or what the parts looked like. On one occasion I needed to buy welding equipment for the workshop. I prayed rather desperately: 'Lord, I know nothing about welding. Please lead me to someone who does and preferably someone who knows about making callipers. This is the fifth shop I've tried and I'm getting tired!'

Sure enough, there was a man who had been a calliper maker in Nairobi. He was incredibly helpful.

"You come with me. There's another shop just along here; they have the things you need."

I followed him. Examining my list, he grabbed the items from another store, told the surprised shopkeeper the price I should pay and then asked if I needed any help in setting up the equipment. A few weeks later he arrived at Kumi and worked for most of a day teaching the men in the workshop how to manage both gas and electric welding. Such encouragements made us all realise that if we tried our very best, then God would increase our efforts in surprising ways.

There were usually about twenty roadblocks between Kumi and Kampala. To make it easier to pass through them we decided to paint all seven of the Kumi vehicles with our special sign. It depicted the leafy branch and fruit of the hydnocarpus tree, the oil of which had been used in the treatment of leprosy many years ago, and this was surrounded by the words: 'Kumi Leprosy Centre' and the address. Although the soldiers at the roadblocks were often drunk, as well as appearing to be illiterate, they were very frightened of leprosy and the words could be read out to them so that they quickly understood our business.

If we actually had patients in the vehicles, any officials waved us along speedily and we sometimes used this trick to get our supplies through from Kenya. There was a leprosy hospital in Kenya very near to the Uganda border. Our drivers would take all the goods purchased in Nairobi and leave them there. They would then pass the border with an empty vehicle without any delays. A few days later someone would drive to the leprosy hospital with some leprosy patients who supposedly needed special treatment. Some hours later the return journey would be made with all the goods and the patients. No one ever liked to check what was being carried on such trips. It was naughty because we were really trying to educate the general public that no one should fear leprosy. We were causing extra problems for ourselves, because the widespread fear of leprosy made our work difficult and frustrating.

When an elderly and badly crippled patient, Yakobo Lolem, was ready to go home, I had the job of taking him to the bus in Mbale. He was clean and tidy, dressed in good second hand clothes which we had been able to provide, and he was excited about returning the hundred miles or so to rejoin his family. Leaving him at the bus park, I promised to return later to see if he had got away safely. Three hours later he was still there, sitting in splendid isolation. He was happy to see me.

"They have refused me completely!" he said.

Apparently when the other passengers had noticed his shortened, twisted fingers, paralysed face and special 'leprosy shoes', they had said that if he were allowed on the bus they would all get off. Indignantly I took the old man to the office to get the officials to see reason, which, to my surprise, was achieved quite easily, making me feel ashamed that I had been so angry. However, my explanations apparently paid off, for the following week Yakobo was allowed on the bus without further argument.

Livingstone sometimes sat and watched me as I tackled the long job of painting the signs on our vehicles. He was often sad in those days. He hated what Idi Amin was doing and the way so many expatriates were leaving. He would read the Uganda Argus (the national newspaper) in the workshop after lunch when he had managed to borrow a copy from one of the staff. I often heard him muttering his disapproval:

"Very bad man...But God will punish him one day!"

By this time whenever the President was mentioned in a newspaper or on the radio he was named in full as 'His Excellency Field Marshall Al Hadji Dr Idi Amin Dada, VC, DSO, MC, CBE, Life President of the Republic of Uganda'. The titles were bestowed on him by himself. CBE actually stood for 'Conqueror of the British Empire in Africa and in Uganda in particular'. It was funny in a way but it was also scary. Some British people had lists of what they would take with them if they were expelled with only six hours to the deadline of a day or two days. In the nursing superintendent's office where we gathered each morning for tea, the senior staff would try to reassure the British people, for we were the ones who Amin appeared to dislike most.

"No, he will never expel the British! He just wants to make a big noise. He likes his name to be in the headlines all over the world – that's all."

Although they were all sad and worried about the state of their country they would roar with laughter at the latest crazy remarks that their President was reported to have said. Fortunately two thirds of our expatriates were Dutch. If the few remaining British people were expelled the work still had a reasonable chance of carrying on. These were great times because of the unity we felt in supporting each other. As Charles Dickens wrote in 'A Tale of Two Cities':

'It was the best of times, it was the worst of times', and 'It was the season of Light, it was the season of Darkness'.

Easter was a very special time. We sang hymns and songs around the Centre at dawn, preached at packed bush Churches and watched the children perform very moving Easter plays. It was all Light. Then suddenly there was a great Darkness. Over one weekend something terrible happened.

I was woken in the very early hours of the morning by a call on our internal telephone. It was Bert. His voice was urgent and desperate:

"We are in the theatre – there are some emergencies – can you go quickly and bring oxygen from the workshop – there is none in the hospital – it's worth a try…"

I struggled into a few clothes, grabbed my bike and cycled as fast as I could along the rutted road in the darkness. Rousing one of my staff on the way, we collected an oxygen cylinder from the workshop and carried it between us to the theatre. Bert and Migchiel were desperately trying to save the life of one of our young dressers, Patrick Okwi. We were too late. With them I watched Patrick breathe his last breath. Two other junior staff members had staggered in earlier with the same symptoms as Patrick. They too had died. One had been a Church teacher and the other had worked in the dispensary. Bert and Migchiel looked exhausted. Just what had happened?

Sitting despondently over mugs of coffee they told me the dreadful story. "They all took methylated spirit from the dispensary on Friday evening. Apparently they have done it many times – we never knew! It makes people intoxicated. They didn't realise that the methylated we have in the dispensary just now is double the usual strength and they drank too much. How could the dispenser allow this to go on?"

I felt terribly shocked. As we walked home from the hospital the sun was just beginning to rise but I shuddered in the still, cool air. I could not believe what had happened especially to such young men. We had known Patrick Okwi ever since he had been in our school as a small lad with leprosy. Who was going to die next? It felt as if the devil had let loose some horrible evil. The bodies were left in the X-ray room, a fairly cool place, until we could arrange the difficult task of driving each one to his family home. The whole event was a severe warning to all the staff and those directly concerned must have felt desperately ashamed.

It was good to get away for a break. One weekend I managed to go to Amudat Hospital in a remote part of Karamoja District, 200 miles to the north-east. Ruth Stranex and Anne Wright were British missionaries working there and they had invited some other British people from Ngora Hospital, so it was a valuable time for sharing our concerns. Some of the party felt like letting off steam:

"Blow Amin and all his threats! Look, Ruth has all the 'Last Night of the Proms' on tape! Let's play them and show him that we don't intend to run away!"

We did not dare to play the tapes too loudly but we were soon mischievously enjoying 'Rule Britannia', 'Jerusalem' and all the other patriotic songs, quietly expressing our defiance at the current situation. On the Sunday evening we gathered in more sombre mood for a simple and very meaningful communion service using bread, which had been specially saved and orange juice.

We all departed on the Monday morning feeling strengthened. I had a friend from Mbale with me and I was driving a borrowed VW Combi. After a few miles it seemed that there was something wrong with the vehicle; it would not pull – it felt as if it would die on us. I turned back to Amudat. We asked our friends at the hospital if there was anyone who could help.

Amudat was such a small, remote place. Apart from the hospital, church and primary school there were just two rows of '*dukas*' at the side of the dusty main street. All around were scrubby thorn bushes with occasional small herds of scraggy cattle and ragged herd-boys meandering around in the sandy soil searching for some sort of grazing. Ruth said there was a man named Daudi who was sometimes at the post office who knew about cars. Not feeling very hopeful, we went to look for him.

Amazingly the man was there! He lifted the bonnet of our car and after a short time removed the distributor cap saying that it was cracked. Silently he ambled into the small mud house and reappeared with another part, clipping it into place and saying that we should now try the engine.

It was mended! We were utterly amazed. "How much do you want for it?"

Daudi did not seem too bothered: "I took it out of another vehicle last week," he said in a matter of fact way, as if for him miracles happened every day.

We gave him some shillings and a great deal of thanks and made our way home. I made sure that the next person who went to Kampala had: 'Distributor cap for VW Combi' on the shopping list, together with the number of the part and the year of the vehicle. It was unobtainable. Someone tried in Nairobi and came back with a distributor cap which did not fit. Several years later when I left Uganda the Combi was still running well with Daudi's distributor cap firmly in place.

One day an old Ugandan gentleman turned up at the Centre. Bert was away at the time and I seemed to be coping with problems from every section of the hospital. I told the visitor how busy we were and he gave me a knowing and slightly amused smile. He was Onesimus Busimo, who had worked at the Centre in the very early days. Some of our older staff rushed out to shake his hand, obviously feeling great respect and affection for him. I felt our problems shrink into proportion as he began to talk:

"I was here from 1932 till 1956. Sometimes I was the only person dealing with 700 patients. I started with prayers for all of them at 5.30 a.m. and then I got them into groups to do the work. I don't know how I managed – but God helped me."

Certainly that was the key for us too, in so many situations.

Chapter 11
Time to move on

I was off on my travels again. It was 1974 and I was exactly half way through my third three-year tour. I had been invited to present a paper at the 6th World Federation of Occupational Therapists' Conference at the University of British Columbia in Vancouver. I planned a five weeks' itinerary and spent the first two in England giving me the opportunity to rest, as I had not been well for some weeks. Maybe this was just because of overwork and stress, for I was soon refreshed and ready for the flight to Canada. My mother had kindly given me some money to help with the fare. She did not really like me continuing to work in Africa but she wrote regularly in reply to my fortnightly letters and the postcards that I sent when I was on holiday. She carefully kept all these and when I browsed through them, the impression they gave was that I was having a pretty good time. I never mentioned things that were particularly difficult or scary.

On the plane I sat next to a young woman who started chatting and she soon discovered that I worked with people who had leprosy. I was sorry I had told her; she did not talk any more and I had the feeling that she was not comfortable to be sitting next to me. Even *I* was stigmatised! However, at the conference there was considerable interest in my work. Many people asked me questions and my slide presentation was well received. I was amazed to meet the now elderly principal of my old training college, especially as she seemed to remember me.

"Yes, I'll come to your presentation," she promised, giving me one of her rare smiles.

As I began my talk I noticed her right in the centre of my audience. Later she found me to offer her congratulations.

During the conference meals were provided in a large restaurant on the university campus. Delegates selected their food from a huge display of dishes. I was not used to such choice and, on the first occasion, as the queue moved along I was unable to decide what I wanted. I nearly reached the end with nothing on my plate. Quickly pulling myself together, I copied someone else's choice and, in a slight daze, found my way to a table. 'Will I ever be able to cope with such luxury?' I wondered. Suddenly I realised that I was more at home in Africa than in the 'developed' world. It was difficult to enjoy fully things that appeared to be extravagant and it seemed wrong to be part of them.

During the week-long conference, I joined a group of delegates for a visit to a rehabilitation centre on Vancouver Island. Each client had a single room with a carpeted floor, a television set and doors that opened automatically as the wheelchair approached. I thought of our patients at Kumi. Many of them slept on concrete blocks or on the floor in overcrowded little houses. Before I left there had been a problem with rats: they nibbled the toes and fingers of the patients who had loss of feeling, while they slept. I expressed appreciation of the beautiful rehabilitation centre without much enthusiasm, keeping my real thoughts to myself. None of these delegates would be able to understand; they all worked in similar affluent establishments; they belonged to a different world.

I tried to attend the most relevant sessions at the conference but the papers were complicated and wordy. By the end I was glad to be collected by Ailsa, a friend of Janet Lea, who had emigrated to Canada some years before and was working as a medical practitioner in a scruffy suburb of Vancouver. She kindly took me on a trip to a friend's home at Kelowna, right on the shore of a beautiful lake.

"We'll come back through Kamloops and the Fraser River Canyon," Ailsa told me, "Then you can see how they catch the salmon. It's dramatic scenery."

How generous she was! She did not belong to a Church but one Sunday she arranged for me to go and came along too. When she finally saw me off at the airport I was considerably embarrassed when she shouted after me:

"I do have a God, but he's not quite the same as yours!"

I wondered what she meant; I hoped that my descriptions of the work in Uganda had been some sort of blessing to her in return for her warm hospitality.

I spent a few days in Holland on my way back to Uganda and stayed with Dick and his wife Ella. They took me to see some of the other Dutch people who had been at Kumi and I shared the latest news from Uganda. They were interested but they all seemed happy to be home again, settling into jobs.

Bert met me at Entebbe. With him was our new Dutch physiotherapist, Wim Brandsma. I found myself wondering how long he would stay, for he and his wife, Mariet, had two little girls, Marit and Lisa, but he was relaxed and committed and this was the start of many years of leprosy service for his family in several different countries. Wim was interested in reconstructive surgery and Bert and Migchiel were spurred on to tackle operations, knowing that he would be able to provide the essential post-operative treatment.

In October 1974 Bert finally returned to Holland. It was a hard decision for him but he knew that if he stayed any longer it would be difficult to re-enter the medical profession at home. Migchiel took over as Medical Superintendent at Kumi. He and his wife Greet were prepared to stay for two years.

I accepted Bert's departure as inevitable but it was with very mixed feelings that I helped him pack. True to form he was frantically busy right to the end with his meticulous mind still organising and planning. While securing a wooden crate I scratched my leg on a piece of wire. The small wound developed into a nasty, deep little ulcer, which only healed after three weeks' rest. It was a time to contemplate. So many of my friends had left the country and very few visitors came our way. I was, for a time, the only member of staff supported by a Mission. Edith Evans, my great friend who had been teaching in Mbale, had left and I missed her greatly. I often recalled some of the adventures we had experienced together.

Edith, being a Government employee, not only had a lovely house and garden but also a smart car. On several occasions I had joined her with other friends for holidays in Kenya. We explored the Amboseli Game Park, thrilled by the distant view of snow-covered Kilimanjaro and enjoyed early morning safaris to watch animals in the cool of the day. Usually we headed for the coast near Mombasa and stayed in a hired cottage right on the white, sandy shore of the Indian Ocean. With great delight we snorkelled among the coral beds to see myriads of different, brightly coloured fish. Friendships were bonded closely, especially when we found ourselves in difficulties.

On one occasion Jean Hurford, a teacher from Western Uganda and myself were stranded with Edith in her car on the Rift Valley Road some miles west of Nairobi. The car had not been performing well but Edith had hoped that it would somehow get us home. Wear and tear on cars was considerable and we had travelled many miles on corrugated murram roads that shake even the best of vehicles mercilessly. A main spring was broken. There was no way of moving the car any further and it was getting dark.

"I'll try and hitch a lift to Naivasha," Jean offered bravely. "It can't be more than twenty-five miles. I might find someone willing to help..."

There were not many vehicles on the road but very soon the driver of a small truck drew up in response to our signals and Jean was on her way. Edith and I did not expect her to return that day, so we ate a little of the food that was in the car and settled down as comfortably as we could, with all the doors locked, to try to get some sleep. Before doing so we prayed together that the Lord would keep us safe because the road was high on the uninhabited escarpment – a wild area where robberies often occurred.

We must have slept a little for I woke to the sound of a heavy vehicle. Peering anxiously into the darkness I could see a huge lorry drawing up beside us. Edith stirred uneasily.

"What's happening?" she asked.

Just then we could see three young Indian men together with Jean. She had only been away for three hours! Skilfully the Indians attached Edith's car to the lorry and we were towed at an alarming speed to the small town of Naivasha. By then it was about 11.00 p.m. The men happily offered to accommodate us at their home; there was some delay because, as we discovered later, some elderly relatives had to be turned out of an enormous bed. When it was remade with clean linen we were shown to 'our' room and the three of us piled thankfully into the bed, weary, but marvelling at such casual hospitality

"We have to get a spare part from Nairobi for your car," the Indians explained next day. "No problem! You just rest and make yourselves comfortable."

The day drifted by but late in the afternoon the Indians announced that the car was ready. Their price was fair and we were soon on our way.

"See how well the Lord cares for us," Edith murmured.

She was always positive and I missed her but when I felt particularly gloomy and in need of encouragement, then something would usually happen to lift my spirits:

There was the visit of the new Archbishop of Uganda, Ruanda and Boga Zaire – Janani Luwum. He was carrying out a tour of visitations in Uganda and when he came to Teso he actually visited Kumi Leprosy Centre itself.

I first met Janani when I was staying with Janet and Maurice Lea in Gulu. He was then Bishop of Northern Uganda and Janet helped him with his secretarial work as his house was very near to hers. One evening Janani came to supper with the Leas. He was well built and tall with a very gentle manner and a cheery sense of humour. His round and very black face with its lovely smile put me immediately at ease. An aura of Christian love seemed to surround him. The Leas knew he was a very special person and I could only agree.

When Janani was asked to be Archbishop he accepted with a heavy heart. Being from the north of Uganda he knew he might not be well liked by people from the south or west. Mary, his wife, was fearful of the move. However, he was duly enthroned in June 1974. I was fortunate in being able to go to Kampala with some of our senior staff for the service in Namirembe Cathedral. The building was packed with Christians who had come from far and near and the atmosphere was one of tremendous praise and love. There were dozens of robed clergy, large groups of uniformed band members and several choirs. Idi Amin was expected to attend but he had not arrived when the service started promptly at the appointed hour. The sermon, preached by the Archbishop of Kenya, had just begun when the television cameras were turned in the direction of the main door, recording the President's entry. The congregation continued to listen attentively, and no one stirred, as Idi Amin, who was holding the hand of one of his small sons, was shown to his seat. I wondered what he was feeling as he joined that mighty crowd of Christians, he himself being a Moslem. After taking communion I made a deliberate detour on my way back to my seat, so that I passed within a few feet of Idi Amin. His expression was a mixture of evil and bewilderment and his huge figure looked incredibly powerful in his medal-bedecked uniform.

All the patients and staff turned out to greet their Archbishop when he arrived at Kumi. He talked to us all under the trees between the wards. I shall never forget what he said. He was critical of our apathy but at the same time he was so loving. His text was Revelation chapter 3 and the second part of verse 1: '…you have the name of being alive, but you are dead'.

"You know how chickens behave," he said. "They peck around in the same piece of dusty ground day after day, never expecting anything new. Don't be like chickens! Don't keep looking down at the dull daily round as if you must live for ever in the same monotonous way. Look up, listen and receive all that the Spirit has to give you!"

He went on to speak very beautifully about Jesus as the bright morning star and encouraged us with the words:

"...let him who is thirsty come, let him who desires take the water of life without price." (Revelation Chapter 22 verses 16 and 17.)

It was a relevant message for patients and staff, Africans and Europeans alike. Janani was a real man of God.

Sitting in my house in the cool of a Saturday morning about a year after Bert had gone home, I wondered seriously about the future. 'Have I really got the courage to come back for another three years?' I asked myself. I was soon due for home leave and a decision had to be made. Suddenly the answer came quite simply and strongly: 'There is no need to return; it's time to move on'. I felt a great sense of relief and a certainty that this was right, hard as it would be to leave the work as well as the staff and patients who hated watching people depart.

As I thought of leaving Kumi, I realised that many of the aims for which we had worked so hard had been achieved. The posts of Administrative Secretary and Nursing Superintendent were now filled by Ugandans and, at last, a Ugandan Rehabilitation Officer had been appointed to take over all my work. With him, the staff totalled twenty in the orthopaedic workshop and rehabilitation section. All five orthopaedic technicians had completed intensive courses on artificial limb making, calliper making and shoe making at the A.L.E.R.T. centre in Addis Ababa. The new workshop was finished and running smoothly and there had been encouraging verbal promises that the Government would take over the funding of salaries for the qualified staff which would mean better pay. Peter Kityo who supervised patients working in the bougainvillea nursery and the vegetable garden and Margaret Akello, my former Girl Guide, had both completed courses in rehabilitation at Entebbe. They and their helpers were now responsible for all the patients who were not in the wards, totalling about 170.

We had seen some signs of spiritual revival too. John, the Pastor's eldest son who worked in the administrator's office, and Mark who worked in the lab, both came back from a Christian conference in Nairobi filled with the Spirit. Michael Onoria, a dresser who assisted in the theatre was wonderfully converted: he had been a tiresome fellow with whom I once had a serious argument because he had refused correctly to dispose of an amputated limb. His stubborn rudeness completely vanished and he became a happy and dedicated worker. It seemed that as the 'economic war' continued to bring more hardships, people were appreciating the things that really mattered.

I wrote to Bert telling him that I believed God wanted me to move on. His reply made me a little resentful and uneasy. He wrote:

'I feel sad about your decision to leave; but of course there is not much I can say as I left myself. After you have gone people will discover your importance. I feel that the light of Kumi is slowly getting dim. I know Nathanael (the Administrative Secretary) regards you as the only dedicated person. He does not think highly of the others.'

Bert went on to say that career-wise he had done the wrong thing by remaining at Kumi for a second tour but he knew that by staying on he had provided some very necessary continuity so that the place could develop. He wanted *me* to provide some continuity now. He continued:

'I wonder if it is right to say too soon that we know what God wants. I have a feeling that the interpretation of God's guidance is not always without a personal touch. When Abraham was told to depart, and when Jonah was asked to go to Nineveh, they were called to leave their precious homes and move on to serve God. I believe you are at Nineveh now. To find people for service in Uganda is virtually impossible; you will find them for Kenya...'

He appealed to me not to leave because I felt I was no longer needed.

'You have been for many years the salt in the boiling brew of the Centre without which the place would not have been very tasty. For the staff you have always been a mark on the land or a beacon from which they adopted or adapted their standards. I feel sorry for you because I know what such inward struggles mean. It can take a night's rest sometimes and what you want is a person to talk to.'

Finally he recommended that I made a firm decision soon so that 'your heart will stop worrying'.

Of course I had already made the decision and I felt that Bert's arguments were rather unfair even though I had always tried to be guided by what he wanted, within reason. But now it was of the utmost importance to be safe and secure in the Lord's will, otherwise I would not be able to draw on His strength and protection.

The Board of Governors accepted my resignation but asked me to stay on for an extra two months for reasons that now escape my memory. Perhaps it was because C.M.S. were sending us a mechanic, John Mattison, who might be glad of help to settle in. John was from Yorkshire. He was a strong Christian who was to give great service in East Africa for the next twenty years.

Zebedee Tayoleke, the man appointed as my successor, needed to learn to drive. I set about teaching him and became irritated when he was slow to grasp the necessary skills.

"I'll let him take the test," I told Nathanael, "He's sure to fail and then he'll realise he has to try harder."

Very unfortunately Zebedee passed! We had just acquired a new VW Beetle for the follow-up of discharged patients and Zebedee was very happy to be able to use it. In view of his inexperience he was far too confident. One evening, a few days before I left, he skidded off the road and damaged the car quite badly.

I was deeply saddened by something else that happened in those last days. I discovered that Lawrence Angatai, the technician in charge of the orthopaedic workshop, had pocketed a considerable amount of money from the sale of shoes instead of paying it into the office.

"I'll pay it back," he pleaded. "I only borrowed it."

I was exasperated. He was a very good technician and I had worked hard to get him trained in every aspect of his job. He was the one who had introduced workshop prayers; why had he been so foolish? It would take him many months to pay back the 'borrowed' money.

In the end we decided he should be dismissed. The workshop had to be staffed by people we could fully trust. I have always felt bad about the decision but in the end his skills were not wasted. He was accepted for employment at the big Catholic leprosy hospital at Buluba in Busoga District, (his home area) where he has remained to this day.

It was on March 20th 1976 that I flew out of Uganda. Idi Amin was actually in a jeep on the tarmac at Entebbe airport when I left. I was so thankful to have got away safely with all my luggage (the same three tin trunks). After a few days in Nairobi, the A.L.E.R.T. Centre in Addis Ababa and Holland, I arrived in England, happy to see the familiar green, pleasant land as we flew over Kent and into Heathrow.

Chapter 12
A new job and a house
to call my own

It took me several weeks to unwind and as I unpacked my trunks and looked at the presents and cards I had received from so many people, I felt a renewed affection for my friends in Uganda. There was the Bible that the Pastor had given me on behalf of the Church Council in recognition of ten years' service as a member. He had added a text: Romans ch. 16 vv 1 and 2:

'I commend to you our sister... that you may receive her in the Lord as befits the saints, and help her in whatever she may require from you, for she has been a helper of many and of myself as well.'

How generous these Ugandans were! The workshop staff had made an 'akongo' (thumb piano) on which was inscribed my name and their thanks, and they had also given me a beautifully made miniature artificial limb. From the expatriates were some lovely books of East African wild life and I had a few treasured items: Karamajong stools, a spear, some pieces of weaving from the workshop and some of Livingstone's paintings. I had several volumes of photographs and about a thousand slides. How could I ever forget Uganda?

I set out in a new Mini to visit all my 'Link Parishes' for the last time, including many friends who had supported our work and my few relatives, in carefully planned circular tours. This took me to various places in Surrey, London, Buckinghamshire, Cambridge, Portsmouth, Bournemouth, and Cornwall. There were C.M.S. gatherings and interviews to attend and as I discussed the future with the Home Staff I had to face realities and make some clear decisions.

"There were two Ugandan Bishops here the other day," one of the C.M.S staff told me. "They said that you shouldn't have left Uganda – that Kumi still needed you."

Do not unsaddle your horse

I was already feeling unsettled and that remark didn't help.

"Well, I *have* left – and I felt it was right. I have to look ahead," I said, wondering if the comment had been made because it was difficult to find a new sphere of work for me. It seemed there were no suitable openings.

"What about working in Sierre Leone with spastics?"

I screwed up my face in exasperation. That didn't seem right at all.

"I would like to use the experience I have of leprosy," I said; but it looked as if that was going to be difficult.

I decided to find out if The Leprosy Mission had any suggestions and spent a useful day at the London headquarters. No one tried to persuade me in any way but the directors listened sympathetically to my ideas.

"I met some people from the States when I was at that conference in Vancouver," I said. "They're still trying to persuade me to do a Master's Degree in health education or public health in Detroit – and there's another possibility at Reading University. It would be hard to do all that studying but if I want to get any further qualification I suppose it's now or never."

I was still wondering what was best when I left the headquarters. Could further study really be the way forward? It would fill a gap, because, like C.M.S., The Leprosy Mission did not appear to have anything to offer me, but I had no great desire to become a student again. Then after a few weeks, to my great relief, a letter came saying that some new work was to be undertaken in Lesotho and was I interested.

Where exactly *was* Lesotho? I found it on the map in the south-eastern corner of Africa, surrounded by South Africa. Apparently the South African Leprosy Mission had been keen to assist the Lesotho Government with leprosy work for some time and had finally persuaded the directors in London that it would be a worthwhile development, even though the prevalence of leprosy in Lesotho was low. So now the mission was looking for two experienced workers to go and assist with the control programme.

When I discovered that the other person who had been approached was a nurse I was rather disconcerted. I felt very strongly that a doctor would be needed. The nurse was from Holland and she had no experience of leprosy. She had, however, previously worked in Southern Africa, (in the Transkei) in a mission hospital run by the Dutch Reformed Church. Her name was Corrie Legemate.

I wrote to Bert telling him about the possible new opening. His reply was realistic and somewhat discouraging:

'It will be a case of out of the frying pan into the fire! The situation in South Africa is very volatile and it will surely spill over into Lesotho.'

I realised this. I also knew that I had received no particular guidance to draw me to Southern Africa but there did not seem to be much choice. All I wanted was to be able to make use of the skills that I had acquired in Uganda, which, though not very profound, were both unusual and practical. So I offered to go.

The Leprosy Mission directors were happy for me to transfer my services, so I had to officially resign from C.M.S. Alan Waudby, the personnel director, kindly went with me to their headquarters. As we zoomed across London in a taxi, the implication of what I was doing suddenly seemed very traumatic. C.M.S. had looked after me well and had provided me with a family of friends and I was glibly saying goodbye to all that security.

"Take it as it comes," Alan advised quietly.

I felt reassured. I was glad he was with me.

Everyone at C.M.S. was very friendly and encouraging and during a meal in the canteen the general secretary, who happened to be at a nearby table, spotted us and expressed his happiness at 'being in on the hand-over'.

Plans then went into full swing for the new Lesotho project. Corrie was to come to England for the Keswick Convention in July and I was to meet her there. In October we were both to attend the 'doctors' course' on leprosy at ALERT, Addis

Ababa for six and a half weeks. We would arrive in Southern Africa at the end of January 1977.

Corrie was a chatty and optimistic person. Although her English was far from perfect, it did not prevent her from fully joining in all the conversations. I got to know her a little at Keswick. She had spent some time at Bible College in Belgium and knew the scriptures well. In addition to her basic nursing training she had a qualification in public health.

During the course at ALERT we helped each other along, comparing notes in the evenings as we tried our best to learn. Almost all the participants were doctors, – a mixture of Africans and expatriates. Among them was a young Dutchman who had been accepted to work at Kumi Leprosy Centre. Some of the lectures were difficult to follow but I found much of the course wonderfully helpful, because I was already very familiar with leprosy but had never had any formal teaching. Aspects that had often puzzled me were now suddenly made plain. There was plenty of practical work too because of the large number of both in and outpatients.

Several of the staff went horse-riding in the evenings and as it was likely that we might need to use horses in Lesotho, the mission had advised us to try to get some practice. It was easy to arrange, but because the people with whom we went were experienced riders, we had to go faster than I would have liked. We always had to get home before dusk, as the local people were not always very friendly: they had been known to throw stones at the horses.

I had never had the opportunity to do much riding and I was not very confident. One evening as it was getting dark my horse stumbled and I was thrown off, badly jolting my back. I jumped up quickly, partly to make sure that I could still walk and partly to shout to the next rider who was rapidly disappearing ahead of me. I was scared and very sore and I walked most of the way back, painfully leading the horse over the rocky ground.

"Could I possibly have a bath at your house?" I asked Jane.

The students only had the use of showers and I needed to soak my bruises. Jane kindly sprang into action. There was some hot water in her tank and when it ran out she heated some more on her stove, pouring it over my back from a big jug. It eased the pain but for some days I walked very gingerly wondering what damage had been done.

The results of a written test at the end of a month showed that my knowledge had improved very considerably. I also gained 80% in a practical test, which I knew would please The Leprosy Mission, because they had decided that I was to organise the field control of leprosy in Lesotho, which would involve diagnosis and treatment. It was hardly the sort of job for an occupational therapist but I now felt more confident about the prospect, especially as we were staying on for two more weeks in Ethiopia for field work exerience.

Jane spoke very highly of the two Ethiopian field workers with whom we were to travel. They were senior men and very experienced.

"You'll be away for four nights at a time," she said, "so you'll be staying in some of the local hotels. They are very primitive. Make sure you check for bed bugs and fleas before you go to sleep."

She was right. I had never stayed at such places before. The guests' rooms surrounded a small cobbled courtyard and resembled tiny horse-boxes. The upper half of the door could be left open for daylight. There were simple toilets at one side of the courtyard. At the evening meal, eaten in the courtyard, I was careful to avoid meat, as I suspected it would be very tough. The alternative was eggs, which were usually provided in fours and served with vegetables and stale bread. No one seemed very friendly at these noisy brothels and we were glad to be out in the countryside all day visiting clinics, although every time we stopped we found ourselves surrounded by groups of scruffy children who also appeared hostile as they

---

Do not unsaddle your horse

chattered and pointed at us. I never found Ethiopia a very friendly place especially when I compared it to Uganda.

* * * * *

It was late November when I arrived back in England. Earlier in the year I had met Jim Findlay who was the director of the England and Wales Auxiliary of The Leprosy Mission. In the course of conversation he had enquired whether I had a house of my own and had urged me very strongly to purchase one.

"You must be realistic about the future," he said. "Missionaries often forget that God doesn't want them to miss out on the things that everyone else considers essential. If you can find some suitable places, I'll come down help you decide what's best."

Now was my chance. I had just over two months before leaving for Southern Africa, so, encouraged by Pam, I started to look at a few properties in and around West Malling. I found two possibilities and invited Jim to come and advise me. The night before he was due to come I was relaxing with Pam and Graeme in their sitting room.

"You don't sound very enthusiastic about either place," Pam remarked.

"I'm not," I replied. "They aren't really what I had hoped for but there's nothing else in the price range."

Graeme threw the local paper over to me and suggested I checked it through again. One of the houses I had arranged to see was in Police Station Road and looking carefully at the paper I noticed that there was another one advertised in the same road. It was rather more expensive but it sounded promising.

"I'll go and see just where it is early tomorrow before Jim arrives," I said.

Walking up and down Police Station Road searching for number 26 was embarrassing. The owner of the house I had arranged to see was watching me from his window, no doubt wondering what I was doing. I couldn't find number 26 – some of the numbers seemed to be missing. I gave up and went back to the Maclennan's to wait for Jim. By the time he arrived I had realised that the missing house must be along one of two small paths that lay at right angles to the road. Jim suggested that we should try to find it first and this time we were successful.

A rather breathless lady let us in. She had a weak heart and needed to move to a bungalow. She obviously loved the cottage and was sad at the prospect of selling it. It was at the end of a row of six that had been built in the 1830's, probably for farm labourers. Downstairs was a living room and kitchen with a bathroom built on at the back and upstairs were two bedrooms. There was a small garden, and, like the house, it was nicely kept, with rose trees and a patch of lawn. As soon as I walked into the place I felt sure it was just right and Jim agreed. We never went to see the other houses but called at the estate agents to make an offer of £11,250.

Then came the shock: I was unable to get a mortgage! Apparently it was impossible because I was going to rent out the house. The bank officials almost laughed at me and I felt stupid and confused. Had I been wrong, after all, in trying to buy a house? Was it just a repeat of what happened before I went to Uganda? Pam felt sure there must be some way round the problem but I couldn't think of any solution and was tempted to let the whole matter drop.

Then came one of those rare miracles. A letter arrived from some friends who had worked in Uganda and were now living in the North of England. They had heard that I was short of money for buying a house and were offering me an interest free loan of £3,000. I was utterly amazed. I never discovered how they had heard of my need. They were certainly not wealthy and they had three young children. My mother lent me £2,000 and I was able to pay the balance myself. I was very excited.

"You'll never get everything completed in the time!" people told me. "Christmas is coming and then the New Year. No one works then. Even at other times of the year you'd need at least two months – and that's if everything goes without a hitch."

But their predictions were unfounded. I moved in to the cottage on January 15th 1977, less than six weeks from the day I had first seen it with Jim! Pam had some furniture stored in her garage that she did not need and when we were sorting out some chairs, beds and a table she also found pieces of kitchen equipment, all of which could be spared. I had brought some of my plates, cups and saucers from Uganda and many friends offered useful items:- an old but reliable fridge, another bed, bedding and linen. The previous owner had left behind a good electric cooker, the carpets and some curtains. In the end I had very little to buy. I borrowed a sewing machine and made more curtains and bed covers, working late into the night. Then I cleaned the cottage until it was spotless. It was looking very attractive.

My advertisement in the local paper resulted in a large number of letters from people wanting to rent the house. It was difficult to judge who would be the most reliable tenant but in the end I chose a young girl who was working at an agricultural research station in the next village. I gathered later on from kind friends, who kept an eye on the cottage for me, that it had been an unwise choice. Very soon other people moved in with the girl and the neighbours grimly tolerated their noisy parties. Fortunately the tenancy soon changed and a more mature lady took up residence. There were still some problems but at least the rent was being paid. That was all that mattered for the time being.

One final job before leaving for Southern Africa was to find a buyer for my car. I had bought it new, so I felt I should get a good price for it but when there were no replies to my advertisement, I wondered what to do. Our Vicar needed a new car but he could not afford to pay very much.

'I need to pay off my debts,' I told myself, 'But then, God has been so generous to me. Maybe I should also be generous.'

Reading in my Bible I came across a passage in 2 Corinthians ch. 9 which confirmed my thoughts:

'God is able to give you more than you need, so that you will always have all you need for yourselves and more than enough for every good cause. He will always make you rich enough to be generous at all times, so that many will thank God for your gifts which they receive from us.' (verses 8 and 11 – Good News Bible)

Malcolm was happy to pay a greatly reduced price for the car and I was well pleased with the solution. God had blessed me so much and I had been able to give Him something in return.

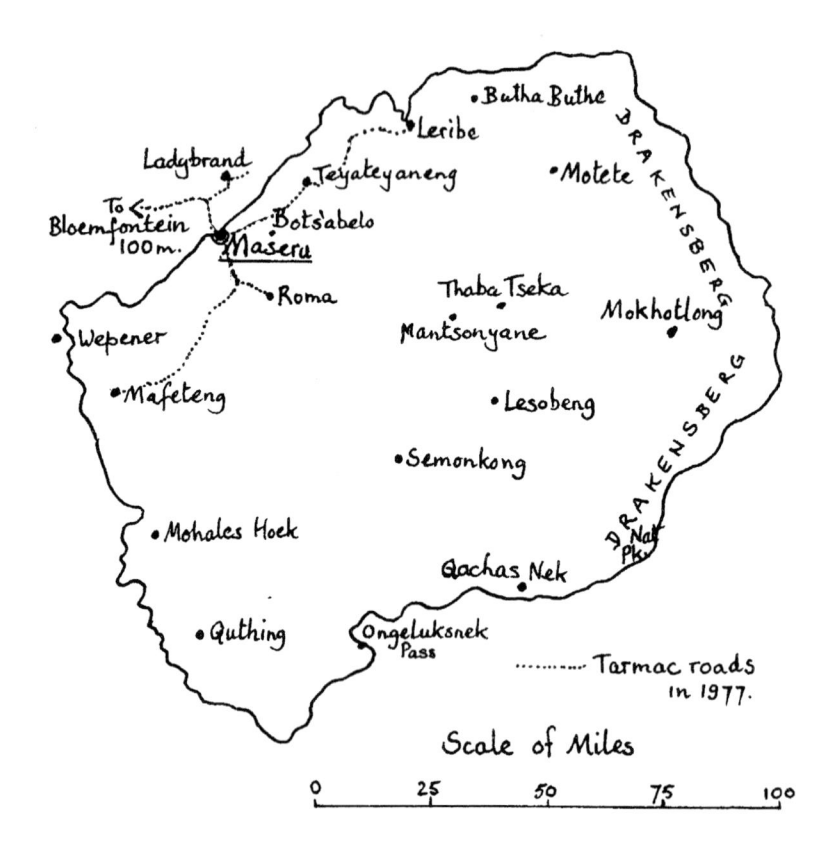

Map of Lesotho

Chapter 13
Bots'abelo – place of refuge

It was early February 1977. There I was at Heathrow, together with Corrie and one of The Leprosy Mission staff who had come to see us off. The bustling airport had succeeded in severing my thoughts from home and all the work and organisation of the past few weeks and I was suddenly focussing on all that lay ahead.

We were flying to Johannesburg to stay a few nights with Walter Maasch and his wife, June, in one of the White suburbs. Walter was the General Secretary of the South African Leprosy Mission. We were treated to some warm hospitality and then driven to Bloemfontein where we were to study the Sesotho language for some weeks. I was not looking forward to this. Solid language study was going to be a hard test but Corrie was much more positive about it. She was feeling reasonably 'at home' in South Africa because of having worked in the Transkei. I was not at ease in the same way. The white people who were taking us under their wing seemed to have no black friends. The only black Africans with whom they had any contact were their maids, gardeners and the boys who carried their groceries from the shops to their cars.

On one occasion someone asked me, "How do the Blacks in South Africa compare with the Blacks in Uganda?"

I didn't know what to say. We never called people 'Blacks' in Uganda and I had not met any well-educated black people in South Africa, so it was impossible to make a comparison. I dodged the question and changed the subject.

However, one thing was becoming clear to me: the white South Africans loved the people who worked for them as if they were their children. At Bloemfontein Corrie and I were taken to a spacious bungalow in a smart white suburb where we were to stay. The bungalow belonged to an elderly man whose wife had recently died. He himself had moved temporally to his daughter's home nearby and he was generously allowing the Mission to use his house. With the house went his maid, Mary. In the early morning the old man frequently returned and pottered around in the garden, coming in by the front door and leaving it open. Corrie and I were usually in the kitchen having breakfast.

One day when I went to my bedroom after breakfast to collect my books for the day's language study, I found that my handbag was missing. Corrie and I jumped to the obvious, but incorrect, conclusion that Mary had taken it. She had, we thought, been in her room that adjoined the garage and it would have been possible for her to have sneaked in and given the bag to someone else to get it off the premises. On suggesting this to the old man, his relatives and the mission staff, we were severely reprimanded. For them such an accusation was verging on blasphemy.

"Mary could not possibly have done such a thing," they declared. "She is part of the family – she has been with us for years. There's a boy who has been seen wandering around the neighbourhood. He is probably the one. You know, these Blacks are so quick. He could have taken a chance and come in while you were in the kitchen."

Fortunately my passport was not in the bag but I had lost some money, my address book and the usual useful things that I carried around. I was very upset, but the increasingly large group of white people who were looking after us rallied round. They were very generous. They replaced everything they could and I was able to send home for an old address book without having to say what had happened.

We had as our tutor a young white South African who lectured in Sesotho in the University. He was a good teacher but he didn't know whether the people in Lesotho spoke South Sotho or North Sotho. Unfortunately we learned the wrong one, and, as the spellings are different, we had to do some re-learning later on. The days and weeks dragged by but Corrie enthusiastically labelled everything in the house with the Sesotho words and we struggled through the grammar sharing any difficulties. I was very impatient to get to Lesotho but it seemed that the Mission was not in a hurry. The houses that were being built for us at the leprosy hospital were not completed.

The area secretary for The Leprosy Mission lived a short distance from our bungalow with his wife and family. They were homely people and very committed Baptists, and we always enjoyed visiting them. Like many sincere South African Christians, they struggled to see how black and white people could live and work together as equals. Norman attended a course that highlighted the problem and he reported to us, with a sense of real discovery, what had been said:

'You people just see a black person as the extension of the petrol pump that fills your car. You need to realise that it *is* actually a human being, a *person* like yourselves, who is doing the work.'

"It's true!" Norman exclaimed, "That's exactly the way we think about Blacks."

On another occasion when we arrived at Norman and Joy's house feeling in need of a break, Joy showed me a newspaper that she had been reading.

"There's a story about an Archbishop in Uganda who's been killed," she said.

As I read the account tears were welling up in my eyes. Janani Luwum had been killed, probably by Idi Amin. Janani! He was one of the most wonderful Christians I had ever met.

"Do you know him?" Joy asked.

I tried to explain: "He was just so loving and yet so bold and great…"

Joy took another look at the paper, reading a little more carefully. Then she said:

"But was he a *black* man?"

She seemed to imply that it would have been a far greater tragedy if he had been white. I felt alone in my sorrow, unable to discuss the event any further.

Eventually, after more than two months, we were taken to Lesotho, to the leprosy hospital, Bots'abelo, which was situated two miles outside the capital, Maseru. Two small prefabricated bungalows had been built at the edge of the very extensive grounds. They overlooked the sprawling outskirts of the town and, being at the top of a hillside, they could be seen from a considerable distance. Electricity had not yet been installed, but for the time being we could manage with candles and camping gas for cooking. The friends from Bloemfontein had provided us with much of the furniture and equipment and the rest had been purchased. It had all been brought across from South Africa. I was glad to have arrived.

Lesotho can boast of being the highest country in the world, as it has no land of less than 4,000 feet. On its eastern borders are the Drakensberg Mountains. The tarmac roads were limited to the western fringes and many villages in the mountains were only accessible by horseback or on foot. My leprosy control work would necessitate travelling to all parts of this barren but beautiful kingdom, and I was anxious to make a start before the winter set in. Already the mornings had an autumnal feel to them.

We spent a reasonably comfortable night in the houses and the next day Walter arrived from Johannesburg to take me to collect a large diesel Landrover that was being stored for the Mission at a place just north of Lesotho in South Africa. All afternoon I drove the strange, heavy vehicle back along the road to Lesotho, arriving at the border after dark. It had been a rather tense drive and by the time I reached Bots'abelo I was very tired. In my weariness I couldn't immediately find the track to our houses that were in semi-darkness because of having no electricity. I chided Corrie for not listening for the vehicle, but we were both happy to have our own transport; it was a cause for rejoicing.

Bots'abelo was typical of many old-fashioned 'Leper Asylums' that sprang up to meet the needs of leprosy sufferers before there was any proper treatment and when the disease was considered to be very serious, frightening and contagious. The Asylum opened at the end of 1913. It was sited on 1750 acres of land in which two large compounds were set up, 500 yards apart, one for 350 female patients and the other for 350 males. Lesotho was a British Protectorate in those days, known as Basutoland, so the senior staff were European. They comprised a Matron, three staff nurses, two compound managers, one mechanic, one electrician, one storekeeper, one farm bailiff, one chaplain and a first grade clerk as second in command under the Medical Superintendent.

Before the end of 1914 there were 693 patients at the Asylum and chiefs and headmen had driven most of them there. The name 'Bots'abelo' actually means 'Place of Refuge', but the leprosy sufferers were led to believe that it was a hospital and that they would be cured and go home. When they discovered that it was a place of detention, trouble developed. They did not like being herded together. There was considerable discontent and frequent desertions. Then there was a serious riot. The Superintendent and the compound managers and chaplain were attacked. Order was restored only when the Basutoland Mounted Police were called in. The number of guards was then increased and they were armed with carbines that were only to be used if the staff was attacked. At his request, the Superintendent was given leave to recuperate; the chaplain had been injured and he resigned. It was then that a new Medical Superintendent took over – a Dr N.M. Macfarlane – who recorded the above events in a booklet, printed in 1934, which I discovered as I browsed through some old records. On his arrival 100 patients absconded but he held a meeting for the 300 men and women who remained and they agreed to co-operate. The military discipline was somewhat relaxed and a 'native court' was introduced.

It was easy to imagine such events as I walked around the dilapidated Bots'abelo. The old buildings were all still there, although there were only 135 patients. There was even a prison with eight cells. Until the 1940's injections of hydnocarpus oil had been used for treatment and some of the old tables in a room called the 'injection room' were impregnated with this oil, its very strong smell still lingering there. Other buildings included three churches, a huge, derelict laundry block, two large dining rooms that were no longer used with doors and windows open to the four winds, a school, a post office and a big store where patients were allowed to buy small items if they had any money. All these buildings were primitive, being constructed almost entirely of corrugated iron sheets that had been brought from Bloemfontein when an old Boer War barracks had been dismantled. The iron sheets had been painted olive green and the roofs were a dull reddish colour but everything was now very shabby and in need of repair. The place resembled a squatters' camp, providing no real comfort for the patients. The male and female compounds were identical, with a quadrangle of 'rooms' and a hospital building in the middle. There were coal stoves in the hospital bocks but there was no heating in the 'rooms' and the patients who had been in residence for some time usually managed to acquire coal braziers that could be smuggled inside at night, (a dangerous practice as the floors and inner walls were wooden). Beside each hospital building was a shed with rows of rusty iron baths. The toilet blocks were near the fences and consisted of cubicles and buckets, known as night soil buckets. These were taken regularly to a site just below our houses where buckets from most of the smaller houses in Maseru were emptied. A lorry passed our houses several times a day for this purpose, the smell and dust lingering in the air for a while as it disappeared down the hill. It was apparently considered unsafe for this lorry to collect the Bots'abelo buckets, so the hospital guards had this job, which they did with the aid of an ox cart.

At the entrance of Bots'abelo stood two ancient notice boards, at the side of a dilapidated gate. The writing on each notice said the same thing but one was in Sesotho and the other in English. It was still possible to decipher the instructions. They read:

BASUTOLAND LEPER ASYLUM

No persons admitted without a written permit, which may be claimed at the office of either the Government Secretary, the Principal Medical Officer Maseru or the Superintendent of the Asylum. Permits must be handed to the gatekeeper when leaving the premises.

NO DOGS ADMITTED

DRAUGHT ANIMALS may not be outspanned, or horses unsaddled within the precincts of the Asylum without special permission from the Superintendent.

ANY UNAUTHORISED PERSON found within the precinct of the Asylum is liable to arrest and to be dealt with according to the terms of the LEPROSY PROCLAMATION No 41 of 1913.

BY ORDER

The outdated patients' accommodation at Bots'abelo

Having made it difficult for anyone to enter Bots'abelo, I supposed it was logical that the fences around the patients' compounds were designed to keep the patients *in*, not to keep outsiders *out*. I noticed that the high wire fences, draped with barbed wire, sloped *inwards* at the top but there were now many holes through which people could easily pass. No doubt the gates to the compounds were once firmly locked every night but now they were dilapidated and permanently open and the guards huts by each entrance were empty. That was fine, but the whole place was so overgrown and poorly maintained. It was depressing.

It was intriguing to find that the medical records of all the patients admitted to Bots'abelo since the very beginning, were still preserved. There were ten or twelve huge leather bound books that had been used for the first thirty-five years or so. They were carefully filled in by hand with two big pages allotted to each patient. As I looked through the books I felt I was back in the Middle Ages. Almost all the patients were under forty years of age and many died at Bots'abelo after just a few years. The recorded cause of death was usually 'leprosy and exhaustion'. In addition to these books were record cards for the later years. I soon made a start at sorting through these, buying large-scale maps of the entire country and grouping the cards in areas.

As I talked with various people in the health department I began to sense a great fear of leprosy. It was a much greater fear than I had experienced in Uganda, where the prevalence of the disease was much higher. Because leprosy was not so common in Lesotho, people were much more ignorant about it, so they let their imaginations invent strange reasons for its cause, elaborated on the horrendous deformities and exaggerated its infectivity.

Never having been responsible for the control of leprosy before, I was not sure where to start. I contacted a Mission Hospital in the centre of the country.

"Leprosy?" the surprised doctor shouted over the radio call, "We don't see that here."

"Well, can I come and check?" I called back, "I've got to make a start somewhere."

Corrie came too and we set out in the Landrover with a Health Assistant to show us the way. It was our first experience of the mountains. The roads were rough and rocky but a few of the very steep places had tarmac. There were sharp bends, sheer drops at the sides of the road and several wrecked cars could be seen lying close to little streams at the bottom. The sun never penetrated some of the deep valleys and we noticed small waterfalls that were frozen solid even though it was not yet winter. Various high points were marked with road signs: Bushman's Pass, God Help Me Pass and Blue Mountain Pass and at each of these places the views were beautiful and daunting. The wide-open spaces excited me but the mountain ranges seemed endless. Blanketed men and women on horseback, small boys herding sheep and mohair goats, people leading loaded donkeys – these were new and interesting introductions for us as we slowly discovered a little about the lives of the Basotho.

We didn't find any leprosy sufferers during our visit to the hospital but we had the opportunity to talk to the staff. They thought there *were* some people who had leprosy in a certain village, but it was a hard day's horse ride away. We doubted if they would be interested in following up their suspicions. They had more pressing problems: TB was common, gastroenteritis was a killer and they were busy with vaccination programmes for preventable childhood diseases. They were obviously fearful of the disease and knew very little of the early signs and symptoms or of how it should be treated. As far as they were concerned, Bots'abelo was the place for leprosy patients and if they found any they would send them there without delay.

"In fact," the expatriate doctor suddenly volunteered, "We *did* send one lady there earlier this year," – and he produced her name for us.

But when we checked this at Bots'abelo no one had ever heard of her.

* * * * *

We were slowly getting to know the Matron of Bots'abelo, a shy but capable Mosotho lady of about our age, who, over the years, we came to greatly respect. Her position was not easy. Her staff consisted of a dispenser, about four staff nurses and some nurse assistants. She had to take some of her orders from the Superintendent, a non-medical man, who always seemed to view Corrie and me with suspicion; perhaps our presence seemed threatening. I am not sure what qualifications he held. He had been appointed after the previous man had committed suicide. Apparently his post was sometimes given as a punishment for anyone who had not performed well in some other health department. At lunch time he could be seen sprawled out on the grass in front of his office, basking in the sun. He was a heavy drinker. His duties included the supervision of the non-medical staff: the guards, who numbered about eight, two carpenters, a storekeeper, office workers and a telephonist who sat at the old post office. Her job was important because the telephone was extremely difficult to operate. She always did her best to help us, but her job was very frustrating and often she failed to connect us even to local numbers.

On the whole the staff members were pleased to welcome us once their initial apprehension wore off, and Matron gradually introduced us to all the patients, explaining their individual histories. They were a mixture of recently admitted and severely disabled people and most of the latter had been at Bots'abelo for many years.

"How long has this lady been here?" we asked, as we examined a few open sores on her fingerless hands.

"Since 1925," Matron replied. "She has a big ulcer on her foot – it's been there for fifteen years and she says that if it ever heals she will die."

Next was a grossly disfigured lady with lepromatous leprosy sitting on the doorstep of her room.

"This is Puseletso," Matron said.

The poor woman had features described in old textbooks as leonine or lion face. I had never seen such a severe case. Her face was a mass of lumpy infiltrations. When we got to know her we found that she had a lovely character but she believed she had been bewitched because her leprosy was worse than that of any of the other patients. She had been very irregular in taking her treatment over many years and was now obviously resistant to the dapsone tablets.

Corrie put her arm around her: "We will get some different, new drugs to help you," she told her.

I noticed tears of gratitude in Puseletso's eyes as Matron quietly translated the words. We had given her a glimmer of hope. With time she did improve but the disease had been neglected for so long and she was often poorly with reactions. She died after a few years. Of all the patients I have known, she was the only one of whom I could say with certainty, 'she died of leprosy'.

Corrie with Puseletso at Bots'abelo

The Leprosy Mission had given us job descriptions as a rough guide. Corrie's duties as a nurse were based within the hospital. She was to supervise the work, introduce better treatment and some simple physiotherapy and assess the buildings. My brief included visiting health centres and hospitals throughout the country, following up discharged patients, planning training for health staff and providing health education for the general public. We were both to continue with language study engaging the help of local people, and establish relationships with all medical personnel from the Minister of Health downwards and with Church leaders. We were also to find and train local staff to assist us with developing the work, consulting closely with Walter Maasch on all matters.

Walter had arranged with the Lesotho Government that there would be a Management Committee that would meet regularly in Maseru. He planned to come to Lesotho every few months so that he could chair the meetings. The Permanent Secretary for the Ministry of Health, the Chief Medical Officer of Health and Dr Jaques (the Government doctor who visited Bots'abelo once a week) were all members of the committee. Dr Jaques was a white South African. He was of retirement age and a charming, gentle person with many years' experience of medical work in Lesotho. He had the unenviable task of seeing to the needs of endless queues of outpatients at the big hospital in Maseru, but on Friday afternoons he would drive the short distance to Bots'abelo, do a ward round, see the new patients and quietly listen to any problems.

I tried many times at our committee meetings to get the old Leprosy Proclamation of 1913, that featured on the notices at the gate, revoked. In theory it was still law to keep all leprosy patients at Bots'abelo under strict isolation but since the introduction of dapsone treatment in the 1940's this policy had not been followed. The fact that we never succeeded in abolishing the Proclamation was a reflection of the fear the very senior health staff had of the disease. They wanted to keep the law just in case it might be useful in some way.

The Permanent Secretary of Health once confessed his fear to me:

"When we were at school we used to come to Bots'abelo to sing for the patients as an act of service. Before we came we were always told: 'Don't touch anything. Don't even pull a piece of the long grass and put it in your mouth; and when you get home have a good bath'."

He also told me that one day their school had a health check and a boy was found to have leprosy.

"He was a *big* boy," the Permanent Secretary said, "And he was crying. The sight of him being taken away in a van to Bots'abelo remains with me to this day. It is only when I hear you people talking about leprosy that I begin to realise that we shouldn't be scared but I still don't like visiting Bots'abelo."

One Sunday morning I was having a 'lie-in', listening to the local radio. It was 'Leprosy Sunday', a day marked by Churches in many countries. Church notices were being given out and suddenly the announcer said:

"The Bishop of Lesotho will be celebrating Communion at the Anglican Church at Bots'abelo to-day. He asks all Christians to pray for the poor, crippled lepers."

I was planning to go to the Anglican Church that morning and as I dressed I muttered indignant thoughts to myself:

What a bad impression to give everyone! Couldn't they have said: 'Let's praise God that the majority of leprosy sufferers get cured without any deformity, and let's pray that people who get the disease will come early for treatment so that they may be cured and not spread the disease'?

The Church was reasonably full for the Bishop's visit, with more than the usual number of local people as well as a few of the patients. Everyone was happy to be greeted outside by the Bishop when he had finished conducting the service. Embarrassed by the patients who obviously wanted to be greeted as well, the Bishop turned to me and asked:

"Is it all right if I speak to that patient?"

'Me Kao, the patient in question, was sitting in a heap on

Do not unsaddle your horse

the ground with a lovely smile. She had no fingers and one leg was amputated; the other foot dragged along the ground when she moved around with her crutches.

"Of course you can speak to her," I said.

"And should I shake her hand?"

"Yes, that's fine."

'Me Kao's eyes sparkled as he moved towards her, greeted her and took her hand. He had made her day!

Concerned that the Bishop should be so wary of our patients, I suggested to him that I might perhaps talk to his clergy.

"People who expound the Bible," I explained, hoping that I was not offending him, "Often compare leprosy to sin, and that's very hurtful for any leprosy sufferers who may be present."

It so happened that a clergy conference was due to take place near Maseru the very next week, so then and there it was arranged that I should give a talk one evening.

When I arrived at the meeting the Bishop introduced me very graciously and then he added:

"Recently, when I was conducting a service at Bots'abelo, I was not sure if I should shake hands with one of the patients, but I was assured that it was quite safe to do so; so I did. All seemed to be well: but when I got home I felt a terrible pain in my arm."

I tried my best to allay such extraordinary fears by presenting some facts:

"Probably in Jesus' time 'leprosy' was a word used to cover all sorts of skin conditions. Today it's used for just one disease and that disease is curable. When people have been on regular treatment for some time they are no longer able to pass on the disease. Most people are cured without any residual deformity; it's only the people who come late for treatment who get crippled. There's no need to isolate a person who has leprosy – it only creates more fear and any members of the family that are susceptible will already have been infected. Leprosy is not all that easy to catch and about 85% of the population are immune to it."

The inevitable questions followed:

"Then why have we got Bots'abelo as a special hospital just for lepers?"

Why indeed! There was great stigma attached to the old Asylum and its very existence made it extremely hard to change people's attitudes.

I prepared a set of questions about leprosy to be sent to students at some local schools and colleges and another set for health staff. A total of 225 were returned and I set about evaluating the answers. The results showed great ignorance about the disease, a strong feeling that patients should be isolated until they were completely cured, and that deformities were inevitable. Many respondents thought that leprosy was caused by severe cold or by eating too much fatty meat. All this information was very useful as I prepared the texts for 10,000 booklets and 100,000 leaflets entitled 'Leprosy can be Cured'.

As time went on I frequently took photographs and slides of our patients for teaching purposes. I had some of the best enlarged for a Health Department exhibition in the town. Even though the patients had agreed that their pictures could be displayed, the Ministry of Health was very reluctant to give permission unless the area around the patients' eyes was blanked out to preserve their identity. I argued that this would cause even more fear in people's minds and in the end it was agreed that the photos could be used as they were.

Later I devised posters and picture stories and wrote several series of radio talks that were translated into Sesotho and broadcast on Radio Lesotho's Health Education programmes. Slowly attitudes changed but it was sometimes the Health Staff themselves who remained the most frightened.

"Why are you standing so far back?" I asked a nurse who had been sent to observe a leprosy outpatient clinic.

"I'm scared," she confessed.

I was examining an ulcer on a patient's foot. I stopped what I was doing and turned towards her.

"You know, it's people like you who frighten the patients away," I said. "This man knows he's an embarrassment and he doesn't want to upset you, so next time he may just stay at home instead of coming to the clinic. There's nothing to be afraid of. Try to see him as a *person* who badly needs your help and sympathy."

School children were often easier to teach. When I had Health Assistants working with me we often went into schools to teach with slides, using a portable generator to power the projector. During a repeat visit to a remote mountain area, a crowd of children followed me up a steep path. They were all chanting:

"Leprosy can be cured, leprosy can be cured."

Somehow the message was getting through.

Chapter 14
The challenge of the mountains

Basotho horsemen in the mountains

I had a huge task. I wanted to trace all the leprosy patients who had been discharged over the previous ten years, and I needed to visit each of the eighty-five clinics and health centres as well as the seventeen hospitals. To start with I couldn't be away too much because it left Corrie without a vehicle. I also needed field workers to accompany me on my trips.

Walter Maasch was adamant that any local assistants the Mission employed must be Christians and to ensure this he visited the Pentecostal Bible School in Maseru seeking suitable young men for interview. I also made our needs known at the Ministry of Health, so we had some other candidates as well. One of these was Molemo Mokhothu. He had wanted to be a Health Assistant but he was not of a high enough academic standard to be selected. Walter was quick to turn him down.

"Did you see the flashy tie he was wearing?" he said when I challenged his hasty decision. "He couldn't be right for our sort of mission wearing a tie like that!"

Three of the Bible School students were duly offered the jobs but two of them very soon decided that they did not want to limit their ministry to leprosy patients or to be trained in medical skills, and they left. The third remained with us for some time. He was an albino – a pale skinned African – and his eyesight was very poor. He could hardly see to write. He was a very sound Christian but not very useful for practical work. He too left us when he was offered a job with a Church.

Molemo Mokhothu now had another chance because Walter agreed that we could interview him again. He was a willing young man, tall and pleasant, and he became one of my first assistants for fieldwork. He and I travelled to many remote places on roads that could hardly be called roads, taking with us everything we might need for coping independently in whatever accommodation we could find.

I knew from the records that there were certain places, deep in the mountains, where leprosy appeared to be endemic. One of these was Lesobeng, right in the centre of the country. There was an airstrip in that area but the scheduled flight went only once a week, so for my first visit I chartered a six seater Cessna from Lesotho Airways, taking with me two discharged patients, Molemo and a Health Assistant who knew the area.

The visibility was poor but somehow the pilot found a hole in the clouds and made a dive for the landing strip. A few children and some women gathered around us as we unloaded the plane. They were curious to see who had arrived in such unfavourable conditions. I looked around for horses:

"I tried to arrange for someone to meet us from the Catholic Mission," I explained to Molemo. "See if those women will carry our things. I think it's about an hour's walk."

The women agreed happily enough after they had negotiated a price with Molemo and our boxes of food and equipment were soon travelling smoothly along on their heads. The mountain scenery was awesome as we walked easily along a well-trodden path, but after a while we descended steeply to a small but fast flowing river, which we forded with some difficulty. Having climbed steeply up the other side we could see the buildings of Montmartre Mission in the distance and, on arrival, we found that the promised horses had just been saddled ready to go and meet us.

Seven Catholic Sisters and a Father, all of whom were Basotho, lived at the Mission. Sister Jacintha, a State Registered Nurse, ran the clinic. She spoke good English but the other Sisters were mainly too shy to use the few English sentences they knew. This in no way limited their caring welcome and it encouraged me to use my still limited Sesotho. They gratefully accepted the food that we had brought and used some of it for our meals. It was early spring and the nights were very cold. The Sisters made sure we were comfortable by giving us plenty of warm blankets and hot water bottles when we went to bed. I felt a real unity with them. Their practical generosity was impressive and in our different ways we were all trying to serve God.

Leprosy patients were supposed to have come to the clinic on the day we arrived but only a few turned up together with a boy who was a suspected case. As I examined him I took the opportunity of teaching the Sister and the Health Assistant, neither of whom knew as much about leprosy as Molemo.

"Leprosy can be diagnosed in one of three ways," I explained. "One way is by finding pale coloured patches on the skin which have loss of feeling when you test them with cotton wool; and another way is when peripheral nerves are enlarged,"

With Molemo I demonstrated how to check for loss of feeling and where to feel for nerve enlargement.

"Then the third way is by taking a skin smear. We should do one for this boy because his skin looks a bit infiltrated and I can't find any loss of feeling or enlarged nerves."

Molemo was by this time very expert at taking skin smears

and he efficiently demonstrated his skill by making a small incision in one of the boy's earlobes and spreading the fluid from the cut onto a microscope slide.

"We'll get that checked at the lab in Maseru," I told Sister Jacintha, "You should get the result in about a week's time."

It was not surprising that most of the discharged patients that had been asked to come to the clinic did not appear. They didn't want to risk being sent back to Bots'abelo. The following day Molemo and the Health Assistant set off on horseback to a village called ha Makara to try to find some of them. I remained at the Mission in case any turned up there. What a place it was! It was so quiet that it was almost scary. Half a mile further on there was a primary school for 280 children. 'Where do they all live?' I wondered. It was only later when I rode up the valley with the others that I could see the many little stone houses with their grass roofs tucked into the folds of the mountains. The children certainly had to walk or ride long distances every day.

Local people told us of a family, some of whom, they thought, had leprosy. The place was several hours' ride from the Mission. Visiting deep in the mountains was not easy for me as people were fearful of seeing a white face but I wanted to see for myself how the they lived. On the way we came upon another large primary school and were warmly welcomed as rare and unexpected visitors. This gave us a chance of giving a health education talk to the children. I felt sure it was time well spent, but as we remounted our horses I realised that the hours were slipping by very fast and we still had a long way to go.

We carefully urged the horses along the narrow paths of the mountain slopes and eventually came to the home where we found a small elderly lady who eyed us furtively. Molemo gently introduced us and tried to put her at ease. Then her daughter appeared. She was a known leprosy patient who had spent several years at Bots'abelo and was now home but it looked as if the disease was active again. Estorina, her mother, certainly showed signs of leprosy and an infectious type at that. She admitted she had a problem and that she had sought cures from several 'local doctors' all of whom had charged her heavily.

"If you come to the Mission," Molemo was quick to say, "You could have tablets that would cure you – and the treatment is free."

The little lady swished her blanket more tightly around herself and gave us a shrewd look.

"And how do you think your medicine can help my body if it doesn't cost any money?"

Molemo laughed but I felt exasperated. We could not spare the time to argue with her. It was getting late and it looked like rain. Giving as much advice as we could to the daughter, we mounted our horses and started the long ride back to the Mission. The horses, which had been reluctant to move on the outward journey, now sped along the narrow paths faster than I wanted to go. At the end of the day I was shattered. Was it all worth it? Of course I knew it was. I thought of all those desperately crippled patients in Uganda – disabled because no one had persuaded them to come early enough for treatment, and of my often hopeless task of trying to prevent foot ulcers and amputations. At least I now had the chance of preventing such suffering. If I could only find *a few* early cases and get them to take treatment, then it was worthwhile.

I often remembered Estorina's remark about paying for treatment. It was actually very sensible and plausible. Lesotho was a country where people tended to cry poverty and beg for free gifts and here was a lady living in very meagre conditions who was holding fast to her pride and dignity. It was a full two years before she eventually reached Bots'abelo. Her local Chief had persuaded her to go and she was still angry with him when she arrived:

"He only made me come because he's jealous of me," she declared. "I have more cows than he has."

Do not unsaddle your horse

Her leprosy responded surprisingly well to treatment and she became a gentle, co-operative person before returning home.

I made several more trips to Lesobeng, checking the patients who were on treatment, teaching the clinic staff, talking at the school and examining all the children for signs of leprosy. On one occasion I attempted to get there by Landrover with Molemo. We reached a Catholic Mission that was about two hours' drive from Lesobeng, where we had arranged to spend the night. People in the mountain areas were always very helpful and this time they were quick to point out a problem:

"The road has been spoilt," they said. "It won't be possible to get through to Lesobeng with a vehicle for several weeks."

We went to see. A mile away the road had been washed away by recent rain. A steep precipice remained and it was hard to imagine that there had ever been a road.

I was always determined to reach our destination because the patients who had been called to the clinic had to travel for many hours to meet us and if we did not arrive they were unlikely to make the effort on the next occasion. So early in the morning we drove back to Maseru. By this time Mission Aviation Fellowship was operating in Lesotho and its pilots were wonderfully helpful.

"Tomorrow you can charter a plane at half price," I was told at the hangar, "We have to go that way to collect some passengers."

Marvellous! We reached the clinic just as the patients were arriving. We were encouraged and so were they.

* * * * *

Whenever possible we checked the 'contacts' of known leprosy patients – the people with whom they had lived when they first developed the disease. As the average incubation period is five years, the 'contacts' had often moved to a different part of the mountains by the time we started looking for them and frequently the men were away in the South African mines, where they stayed for nine months at a time. However, our efforts were sometimes surprisingly rewarded:

There was a village called ha Ramotsoane about forty minutes' drive from Bots'abelo. It was the home of a teenage girl who had been admitted to the hospital. Hers was not an infectious type of leprosy but I wanted to find the 'index case', that is, the person who had passed the disease on to her. After chatting to people at the girl's home, we decided to wait for her brothers and sisters who were on their way home from school. While we waited we asked the family if there were any people in the village who they thought might have leprosy.

"Yes," they said. "There is an old lady. But her son is the Chief and it would be difficult to say anything…"

As we waited we slowly tried to persuade them to go and find her. Serious conversation flowed in whispered tones and after a while it seemed they had thought of a tactful approach and someone hurried off. When the old lady arrived it was fairly obvious that she was the person we were looking for and a skin smear confirmed our suspicions. She was admitted to Bots'abelo and, sadly, after a few weeks, she died – not of leprosy, but perhaps the wrench of leaving her home had something to do with it. I feared that the villagers might blame us, but they never complained. During at least one visit after that I was given a chicken.

We continued to check contacts at ha Ramotsoane and by very careful examination we diagnosed early leprosy in the Chief himself, in one of his daughters and in one of her children. Such people were invariably cured without getting any disabilities, so word was spreading that leprosy was not such a fearful disease as everyone had thought.

All the hospitals were staffed with expatriate doctors who knew very little about leprosy. When Molemo and I visited the Government Hospital at Butha Buthe, one of the nine towns or 'camps', we found a young Dutch doctor in charge. He couldn't understand why we wanted to stay and work in his District for a whole week, as he had never seen anyone with leprosy. On a hot afternoon I gave a talk to his staff, and he also attended. Everyone seemed rather sleepy but as I described the diagnostic signs I noticed the doctor's expression change. He was listening intently.

"Come with me to the ward," he said when I had finished the talk. "I have been treating a woman for a chest complaint but she is also complaining about numbness in her feet."

We examined her and found pale coloured skin patches that clearly lacked full sensation.

"So that's leprosy!" he said with amazement.

The next day when he was doing some routine checks for men who were going to the mines, he found another case. A few days later we met his vehicle on our way to a clinic. As we passed he shouted to us:

"I've found another!"

Some years later I came upon the same doctor at a different Government hospital. On seeing me he must have thought at once of leprosy. He quickly approached me with a request:

"Could you just look at a man who was admitted yesterday? He's in the far corner of the ward. I haven't had time to diagnose his problem yet."

When I told him that I thought the man had leprosy he became quite agitated.

"I don't know…this is really weird! Every time you turn up we see leprosy…"

A skin smear once again confirmed that particular man's diagnosis but in the early days I had to be careful not to think that anything that looked like leprosy actually was. Sometimes medical staff would alert us to suspected cases and whenever we could we tried to find them. After spending several hours driving on rocky tracks, precariously crossing rivers, getting lost and finally abandoning the Landrover and walking the last mile or so, it was tempting to believe, before we had even seen the person we were looking for, that he or she *must* have leprosy. Sometimes it was difficult to decide. Negative skin smears did not necessarily mean that it was not leprosy and it was often difficult to be sure about enlarged nerves. I soon learned that there are dozens of different skin conditions and most of them are not leprosy.

Mokhotlong was the most distant town, situated in the eastern highlands close to the Drakensberg Mountains of South Africa. I drove there with Molemo for my first visit, rather then going by air. The mountains were breathtakingly beautiful but the twisting, rocky track was wearisome. Whenever we stopped to ask if we were on the right road, we were told:

"Yes. Just go straight."

The road was anything but straight and it went on and on – so many mountains, so many rivers – eventually we reached the town only to discover that there was no accommodation at the 'hotel' where I had tried to book rooms. Molemo was somewhat concerned because when I got out of the Landrover at the hospital I was sick at the side of the road. After that my eyesight played tricks with me: I was seeing everything double – people had two heads one above the other. It was exhaustion, I knew.

Someone suggested we went to the Catholic Mission to ask the Father if he could accommodate us.

"We usually stay together," I said to the Father when he had agreed to take *me* in, but he was cheerfully adamant in his reply:

"No, no, you can go and eat papa with the Basotho," he said to Molemo.

So while I revelled in luxury, Molemo shared a Health Assistant's small house. It was not a problem for him. He enjoyed our trips and had learned to cope happily in most situations.

Do not unsaddle your horse

The Catholic Father was French and he was very understanding. He could see that I was very weary and he prayed for me asking God to help me, "...because such journeys are tiresome to our bodies."

By morning I had recovered. The Father advised me to take a short cut to the clinic that I was planning to visit some few hours' drive away. Little did I realise what this would involve. After crossing a wide and fairly fast moving river we were faced with an extremely steep climb with very tight hairpin bends. Landrovers are not able to get round tight bends and I had to reverse on some of the corners with vertical drops behind me. I slammed the vehicle into four-wheel drive, prayed and roared my way up and up.

A very large and extrovert Staff Nurse gave us a wonderful welcome when we arrived at St Martin's Catholic Mission. I always found the warmest hospitality at the most remote places. She had done her best to call in the people I wanted to see and she helped examine them and patiently listened as we tried to teach her about leprosy. However, she was especially pleased that we had come because she had seen her chance of transporting some bulky furniture to Mokhotlong. Of course we had to oblige, and the next day the three of us piled into the front seat of the Landrover, the rear space being full up with a large wardrobe, a table and some chairs. I always insisted on carrying our projector on the front seat, (we had used it the previous night to show slides of leprosy to all the school children), and because of the Staff Nurse's bulk it was a very tight fit, making driving even more difficult.

'What's this got to do with leprosy control?' I wondered, as I struggled to change gear; but it was all in the day's work and when we off-loaded our grateful friend and her furniture I could only be thankful that yet another trip had been manoeuvred without an accident.

Lack of transport often made nurses reluctant to work at remote clinics and I admired some of the older women who had stayed at isolated places providing a vital service through thick and thin. It was good if I could encourage them in some way.

After a hard day's drive I arrived at a health centre in the south of the country to be greeted by a surprising degree of happiness. By now I was suspicious of such delight.

"You have been invited to a feast," the staff nurse told me.

The last thing I wanted to do was to go to a feast.

"Where is it?" I asked.

"Oh, it's not far…"

Obviously she wanted to go and my vehicle was her only means of getting there, so we set out. At the appointed place we found a large crowd of people, quantities of cooked mutton and many flies. Being a guest of honour I was expected to eat some parts of the sheep's anatomy that the Basotho consider to be delicacies and which Europeans tend to dread. Somehow I survived. I do not recall the reason for the feast but I was thankful that our staff nurse was happy to leave before the end. The revelry seemed set to continue well into the night.

It was remarkable that we were kept safe from accidents on most of our trips for we often came upon vehicles that had come to grief. On one occasion we noticed two buses near the top of a muddy road with a large crowd of people standing around. Knowing that we would not be able to pass, I parked our vehicle and walked up the slope with my passengers to see what had happened. One bus had skidded into a ditch and the other one could not pass. The driver was furiously revving his engine and the wheels were spinning deeper and deeper into the mud. Nobody seemed to have taken any initiative to help.

"Get some stones," I said to some of the bystanders.

Word spread fast as my orders were translated:

"Majoe, majoe…"

"Watch out that someone doesn't get hit!" I said as people clamoured up the mountain-side and started hurling down large stones. "Now, pack them in all round the wheels."

Do not unsaddle your horse

Before long the bus was back on the road and the driver ordered his passengers to reboard at the bottom of the hill.

"Thank you, thank you," the people exclaimed as they walked down with us.

"That's all right," I said, knowing that we ourselves might have been stuck all day if we hadn't helped.

* * * * *

When Molemo had worked steadily for about two years and it seemed only fair that he should gain some recognised qualification. On our recommendation he was accepted for Health Assistant training – a two year Government course in Maseru. I was happy for him. Meanwhile we were allocated a newly qualified Health Assistant, Mashesha Tshabalala, who now accompanied me on field trips.

Darkness was falling as I drove along the narrow tarmac border on the western side of the country. Mashesha and I were returning from a long day out in the north. Ahead of me I could see little red balls that looked like fireworks streaking across the road. There was often trouble on the South African border at this time but I didn't realise that searchers were being fired into Lesotho. Mashesha was a very bright and intelligent young man.

"What are those?" I asked him.

He may have known but if he did, he appeared to be just as puzzled as me. Perhaps he wanted to get home.

"They haven't closed the road," he said.

So I drove calmly on. As soon as we were clear of the 'fireworks' the lights on the Landrover failed. I knew that the connections on the battery were weak, so fixing it was not a problem, except that we couldn't see. I hadn't expected to be out so late and there was no torch in the vehicle. Mashesha was wearing a belt with a large shiny buckle. He managed to angle it so that the reflection of the moon gave sufficient light under the bonnet for me to reconnect the battery, and we reached home safely.

Next day everyone knew about the shooting from South Africa. The road must have been closed soon after we had passed and it was still closed. People were horrified that I had driven that way.

It was Mashesha who came with me on a week-long trip to Motete – another very remote place. We went round the north of Lesotho and up the very steep escarpment to the high mountains before turning sharply west again. Half way up the escarpment I spotted a very large bird. We stopped and watched it. Mashesha even wondered if it was safe to get out of our vehicle, but then the bird lifted its huge wings and with a few initial flaps glided gracefully across a deep ravine to some distant rocks. I was excited. It was the rare lammergeyer or bearded vulture that measures 40 to 45 inches from beak to tail.

Mashesha was always full of bright observations and as we bumped over mile after mile of rocky track, managing an average speed of only five miles an hour, he suddenly laughed and said:

"Just look at all those tiny birds – how often they flap their wings!"

Flocks of birds were frantically busy flying around in the high moorland pastures but they didn't seem to be achieving anything. I contrasted them to the majestic lammergeyer and longed that we could achieve our goals without wasting so much energy.

When we reached Motete clinic I found that one of the leaf springs on our vehicle was broken. It was not surprising as the journey had been so rough. The other springs were holding it in place but it could easily become dislodged.

We camped in two of the clinic rooms, cooking our own food and seeing a few patients as well as visiting the school, holding a *pitso* (a meeting for all the people) and teaching the nurse. The problem of the broken spring kept worrying me but there was nothing I could do about it. There were no mechanics for many miles around and anyway we needed a spare part.

We prayed before we set out for home. Every so often I stopped to check the broken part, forcing it back into the best position. Slowly and carefully we drove right through the day and when we reached Maseru I offered a huge prayer of thankfulness. Shared experiences like this made me greatly appreciate my young assistants. Their interest in the work and their loyalty were commendable and I enjoyed their company.

As we travelled the country I met many Health Assistants because it was they who ran the leprosy clinics at the Government Hospitals. I wanted to find a Senior Health Assistant who could be my counterpart – someone who could head the fieldwork when I eventually left Lesotho and Ramatla Makong was the man I wanted. He worked at Qacha's Nek in the southeast. He was tall and strong and very kind to the patients and when I came to his area he always looked after me as well as he possibly could.

One winter's day I travelled alone by air to Qacha's Nek in order to do some teaching. To save mission funds I always asked for accommodation at the hospital rather than paying for a 'hotel'. Ramatla settled me in an office beside a blazing coal fire while he made some arrangements. In the welcome warmth I almost fell asleep waiting for him and wondered every so often if he had been called away to some emergency, but eventually he reappeared.

"I'm sorry for the delay, 'Me," he said politely. "There was a small problem but it's solved now."

It seemed that two leprosy patients who had been admitted for treatment for foot ulcers were occupying the room he wanted for me. When he tried to move them into a ward, the other patients said that if people with leprosy were allowed in, they would all go home. So Ramatla had resorted to his only other option. He moved the two men into a unit for mentally disturbed patients.

"But that's terrible!" I protested.

"No, 'Me, they will be all right. The nurses there said they would take special care of them."

I remembered an old file I once found at Bots'abelo entitled 'Lunatics and Lepers'. Our poor patients! Ramatla had made up a bed in the empty room for me, so all I could do was gratefully accept, but *why* was this dreadful stigma so hard to eliminate?

Ramatla did eventually join our team although I had to wait a year for him. He was a good driver and he arrived at Bots'abelo in a Government truck with all his belongings piled in the back. On top of everything was a large sheep with a long-suffering smile on its face. Ramatla had his wife and young children squeezed in with him on the front seat. They were tired by the long, rough journey but they all seemed to have the same expression as the sheep. They were happy to be back in their home area. They had a house in Maseru.

Ramatla was able to undertake some of the field trips for me but there was still plenty to do and when a Leprosy Mission Area Secretary visited us from London it was obviously my job to take him to see some of the outpatient work. I took him to a leprosy clinic and then, together with the local Health Assistant, we went to look for the patients who had failed to turn up. It sounded as if their homes were quite near and it was a sunny afternoon, so I ignored the Health Assistant who was muttering something about the river and not being sure what the road was like, and we set out. Along the way we found a man sitting on a rock under the shade of a large black umbrella. It was always necessary to obtain the village Chief's blessing on any visit done in his village, so we asked the man where we could find the Chief.

"I'll take you there," he responded helpfully, clambering into the back of the vehicle.

The Chief turned out to be a Chieftainess and she was sitting on a low wall outside her house chatting to some people. She wore the usual Basotho grass hat and blanket together with some checked bedroom slippers. For some time she continued her conversation, carefully observing us at the same time. This was a lowland area and people were not as friendly

Do not unsaddle your horse

or co-operative as they were in the mountains. Eventually she gave someone her brief orders:

"Why don't you take those visitors inside?"

We were shown into a beautifully neat little mud and thatched house and when we were all seated the Chieftainess joined us. She listened patiently as we explained our business and found out where the patients lived, trying to allay any fears that were inevitable because we must have appeared to be very affluent visitors and we were concerned with the dreaded leprosy.

Then an old, cured but very crippled leprosy sufferer was brought in for us to see. He had ulcers on his feet and problems with his eyes and a lot of other complaints that he wanted to explain. Everything had to be translated and time was passing fast.

After negotiating some bumpy tracks with plenty of rock and mud we arrived at the first patient's home but she was out in the fields. We arranged to come back later and went to find the second; no one had ever heard of her – but we wondered if they were telling the truth. Eventually we met the first patient. She and all her children appeared to be free of the disease.

Dark clouds were gathering and as we dropped our guide at the place where he had joined us it was pouring with rain.

"Just wait!" he said, "there's a woman with leprosy near by. I'll go and get her."

It was some time before he returned with a very crippled lady. She had a big sore on one hand but she was quite certainly cured of leprosy. She sat in the back of our vehicle while we gave as much advice as possible.

We then set out for the river but the ground was clay and we were soon slithering badly. For an hour we sloshed around in deep mud building a stony platform that eventually enabled me to drive the Landrover out of a ditch, across the river, up a steep scree slope and, thankfully, onto firmer ground...and home, very late. After that I had fresh sympathy for the Health Assistant, who, I had thought could have visited those people on foot. He had also impressed me by graciously pulling handfuls of mud off my shoes every time I got into the vehicle to try to get it moving.

I never seemed to learn! On another occasion, in the south, I was warned that a crossing place on a small river, which flowed steeply down the mountains, had been washed away making the road impassable. I thought we should make the effort to see if it had been repaired. When we reached the place we found that a large group of women had just finished the job – (women were always the road menders, most of the men being away in the South African mines). They all roared their approval as I drove across. However, we soon came to another river and it was far too deep to drive through after recent heavy rain. My two assistants found someone who agreed to lend us a horse and although the water was almost too deep for the animal, we all managed to ride across on its back in turns. We walked the last mile to the clinic only to discover that none of the patients had arrived because the swollen rivers further south were too dangerous to cross.

Women repairing the road across a river

At the end of every Friday afternoon we always tried to gather with Corrie in her office to read the Bible and pray for the work. It seemed odd to do this at the end rather than the beginning of the week, but I often asked the Lord to bless the efforts we had made and in some way make our small achievements bigger by His grace and power. I believe He honoured this prayer on many occasions.

Chapter 15
Frustrations and clashes

From the very beginning I realised that the dilapidated buildings and derelict appearance of Bots'abelo were perpetuating the widespread stigma and fear of leprosy that hindered every aspect of our work. I made many suggestions to the Ministry of Health officials and so often there were promises that something would be done but nothing ever happened. Lack of funding was always the main stumbling block for major alterations but it was sometimes possible to make small improvements.

I had no proper office in the hospital so I did most of my administrative work in my bedroom often working late into the night. I needed a desk in the old 'injection room'. Expatriates from Maseru sometimes visited Bots'abelo, curious to see what the place was like and to catch a glimpse of leprosy patients. Some of these visitors were genuinely interested in helping us, and Mrs Regenhardt, the wife of the German Ambassador, was one of them. Like most people she was suitably horrified by the facilities. She belonged to a ladies' group in the town and at her suggestion they agreed to provide me with the desk that I so badly needed.

Nothing happened for a long time and then one morning Mrs Regenhardt arrived at Bots'abelo in a very agitated mood. She had hoped that by now I would have received my desk but she couldn't get the other members of the group to finalise its purchase. The previous afternoon they had met, but only for a tea party, so the matter had not been discussed.

"Zose stupid English vimen!" Mrs Regenhardt exploded. "How do you think Germany became the richest country in Europe after ze var? – Vith all the vimen sitting around drinking tea? No, I vill do it myself. You go down to my husband at his office and collect ze money from him. You have seen vat you need, so you go and buy it."

So I acquired a desk. I put it in one corner of the room and hung a big map of Lesotho nearby. On this I gradually marked the homes of all the leprosy patients who still needed to be on treatment. There were just over 400.

When I returned from my home leave in 1979 I walked all round Bots'abelo to see if anything had changed. It hadn't. In fact it looked even worse. Gutters were hanging off the buildings, some roofs were leaking and bees had infested the men's ward. No amount of poisoning had shifted them and sick patients lying in bed had to put up with them zooming around their faces. A visitor who was shown around at this time said it was worse than a concentration camp he had been in during the war.

I drew a plan of a thirty-six bedded unit, including single and double rooms, a hospital, kitchen and laundry. There was a beautiful site for building just next door to the female compound. I presented my ideas to the Health Planning department but there was little positive response. However, it was agreed to make the veranda at the female hospital into another ward so that men as well as women could be accommodated. This meant that the whole of the men's compound could be demolished. A small building that had been used for physiotherapy was made into a kitchen, replacing the primitive cooking facilities in a smoke-blackened room near the wards. Two flush toilet blocks were also built to replace the night soil buckets. I viewed all these developments as only temporary. Bots'abelo was still far below the required standard.

Suddenly we noticed that some new buildings were being constructed on part of the Bots'abelo land. We were told that they were to be a piggery and from time to time members of the staff wandered down to see what the place was like.

"It's beautiful," people murmured. "There's even hot water laid on!"

The teacher at our school quickly saw an opportunity. Using another name he wrote a letter to the local paper describing the piggery and saying that the pigs had better accommodation than the leprosy patients. This caused an immediate response. The Minister of Health arrived for a tour of inspection, together with the Prime Minister, the Permanent Secretary for Health, Health Planning Officers and the Health Department Architect. Matron, wearing her smartest uniform, showed the visitors the very worst corners of Bots'abelo that would normally have been kept hidden, and the Prime Minister declared that the whole place must be demolished. We all wondered how this could be achieved but it gave me renewed courage to continue with my plans and suggestions.

The Leprosy Mission agreed to build a Guest House near the two small houses that they had provided for Corrie and me. It was to be prefabricated like our houses, but larger. This type of house was adequate but I was determined that the new one should not face west as ours did, because in summer when the sun set late in the evening the rooms stayed unbearably hot till nearly midnight. If I wanted to rest in the afternoons I would lie on my bed sweating. Experience in Uganda had taught me how important it is to align buildings correctly: I remember altering the new workshop by just a few degrees after the foundations had been dug, to get it exactly right.

My insistence was not popular with the Mission and this led to some reorganisation of our supervision, Alan Waudby visiting us every six months to provide guidance and support. The Guest House was positioned as I requested and it was beautifully cool in the summer, but I had caused some trauma; Corrie would have let the matter drop without a fight.

Vincent Matoase, the Catechist who often led the services at the Anglican Church close to the hospital, admired the work we were doing for the patients. When he heard that we needed someone to make simple shoes and crutches in a small workshop that had been set up, he was very keen to have the job. We tried to dissuade him. He was a middle-aged man whose vocation was clearly in the Church and he was seeking to be ordained. He was also extremely deaf, although he coped with this disability extremely well. When he refused to be discouraged the Mission agreed to employ him. His brief included organising simple physiotherapy exercises for some of the patients and taking daily prayers in the wards.

Everything went well for some time. The patients liked having him around and Vincent was encouraged by their keen interest when he explained the meaning of Bible passages in simple terms. However, it was not possible to give him much supervision and when he used his own initiative rather too freely, there were some differences of opinion.

"Who are you making these for?" I asked him one day when I paid a quick visit to the little workshop and found him at work on a pair of sandals.

He smiled broadly. "For myself! My feet are very painful and I need soft sandals otherwise I won't be able to walk to work."

I frowned and muttered something about working only for the patients. Vincent was a delightful person but this wasn't acceptable and in addition, pressing duties at home or connected with his Church responsibilities were often making him late for work. After a while, feeling our disapproval, he decided to leave. I was sad because he was a wonderful Christian. I met him at the Church on Sundays where his preaching showed his passionate faith, but our relationship became somewhat strained.

The Hospital Superintendents, who changed quite frequently, continued to view Corrie and me with some suspicion. Some of them had worked in South Africa and that tended to make them dislike any white people, regardless of their race. They were always reluctant to co-operate or to discuss our plans and it was difficult for us not to be critical of them.

There was a Catholic Mission at Bots'abelo with a large Church and a school. A very elderly, small and frail French Canadian priest looked after the establishment. His name was Father Labreque. Corrie and I were on good terms with him and he sometimes asked our advice when people sent him gifts for the patients. He had a suspicion that the gifts were not always getting to the patients. So when large quantities of dried milk arrived Corrie would collect them from the Father and assume responsibility for their distribution. This did not make for good relationships with the Superintendent but Father Labreque was no fool. There was certainly a lot of dishonesty and the patients began to confide in us, asking us to do something about it. It seemed that far more food was ordered for the patients than was actually needed and in the evenings they could see that it was being taken off the premises.

"When it happens next time we will call you so that you can see for yourself," one of the patients said to me.

I didn't want to get involved. Accusations such as these, whether they were true or false, sometimes resulted in deportation, because the people who were being dishonest often had friends in high places. At least the patients were not going short of food. Their diet was extremely good.

It seemed as if I was finding difficult people at every turn. I was so determined to press ahead with the fieldwork and all the other developments that I was forgetting the importance of being charitable and forgiving. I should have approached everything in a more relaxed manner but I was used to the way Bert had worked in Uganda, trying to get good facilities and everything running smoothly before we left the country. Progress in Lesotho was so slow. We had a five-year contract with the Government but at the rate we were going we would achieve very little in the time; and would the contract be renewed? Most expatriates had contracts of two years, or at the most, four and in that time they were expected to have taught their job to a local person so that they were no longer needed.

I was finding it difficult to work with Corrie, as she did not tackle with sufficient energy what I considered to be priorities. I am sure some of the things she did were greatly appreciated – the children's Bible class and the time she spent in language study, but I could see a need for a greater improvement in the laboratory work and in the provision of physiotherapy and footwear and we needed some rehabilitation activities for the patients. Instead of sharing responsibilities with her I shouldered too many aspects of the work myself. A year or so after we arrived I organised two four-day national seminars each of which were to be attended by 45 health staff carefully chosen from the areas where leprosy was most commonly found. Dr Stanley Browne, a very senior and well-known leprologist was our main lecturer. At about the same time Corrie parked the eight-seater VW Kombi, that she used for carrying patients, on a slope, without leaving it in gear and while she was visiting friends the vehicle rolled into someone's garden and crashed into a wall. It was one of her many 'mistakes', which she always acknowledged but, because I did not want to delay my work by sharing the Landrover with her, I felt I must take it upon myself to arrange for the Kombi's speedy repair. It was all very exasperating.

I explained my frustration to the Mission Directors when they visited us. They sympathised. It was obviously not unusual for them to have to sort out personal relationship problems but there was a difference of opinion. One person thought that discussion and prayer and more effort on both sides could rectify the whole matter. Another thought the time had come for Corrie to move on. In the end Corrie was asked to leave. When this actually happened I was very shocked, and ashamed that I had complained, but at the same time I felt that the decision was right. It was terrible for Corrie and we both had a traumatic month through which to work before she left.

Corrie was offered a job with the South African Dutch Reformed Church in Malawi. It says a lot for her ability to forgive that we kept in touch. After some months she told me that her new job was just a little better in every way than the one in Lesotho. Some years later she was nearly killed by a hippopotamus while swimming in Lake Malawi. It was amazing that she survived. Her rehabilitation took a whole year and she was left with some paralysis in one leg but eventually she returned to her post. I admired her courage.

All along I was helped by the friendship and support of various expatriates whom I got to know through attending the

Maseru United Church on Sunday evenings. Bill and Nancy Cape had helped me with the hospital plans, and they knew of a retired male nurse called Harry Oram:

"He's just the sort of person you need at Bots'abelo," Nancy said. "He'd be in his element. He's nearly finished building a hospital for the Methodists in the mountains so he should be free soon."

I had never met Harry but from their descriptions he was an unusual and remarkable person. It would be some time before The Leprosy Mission could send someone to replace Corrie, so I was very keen to meet Harry and see if he might be interested in filling a gap. The Capes managed to contact him and a meeting was arranged at my house.

Harry had a broad Dorset accent. He was from a farming family but he had trained as a nurse and then moved to South Africa where he worked in mission hospitals. His wife had deserted him when the youngest of their five children was only a toddler, leaving him to bring up the youngsters on his meagre nurse's salary. He was obviously a very practical person, used to turning his hand to whatever was needed. He listened to my ideas about working at Bots'abelo for a short time and seemed quite interested.

"Aarr, I could put in a few weeks and see how it goes," he said in an unassuming way, "But you'll have to square it with your Mission first. They may think I'm some funny old man...."

His easy manner and sense of humour were refreshing and I was very happy when the Mission agreed to employ him. He soon moved into the Guest House.

Harry possessed a wealth of experience and skill as a nurse and he had many incredible stories to tell. While he was building the hospital in the mountains people came to him from miles around even though medical treatment was not yet officially available there.

"There was an old chap who turned up one day with his wife," he said, "He'd had an argument with her and bitten off her lip. They'd got the lip there in a rusty old tin. I looked at it and thought I'd have a go at stitching it back on – there was nothing to lose – and it worked! 'Corse it weren't quite perfect but I saw her some weeks later and she was quite pleased with it."

It seemed best for Harry to work at some rehabilitation projects rather than nursing. He fenced off a third of an acre of land and made a vegetable garden. Initially some of the guards helped but later it was the patients who worked with him. They benefited from being active, learning to work safely with their various disabilities and earning a little pocket money. We hoped they would try to grow vegetables when they went home.

"We need a simple kitchen where the patients can be taught to cook without damaging their hands when they have no feeling," I said to Harry. "It should be the sort of place they would have at home."

We went to look at one of the small buildings that had been used for a storeroom for the patients and obtained permission for Harry to do some renovations and install a small wood stove. When he had built up the walls to make the roof higher, patched up some holes and made a chimney, we bought some paraffin stoves and local pots and pans. It was ideal because the patients could use whatever method of cooking they would use at home and they could also cook outside on open fires with large stones to balance the pots. We proudly showed the kitchen to some senior people from the Ministry of Health but they were not impressed. They thought the patients should have modern facilities and cook on electricity. They didn't understand our reasons for making it simple and thought we were lowering the standards when we had expressed the need to raise them.

It was a joy to have Harry around. The patients loved his slow, gentle approach. He didn't interfere in any way with the management of the place but very little escaped his attention. He noticed the dishonesty and the laziness of some of the staff.

Sometimes he came to my house after work to drink tea and listen to my frustrations.

"Yea, it's 'opeless, 'opeless," he would agree, shaking his head despondently.

But quickly his mischievous eyes would light up as he shared with me some funny incident that had happened during the day and we would both start to laugh. It was refreshing because my clashes with so many other people were making me depressed. Worry and feelings of guilt often kept me awake at night, although a mild antidepressant drug eased this considerably.

Before long I received a letter from The Leprosy Mission saying that they had managed to find a nurse for Lesotho, detailing her experience and qualifications.

"Is she the sort of person who can see priorities and get on and do something about them?" I wanted to know.

"We have no one else," came the reply. "If you don't want her you will have to struggle along on your own."

So Margaret Wilson arrived. She was from Northern Ireland and was a sweet, gentle person in her late twenties. It was obviously a big step for her to come to Africa and she was proud that she had acquired all the necessary qualifications in nursing as well as at Bible College. I tried to support her as she eased her way into the work in the hospital and the nursing staff made an effort to encourage her as well. She needed to settle in quickly as I was due for home leave just six weeks later. Harry was staying on, so I thought it would not be too difficult for her.

* * * * *

I was fortunate that the tenants in my house were able to vacate it for me when I came home and in between visits to different places and giving talks I was able to get the garden shipshape and smarten up the house. There were the usual visits to The Leprosy Mission's headquarters in London including a medical check up. I had a small, raised pinkish area on my ankle. It had been there for several years but it was slowly getting bigger, so it had to be investigated. There were delays in getting a biopsy and when it was eventually done, and found to be a melanoma (a form of skin cancer), my leave was nearly at an end. I was alarmed by the diagnosis and irritated that I had to cancel all my plans and engagements and speedily be admitted to hospital where I was, rather wonderfully, given a private room. The area around the melanoma had to be excised quite widely and skin grafted and I was in hospital for ten days.

The rest in hospital was actually a blessing. I was happy about the surgery and reassured when the surgeon told me that the trouble would not recur. However, after a few days I realised that my heel and the side of my foot had lost their full sensation. Suddenly I felt devastated. Could God really punish me like this? I had worked all those years with leprosy patients who had loss of feeling and here I was with the same problem. Gingerly I felt my damaged foot with the good one. Well, it was not *complete* loss of feeling, it was just impaired. The sural nerve had been damaged – something that, apparently, could not have been avoided. It was a permanent disability and I would have to learn to live with it.

My leave was extended by two weeks and when I arrived back at Maseru I soon discovered that Margaret had found the past few months very difficult. Harry had left a few weeks before my return. There had been problems with thieves at our houses and being too frightened to remain at Bots'abelo at night time, Margaret had been staying with friends in the town. As she was soon going to Addis Ababa for a course, I felt she would get the break she needed and come back refreshed, but the isolation of Bots'abelo continued to be difficult for her and at weekends she often drove the hundred miles to Bloemfontein so that she could enjoy the shops.

After a while Margaret became ill with acute stomach pains. She was admitted to hospitals both in Lesotho and in Bloemfontein but none of the doctors could diagnose her problem. On one occasion I drove her at high speed to Bloemfontein while she was sedated with pethidine so that she could be admitted before the drug wore off. On the way the police flagged me down for speeding but because they could see Margaret lying on the rear seat they believed my excuse and let me go.

In between her spells in hospital Margaret was cared for by some very special friends of ours at their house in Maseru. Bud and Doreen Isaacs were Canadians who worked with Mission Aviation Fellowship. They had been in isolated parts of Ethiopia for many years and being now near to retirement, they had become 'father and mother' to the families in their own mission as well as to some people outside it. They shared the burden of Margaret's sickness with her and with me in a most supportive way but after six weeks, to Margaret's relief, it was recommended that she went home to Ireland for further investigations. Once home she was admitted to hospital to have her appendix removed. She made a good recovery and took some home leave before bravely returning to Bots'abelo. Ten months later she handed in her resignation and left at the end of 1984.

Was it all my fault? Could I have made things easier for Margaret? I couldn't honestly say but I was now doubly grateful for Harry who continued to return to Bots'abelo for several weeks or several months at a time. It was out of the kindness of his heart. On arrival he would temporarily fix a nicely carved wooden notice on the door of the Guest House where he stayed. It read 'I do bide 'ere.' He actually had nowhere to 'bide' when he finally finished work, but the Methodist Church, of which he was a staunch member, offered him a partly finished house in the Cape on the understanding that he completed the building after he moved in. It was hardly a project for a seventy year old but he accepted the challenge and then went on to build a Church – but that's another story.

Do not unsaddle your horse

Chapter 16
Perpetrators, police and Patch

It was not surprising that thieves had upset Margaret. She was new to Africa and had not experienced such things before. In Uganda I had learned never to put temptation in people's way but even though we all lived very simply, our houses were known to contain things which local people coveted. Elimilech had been very ashamed when someone stole a radio from my house when he had left the front door open. He discovered who had taken it and eventually produced it for me – a completely useless object that had been rescued from the swamp. Because the thief was known he had been unable to make use of it so his only option had been to throw it away.

I also had two wheels stolen one night from a car that I owned for a short time in Uganda. It had been parked a few yards from my bedroom window and before leaving the thieves had neatly mounted the hubs on bricks. Such thefts were never reported to the police but local people sometimes assumed responsibility for meting out punishments. A young man who had stolen a cow at Kumi Township was tied to the animal while it was forced to race around in full view of everyone. The unfortunate fellow was dragged along in the dust until he died and for days his body lay in the road – a brutal reminder of the need to live an honest life.

With all these experiences as well as the loss of my handbag in Bloemfontein, I should have been hardened to such events, but in Lesotho we were particularly vulnerable because our houses were perched up on a hillside in full view of people living in the sprawling suburbs of Maseru. Robberies were often violent and we had no near neighbours to lend a hand if there was trouble. Corrie had a small mongrel dog called Mobebeli, but he had a poor reputation as a guard. He had allowed thieves into her house while she was in the kitchen and had remained asleep when the spare wheel and battery were removed from the Landrover one night.

One winter's evening I was with Corrie in her house, discussing plans, praying about them and doing some Bible study. After some time I went back to my house as I had forgotten to take my diary with me. As soon as I entered the kitchen I was aware of someone inside the house; also the contents of my big potato basket had been emptied on the floor and the basket had gone. I froze, scared to go further and shouted for Corrie. By the time she reached the house the intruder had gone and we ventured into the bedroom to find a broken window and my two cameras, the radio and some other items on my bed ready to be taken in the big basket. We were just in time, but the thief had got away with some money and keys, which was an infuriating loss because so many locks would have to be changed. Still feeling very shaken we went outside so that I could fix a temporary cover to the broken window, and there on the grass we discovered a jacket. There was a notebook in one of the pockets with the name and address of the thief together with those of various other people who were presumably his friends!

Early the next morning I went to the Central Police Station in Maseru to report the theft. The young officer who was sent to the counter to take my statement found writing, especially in English, very difficult but he was unwilling for me to do it for him, so it took a long time. Many words needed to be spelt and there were frequent interruptions. The place was more orderly than it was at night but even so a drunk and argumentative detainee in a cell near the counter was making a lot of noise because he was being treated harshly.

When the statement was completed and I had signed it and handed over the 'exhibits', the police suggested that their fingerprint experts should go with me in my vehicle, as *they* had no transport available. Later I discovered that this was a service they could always provide without delay, although it never seemed to assist them in actually finding culprits. When they had secured the prints, of course, I had to drive them back to base.

It was Sunday and I still had time to get to Church. As usual I met the Mothers' Union ladies and I told them about the theft. They were genuinely distressed about what had happened. As a result of Vincent's persuasive powers I too had become a Mothers' Union member and I enjoyed the friendly welcome the women always gave me. They prided themselves on their striking blue blouses, black skirts and woolly hats and many of them were extremely plump. As the Church had no heating it was exceedingly cold in winter and they wore their woollen blankets over the uniforms. I found comfort in sitting between two of them, warmed not only by their sympathy but also by their blankets. It was like sitting between two polar bears.

After the service the ladies all trooped down to see what had happened to my house. Having viewed the broken window, they all filed inside noting the open cupboard doors and the things that had nearly been taken and what had been left. Then they squeezed into the sitting room to pray and to just sit there, mostly on the floor, for they were many and interested youngsters had piled in too. A little refreshment eventually cheered them on their way and as they left I felt strengthened by their support.

"We know this man," some of them had told me. "The police will easily catch him for you."

I also thought it would be easy, but it was many months before he was brought to court. I made numerous visits to the Police Station to try to encourage them in their search.

"No, the man is not there. His mother is there but she is sick, so we can't ask her. Anyway she said he has gone to Mohale's Hoek" (in the South).

In the end he got nine months in prison and several other thefts were taken into consideration. I attended the court session and was surprised to see that he was a well-dressed and slick-looking young man. Usually petty crime was committed by the very poor who were desperately trying to provide for their basic needs.

Ours was the only transport available at night – at least it was the only transport with drivers, so we were often called if there were emergencies. Someone was hammering on my door late one night after I had gone to bed.

"Who is it?" I demanded.

I recognised the voice of one of the guards. "We are sorry to disturb you, 'Me. We need your help to go to the police."

I groaned, shivered and pulled on some warm clothes.

"What's happened?" I asked him as he joined me on the front seat of the Landrover.

"Someone has stolen one of the chickens. We have caught him…."

The patients were not supposed to keep chickens but some of them who had been at Bots'abelo for a long time had developed this 'initiative'. The thief was a miserable, poor little man and the patients in their fury had beaten him up. He was nursing his arm, which could well have been broken. Many of the patients piled into the vehicle with the thief to make sure he did not escape on the way to the police station. Incidents like this showed that desperate people no longer feared entering Bots'abelo.

All around our compound were little copses of mimosa trees. They were a wonderful sight in winter-time when the bright yellow flowers shone out against the clear blue skies, their strong scent filling the air. Often in the evenings I could hear people cutting down branches and one day I came upon an old man chopping away at a tree.

"Stop spoiling the trees!" I said furiously in my best Sesotho.

He looked up at me patiently and explained in simple English: "Madam, I am just collecting a little wood so that I can make porridge. I am hungry."

What could I say? He looked so thin and tired. By the time we left Lesotho all those small copses had been felled.

Rather against my will I was persuaded to be the treasurer of the Anglican Church at Bots'abelo. After his ordination

Vincent Matoase became priest-in-charge. In spite of his deafness he was very outgoing and charismatic and he attracted a fair number of local people to the services. As treasurer he asked me always to follow immediately behind the two Altar Boys as they returned with him to the vestry at the end of the service. I thought this to be rather unnecessary, but on one occasion when I was slow in joining them, the collection had already been counted.

"Seventy-eight cents," Vincent announced.

"That's funny," I said, "because I put in a Rand."

A tall Altar Boy had carried the plate with the money. Vincent glared at him and disappeared to the hospital, which was a short distance away, to take communion to a sick patient.

"Now look," I said to the boy, "It doesn't matter to me what happened to the money because I gave it to God. But why don't you go back into the Church and see if it fell on the ground somewhere?"

The boy disappeared and soon returned with the 'lost' coin.

"Did he confess?" Vincent asked when he returned.

I nodded. I felt sad that money was such a temptation for everyone.

With the building of the Guest House came even more problems. A large quantity of building materials arrived one day and, because there was nowhere else to put the things, they were piled up against my house. Huge drums of paint were among the items. Everything would probably have been safe for a few days but I thought it wise to ask the hospital guards to walk over several times during the night to check that all was well. The next day two drums of paint were missing. Of course no one knew how this could have happened but secretly I accused the guards and blamed my own naivety.

One Sunday, when the Guest House was completed, Vincent brought the entire Church congregation along to bless the building and pray for its safety. This must have been interesting for many of the people, as they didn't often have the opportunity of inspecting the houses of expatriates. Although

I appreciated the prayer and concern, I was, by this time, not too keen that everyone should be gossiping about our facilities and probably making them seem much grander than they really were.

I worked hard to furnish the Guest House and shortly after it was completed I was away for a couple of nights. On my return I went there to fetch something. On the floor just inside the door I was confronted by a bottle with two dried up fern heads in it – a sinister sign for some tiresome trick, I thought. Sure enough the place had been stripped of most of its contents, including beds and bedding, cutlery, the fridge, electric fire, chairs and tables. Afterwards people said that they had seen the things being driven away one lunch-time in an open truck by men in police uniform.

Obviously something had to be done. The compound was fenced and we locked the gates at night. We had several security lights on tall poles that came on at dusk and we had burglar alarms on our houses. These went through phases of going off for no apparent reason and were, on the whole, more trouble than they were worth. We had our own night guards but we now arranged for them to provide day cover as well, and in addition I decided to get a good guard dog and rather apprehensively made my need known among my friends in Maseru.

One evening in mid-winter when we were already settled in the warmth of our houses for the night, there was a noise at the gate. In the headlights of a vehicle I could see our guard talking to people and then I heard the Scottish accent of the Government Veterinary Officer's wife asking him to fetch me.

"We've got a puppy for you," she called as I ran outside. "She's from the dog's rescue home at Bloemfontein – they found her on a rubbish dump. She's so independent! She wouldn't even sit on my lap in the Landrover."

Over the gate she handed me a squirming white bundle with a soft stretchy skin over a sturdy little frame. I had to clutch the little creature firmly, feeling rather uncertain as to what I had been landed with. I must have sounded rather uncertain as my friends exclaimed:

"Don't you want her?...If you don't, *we'll* have her! Just look at her feet" (they were huge), "she'll be a real guard and a loyal friend, you'll see!"

"Oh, yes, I *do* want her," I said. "It's only that I had never thought of a puppy – but a grown dog…"

I *had* to be grateful. She was a gift from the kennels because they had been told that she was for a Mission. I carried her inside, found a cardboard box and a small blanket and let her settle into it under the kitchen table. All that evening I was very conscious of a pair of eyes watching me. She was only a few weeks old but a black patch over one eye already seemed to give her character. Of course she had to be called Patch. Later, when I had her details I found she was described as 'Boxer, Bull Dog, Bull Mastiff', and as she grew, that description fitted her well.

When I went off next morning Patch was following me towards the gate.

"Stay!" I ordered her.

The little animal sat down in the driveway and remained there as if frozen to the spot. She was intelligent and very quickly became house trained and used to the daily routine, gobbling up any food that was offered to her with great delight. I only once remember her refusing food and that made it very clear that she had bilaria, (a debilitating disease caused by ticks). After a visit to the vet in town she was soon on the mend, but she was poorly just at the same time as Mashesha was recovering from an accident on one of our motor bikes, damaging his thumb, and both he and the dog looked equally miserable.

"It wasn't my fault, 'Me," he complained.

I listened to a complicated explanation of what had happened.

"I believe you," I said, "but you've got to be clever enough to avoid other people's mistakes."

Patch put on weight at an alarming rate. I regularly sneaked her into the 'injection' room and weighed her on the hospital scales. She had to be coaxed into the room with its unfamiliar smell but eventually the undignified performance of being made to sit in a box on the scales annoyed her so much that she refused to co-operate any more. She was putting on about five ounces a day – just how big was she going to become! After three months in the kitchen at night, I decided it was time she lived outside, as that was where she was really needed. I had a large, open, wooden box made for her, guessing the size she would be as an adult, and in this she bedded down beside the guard under the carport.

By now Patch was very much aware of her job. The compound was about an acre in size but she concentrated mainly on the front fence, tearing up and down in the dust or mud, according to the time of year and wearing away a deep little track. It was very unfriendly. Children, taken by surprise by her bark would rush shrieking into the bushes, thinking that the dog would get outside the fence. This, in fact, she never did: the fence was her security too and she always remained inside even if the gate was open.

One of our elderly guards, Ntate Moruti, was very philosophical about Patch.

"It's a good dog, but not a good dog," he commented.

The trouble was that Patch controlled the guards' movements. She did not allow them to approach me because she knew I was the most important person to protect. After all, I fed her! On one occasion I asked Ntate Moruti to hold Patch by the collar so that I could take her photo. It was a stupid thing to do. Patch pulled loose and bit him (not very badly) on his hand. After a few days I asked if the hand had healed and discovered that Ntate Moruti was applying paraffin to the bite 'to clean it'. It was sore and infected. He was a frail old man with a knowing smile and he was proud of the little English he knew. He had been in the army with British soldiers in the Second World War and was very pro-British and polite. Like many Basotho he was also very uncomplaining. I dressed his hand every day for a week and it was soon healed.

Winter came again. The guards had a ration of coal for their brazier at night and we let them saw up dead wood that could sometimes be found. Patch needed a warmer place to sleep and Harry made a smart kennel out of scrap wood from the demolished hospital buildings. Patch was very doubtful about going inside the kennel and another old guard, less fluent in English than Ntate Moruti, spent a long time coaxing her and ordering her, in the language he must have felt she understood best, to get inside:

"In house! In house!" he kept repeating.

After an hour or so, Patch obeyed.

One Saturday morning I was busy in the kitchen when Patch, who was lying outside the open door, started to growl. It was a noise I had never heard her make before and when she refused to be quiet I went to see what was happening. Two yards from the door was a cobra, partly coiled up but with its head erect and threatening. Snakes were fairly common. I got Patch inside, thankful that she had the instinct to leave it alone, and the guard came and helped me kill it.

I was always careful to dispose of dead snakes thoroughly. I once buried a puff adder in a rather shallow hole and later I heard that two men who had been working on the electricity lines nearby had dug it up and eaten it. It was unusual, as most Basotho are very frightened of snakes. My maid, Sebolelo, came upon a snake when, on a rare occasion, I had persuaded her to cut some of the long grass around the house. Terrified, she threw down her sickle and ran home without even locking up my house.

Patch loved to go outside the compound for walks but it was a risky activity. I always scanned the hillside to see if there were any sheep. Sometimes I could not see the animals lower down and Patch would immediately spot them and tear off. She liked nothing better than driving a flock of sheep at full tilt down the slope. Woe betide any chicken that strayed from the patients' quarters. Many a time I had to pay for a dead chicken or a supposedly dead one. The patients always looked very miserable and of course I was furious with Patch, but the owners did very well out of these tragedies, receiving not only the money but also a chicken to eat. On one occasion, at dusk, Patch found a hare. A rapid chase followed and I was sure she would catch it. However, the hare cleverly turned a summersault and Patch overshot it. She was completely baffled.

"Where's it gone?" she seemed to be asking me.

"You lost it," I laughed, "and just as well! Come on, we're going home."

'Work' was such a serious business for Patch that she sometimes landed herself in trouble. We had visitors from the Mission staying in the Guest House and Matron arrived at the gate with a present for them. Either she wanted to come in, or she wanted the guard to take the present to them – whatever it was, Patch put up a terrific fight to prevent the guard from helping. She was so fierce that he lashed out with his stick to protect himself. In the end he cracked the stick against her lower leg and she came squealing to the house. She limped for several weeks but never gave up on her duties.

"Oh you *are* a mess! What am I to do with you?"

Patch had a skin condition and an infection in one eye that kept recurring. It was probably because she was almost entirely white and she was out in the sun so much. The black patch over the other eye protected that one perfectly. I carefully cleaned her weeping sores and fixed a big cardboard collar round her neck to stop her scratching. Careering through the bushes wearing the collar made her seem even more alarming to passers-by. I was desperate to get her well, so one day I bandaged her around one thigh and all over her body. Patch sat looking very pathetic during this process and when I had finished she refused to move from the kitchen floor. It was as if she was saying:

"Now I'm sick, and if you want me to move, you'll have to carry me, 'cos I'm sick."

Do not unsaddle your horse

I coaxed her outside where she sat looking cross and dejected. After a while I could hear a horse and rider galloping down the sandy track. In an instant Patch was up and off and within a few seconds the bandages were trailing in the dust. So much for my efforts! It was amazing that the sores did eventually heal.

Patch was lying enduringly under a chair in my sitting-room one night. I had brought her inside because there was a terrible storm. She was pretending not to be afraid of the lightning and crashing thunder. At such times she was gentle and lovable and always keen to roll over and have her tummy rubbed; but she had become a dangerous animal. She was very strong and had even knocked a nine-year-old boy clean off his feet when he was looking the other way. He and his parents were new to Lesotho and I was showing them round the hospital. The boy fell on concrete and was slightly concussed. I felt very ashamed but Patch was so exuberant. To this day I have a scar on my arm, caused by one of her many enthusiastic greetings when I had my hands full and could not fend her off.

I knew that when I finally left Lesotho Patch would have to be put down. I could hardly bear the idea. I dreaded having to take her to the vet for that. She had been a loyal friend, defending me with her life. Fortunately Harris Waltner, the American Pastor from the Maseru United Church came to my rescue. He and his wife Christine came to Bots'abelo immediately after my farewell party (which I describe in a later chapter) and Harris took Patch, with her mouth muzzled, down to the vet. When he returned the guards buried her in a grave that they had prepared. We stood together while Harris prayed, thanking God for such a faithful dog. Somehow it seemed all right. I could cope. I also had so many things to do just then. When I took Ntate Moruti his flask of coffee later in the evening I found him walking freely around the compound singing hymns to himself. Probably he has never had to manage such a challenging dog since.

When I revisited Lesotho four years later, people were still talking about the fierce, white dog with the black patch over one eye that used to terrify passers-by. But she is gone, and over her grave large, bushy mimosa trees are thriving.

Patch as a puppy

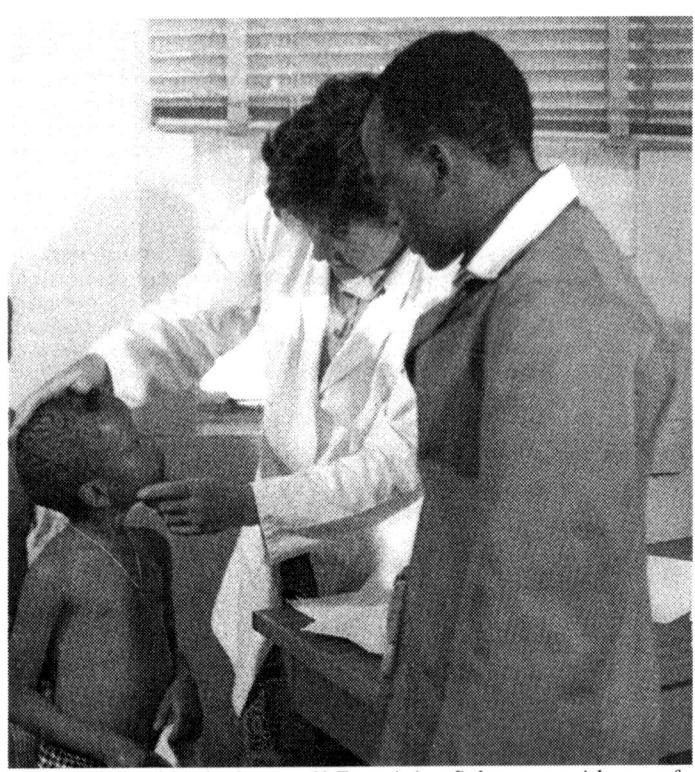

Above: 'Could it be leprosy?' Examining Sebetoane with one of my helpers; Below: Sebetoane settling in at Bots'abelo

Chapter 17
Successes and surprises;
joys and sorrows

I was sitting outside the Minister of Health's office in Maseru anxiously looking at my watch. I had an appointment for 9.30 a.m. and it was already well after that time. In three hours some people would be arriving from England to make a film of our work and despite my efforts over the previous few months I had not yet obtained the necessary permission. What if our request was refused? I shuddered at the thought and prayed hard.

It had not been difficult to provide a story about one of our patients for The Leprosy Mission. Some of our most rewarding work was with children and Sebetoane was the ideal star for a film. He was six years old when the mother of the family living next door brought him to one of the Government hospitals, where she herself attended for leprosy treatment. We knew 'Me Ramouane's family well. Almost all of them seemed to have had leprosy and two of her children had recently been at Bots'abelo for several months. Apparently one of her daughters had looked after Sebetoane when he was a baby and she had now spotted some swelling on his face and was suspicious that he too had the disease.

'Me Ramouane was a clever woman. She watched me closely as I carefully examined the little boy and looked surprised when I said I could not see any obvious signs of leprosy.

"I'll do a skin smear," I told her. "That will tell us if there's anything wrong."

She nodded approvingly. Sebetoane winced as I made the small incisions but he did not complain. A week later we had the results. Sure enough, 'Me Ramouane had been right. Sebetoane had lepromatous leprosy – a difficult type to diagnose in the early stages.

It had seemed terrible to take Sebetoane away from his home and bring him to Bots'abelo with its poor facilities and severely crippled patients but he soon settled in and there were some other children, which helped. His admission gave him the opportunity of going to school – a chance he would never have had at home because his family was so poor. Being the eldest of three children and the only boy, he was already fully occupied herding the few cattle that his father owned. This would have been his job for many years, as girls were not allowed to work with animals.

I looked at my watch again and sighed. I could hear men's voices chatting happily in the office as if they were oblivious of time. It would be such a pity if the film could not be made; it was a good story. We planned to involve a teenage patient who started treatment and refused to carry on with it long enough, and to illustrate the inevitable results of such stupidity, by showing several badly crippled patients waving goodbye with stumpy hands and crooked smiles when Sebetoane was discharged. Suddenly the office door opened and out came some Basotho men in light-hearted mood, one of whom I knew. He was a Chief from Lesobeng, and he had kindly lent me a horse during one of my visits to his area. He recognised me at once and showed no surprise at seeing me there; I had a feeling that the Minister had mentioned me to him and that he had put in a good word for me.

I was soon in the office and permission was quickly granted for the film to be made, with the assurance that the Ministry of Health would co-operate fully, on one condition, that they would see the finished film in due course. I breathed a sigh of relief, thanked the Minister politely, and left his office.

'Praise the Lord!' I muttered to myself.

I had not been heavily involved with the film of Livingstone in Uganda but this time a great deal of the work fell to me. Corrie was away at a conference in India when the team arrived, so Hugh and his camera-man, Brian, were able to use her house. Morgan Derham, from The Leprosy Mission, came for the first week and stayed in my house, as the Guest House was not yet completed. In fact I was supervising the building of the Guest House, so my day started at 6.00 a.m. with the builders. I then prepared breakfast for the team before we all set out for the day's filming. Much of this could be done locally but I also had to arrange a trip by plane into the mountains, two days at Sebetoane's home, a day at the clinic where we first met him and a visit to a school where we were to give health education.

One of our staff nurses was married to an important Principal Chief and she was very helpful in getting him to organise a gathering of his Chiefs, again for the purpose of filming health education. The Principal Chief was rather too enthusiastic for our requirements. He viewed the whole procedure as something very special that needed a colourful ceremony. Wearing an ostrich feathered headdress and holding a flag up high, he led his brightly blanketed Chiefs on horseback at a gallop to the place where we had assembled. He had also invited a 'Rain Man' in an effort to keep the rain away. The man was 'successful' for a while but dark clouds were building up and just as a downpour was about to start he came bounding towards us declaring:

"I can't stop this one!"

Still leaping around he helped us carry all the equipment to the shelter of our vehicle where we thankfully consumed a few sandwiches away from the public eye. Somehow the material was included in the film and Hugh was particularly amused because the Principal Chief, who was never very sober, always addressed him as 'My Lord'.

On another occasion we needed a crowd of people for some of the filming. Vincent had tried to organise this with a local Chief but no one turned up. It was important not to waste time and, realising the urgency, he rushed to the nearby mental hospital and asked for as many of their patients who were fit enough to come and help us. My maid, Sebolelo, and a few other people from Bots'abelo joined in as well and the filming went ahead without any problems, the borrowed patients enjoying their little outing.

Sebolelo was invaluable during the three weeks of filmmaking. Normally she did not do any cooking for me, but she had once worked for an English family in Johannesburg and preparing meals seemed to be quite easy for her. Every evening she cooked an excellent feast for us all.

"It's like a five star hotel," Hugh told her on several occasions.

Sebolelo beamed. She thrived on praise and did not mind how hard she worked to obtain it. I always made sure there was enough food for her as well but often she was so busy that she didn't have time to eat it. She preferred to take her share home with her so that she could enjoy it without having to eat in a hurry, even though it was cold by then. I was pleased to see her so happy because she was intelligent and she normally got bored with the monotony of washing and cleaning.

Corrie returned for the last week of the filming and amazingly it was completed in the available time. We were both included in the story but Sebetoane was the star. He was a charming little boy, always interested in what was going on and delighted when he was allowed to look through the camera. Whether or not he understood what was happening was another matter but he enjoyed watching the completed film as did all the other patients and staff who took part in it. The film won an award and in the months and years that followed, Sebetoane's bright little face was seen in many countries as mission staff encouraged people to pray and give.

On the day we filmed Sebetoane's discharge from Bots'abelo I insisted that this must be the real thing and that he should now remain at home and get outpatient treatment at his nearest clinic. I felt it would be too unkind to take him back to Bots'abelo again, but it turned out to be a foolish idea. Sebetoane had a type of leprosy that was difficult to treat and he was sometimes poorly with reactions. After a few months I visited his home to see how he was, only to discover that he was not getting his treatment.

"The tablets got left in the sun and they went a funny colour," his mother told me. "I got some Holy Water from Church. We thought that would be better."

I was horrified. Sebetoane did not look well and I knew I had to take him back to Bots'abelo. His mother agreed and Sebetoane did not appear to be worried.

"Are you hungry?" I asked him as he sat beside me in the Landrover.

He nodded. I had a banana and a sandwich left over from my lunch and he gobbled them down ravenously. I found him a peach as well.

Sebetoane stayed at Bots'abelo for several years. Fortunately in 1982 we were able to use much more effective drugs that had been tested by the World Health Organisation and approved for careful use. The new treatment, known as multi-drug therapy, involved the combined use of Rifampicin and Lamprene (clofazamine) with dapsone and these reduced the period of treatment very significantly. Sebetoane responded well to the new drugs and when he was finally discharged in 1985 he really was cured of leprosy.

"Will he be able to go to school?" I asked the family when I took him home. "He has done very well and it would be very sad if he can't continue."

The parents assured me that they would send him – there was a primary school very near to the home. But perhaps they were too proud to admit that it would be impossible for them to pay the fees. Some months later I heard that Sebetoane was once again herding cattle.

Fortunately I knew the organiser of Save the Children Fund and was able to persuade her that twelve-year-old Sebetoane was a deserving case for sponsorship. I was so determined that he should get to school that I took him with me to buy his school uniform and some necessary books. Save the Children co-operated well and saw him through school as far as his GCSE exam. After that he worked as an unqualified teacher for a couple of years until Save the Children agreed to sponsor him again for teacher training. When I last heard of him he was doing well in his final year.

It was during the time that we were making the film that news came from home that Pam Maclennan had died. Pam had become my closest friend; she was like a sister to me and her regular letters were a source of great encouragement. She always commented in detail on my news and then gave her descriptions of small or big happenings so vividly that I could imagine that I had been there myself. Often she was very amusing but she was also wise and practical and very special.

Pam had visited me in Uganda and we had gone together to Rwanda for a holiday. She had also come to Lesotho with our friend Joy Reynolds. On that occasion she had miraculously been declared free of the cancer that had been diagnosed the previous year. She had a tremendous testimony of how the Lord had answered the prayers of a group of friends who, unbeknown to her, had decided to pray for her throughout a certain night. At about midnight they had felt clearly that there was no need to pray any longer and they all went home. It was exactly at that time that Pam felt certain that she was cured and this was confirmed at her next medical check up.

Sadly the disease recurred some months later and during my leave in 1979 she was poorly. She did not want to undergo any treatment, still trusting the Lord to heal her. She bravely drove me to Heathrow for my flight back to Lesotho, which must have exhausted her. Her 'Goodbye' at the airport really was goodbye. It was the last time I saw her.

I was so busy when the news came. I felt I should be grieving for Pam but her death hardly seemed to register in my mind. People wrote to tell me what a wonderful funeral it had been and how much she was missed but I couldn't take it all in. It was a full two years later when I was again in England that the loss became real. I drove home from church one Sunday, making a detour so that I could pass by Pam and Graeme's home. Suddenly I found myself sobbing with grief. It was true, what I had been told; she was no longer there. Graeme was carrying on alone bravely coming to terms with his loss. I had to begin to do the same.

A considerable amount of money was donated in memory of Pam and I was told that half of it was to be used in some way for my work in Lesotho. Someone wrote to me:

'We hear you have had a portable generator stolen. Would you like to use the money to buy a replacement?'

'Certainly not!' I thought to myself. 'That's not a worthy cause. If I try hard enough I can get the Ministry of Health to get a new one.'

But what would be a really special thing to do? Something that Pam herself would have applauded? One idea kept presenting itself to me: – that Malcolm and Charmian Bury (our vicar and his wife) should visit Lesotho. Pam had on several occasions collected money so that they could have a holiday. The problem was that the money was not nearly enough for the air fares.

As I had no other ideas, I sent my suggestion to the folk at Ryarsh. They thought it was a brilliant plan. Very generously all the necessary money was raised including pocket money and Malcolm and Charmian duly arrived for a two weeks' stay. The time together was richly blessed. I took them with me when I visited some of the mountain clinics and when I was able to take some holiday we flew to Semonkong, high in the mountains, and stayed a few nights in a lodge close to the Maletsunyane Falls (the highest waterfall in Southern Africa). Malcolm particularly enjoyed watching what he thought were eagles soaring around between the escarpments and we all revelled in the grandeur of the bare landscape.

During my home leave in 1982, Malcolm and Charmian suggested that we had another holiday together and we decided to go to Ireland. We hired a car at Dublin airport on the first day and went to Killiney to find the house where I had lived as a child. It was not difficult to locate and we drove up to the front door and rang the bell. A lady who was probably a housekeeper greeted us.

Do not unsaddle your horse

"Mr and Mrs McClenaghan are out," she explained apologetically.

Suddenly I felt aghast. Someone called Ken McClenaghan had caused some confusion in Lesotho. He administered an Irish leprosy association and there had been an understanding between him and The Leprosy Mission that he would not send any workers to Lesotho because it was a small country and it was easier for just one organisation to give the necessary assistance. However, we had only been in Lesotho for a few weeks when we learned that an Irish doctor was to be sent. As it happened the doctor was an understanding young lady with whom it was easy to work but Ken McClenaghan often turned up unannounced at Bots'abelo and because I felt threatened I sometimes greeted him abruptly. Could it be possible that he now lived in 'my' old house?

I must have looked stunned.

"What's the matter?" Malcolm asked

Just then a car came up the drive and out stepped Ken.

"I know him," I said.

But Ken did not recognise *me*. So without any introductions I explained why we had come and showed him a few old photographs of the house.

"That's amazing," he exclaimed enthusiastically. "You see I bought the place just a few months ago. Of course it's all in scaffolding – needs a lot doing to it – but we are trying our best to make it nice."

Still hardly believing to whom I was talking, I asked falteringly:

"But do you sometimes go to Southern Africa?"

"Why, yes!"

"And Lesotho?"

"Yes."

"Well I'm Margaret Phillips," I said.

With that he flung his arms around me and gave me a kiss. I was in a daze.

"You must come in and see all round the place!" His genuine happiness challenged my embarrassment.

"Oh, yes please," I said.

We ate our sandwiches on the steps leading out of the old garden room onto the grass. The laburnum trees had all gone and the garden was just areas of rough grass. It was a place I had loved so much and it was now neglected and shabby. I wanted to stay longer and absorb the changes but time was limited. What a small, small world it was!

The world was getting smaller for me in other ways too. In 1984 The Leprosy Mission invited me to attend the Twelfth International Leprosy Congress in Dehli, North India. It was a busy and useful time but a real highlight was the unexpected arrival of Mother Teresa at the opening session. She had heard of this gathering of 1,500 delegates from all over the world and had decided that it was too good an opportunity to miss. A small wizened figure, she stood there on the platform and gave her brief challenge with great clarity:

"We have just to be channels for God so that His love and caring can flow through us to needy people."

I felt she had set the right tone for an important gathering of people who were certainly not all motivated by a desire to serve God.

From India I took the opportunity of visiting Mary and Philip once again in Australia. It was a short holiday and soon I was once again back at Bots'abelo.

Sebolelo, my maid, was usually a great help to me although she was sometimes a mixed blessing. If I went away I left plenty of jobs for her to do so that she was kept busy. On one occasion I returned from a field trip to find the house in the same state as I had left it a few days before. There was a pile of dirty dishes, my bed was not made and the ironing was not done. Where was Sebolelo?

The next day a young woman arrived at my house. Sebolelo had given her the key of my house and had told her to do her work. She herself was in prison. I was shocked and angry. The woman did not seem able to explain what crime

Sebolelo had committed and I did not feel like trusting her. I took the key and sent her away.

Over the next few days other people confirmed that it was true that Sebolelo was in prison, so I telephoned to ask what she had done to deserve such punishment and how long she would be there.

"She's here for bad language," the officer told me. "She could have paid a fine of twelve rands but she preferred to come in for a month."

I later discovered that cattle had strayed on to Sebolelo's land and she had verbally abused the owner who then complained to the authorities.

It was less than a month when I heard that Sebolelo was home. Apparently her grandmother, with whom she shared her house, had died and she had managed to get out of prison earlier than expected. Once or twice I saw her in the hospital grounds but she never looked at me. Probably she felt too ashamed.

Then one Saturday morning Sebolelo appeared at my gate. She was very smartly dressed. I called Patch inside and shut her into my bedroom before telling Sebolelo to come in. She was very much on her best behaviour, as she had, of course, come to ask if she could start working for me again. I was not too keen. I had been managing quite well with another woman on a parttime basis but I told Sebolelo I would consider her request and let her know. Encouraged by my response Sebolelo said:

"Let's have a nice cup of tea!"

So of course we did.

At Church that weekend I met a Canadian lady who ran a Bible class in the women's prison. I was interested to hear about her efforts in evangelism and I told her about Sebolelo and her brief stay in the jail.

"She's about my age and size and she speaks English quite well. She's a capable woman – a leader really…"

"Yes, she was there!" my Canadian friend replied, "She was very helpful and interested too. She made a commitment and accepted a simple Bible study course that she could do at home. You *must* take her back. She will be useful to you now."

So Sebolelo was reinstated. It was good to have her with me again and she had certainly gained something from her stay in prison although she did not talk about it. I compared her to Onesimus, the slave who Paul had asked Philemon to take back into his service because he had been his spiritual father while they were been in prison together. My Canadian friend was Paul and I was Philemon. Working for me was boring, but Sebolelo continued to give loyal service to the end of my time in Lesotho, and I struggled to settle her in a new job before I left, feeling that I could genuinely recommend her as a useful person.

* * * * *

Bert Landheer used to tell the Leprosy Assistant students in Uganda that they would never be good workers until they dreamed about leprosy. If that was true, then I was becoming a good leprosy worker. The patients, their treatment, their families, the field work, – these things were constantly on my mind and it was never a problem to explain how we tried to control leprosy to any interested enquirers.

The Maseru Rotary Club was interested in buying radios for the wards at Bots'abelo. Some of their members visited the hospital from time to time and after showing them round I would chat to them in my house. Unbeknown to me they were looking for someone whose work showed dedication and commitment on whom they could bestow the Paul Harris Fellowship award. I felt honoured when they chose me, especially as it was the first of such appointments that the Maseru Club had made. For the presentation I was invited to one of the Club's lunches.

"Do I have to make a speech?" I enquired of the secretary beforehand.

"Oh, no," he replied vaguely. "You just have to say 'Thank you'."

I had been a guest speaker at the Rotary Club on two previous occasions, so I was familiar with the way they conducted their meetings. After the meal the presentation of a medal and a certificate was made. I thanked the assembled members for the honour and sat down. After a few announcements the chairman came to the final item – the guest speaker – and he happily announced that I was now going to speak. Unexpected as this was, there was only a short hesitation before I was able to launch into a few stories of patients who had been helped and of how our work was reducing the fear of leprosy in Lesotho.

I might well have described how a man who worked in a platinum mine near Pretoria turned up at Bots'abelo one wintery afternoon with his wife. We immediately noticed his infiltrated face. He had been to several doctors and each one had told him to go to Bots'abelo. Now that the signs of leprosy were so obvious, he had finally plucked up enough courage to follow their advice.

The field workers talked with him in Sesotho for a long time that afternoon. Slowly he explained his symptoms and his fears:

"I am Mosalla Lekaka," he told us. "I'm thirty years old and I live just down there," he pointed towards Maseru, "I have to go to the mines to support the family. If I do have leprosy the people at the mine must not know – otherwise I will lose my job and I have to report back next week or they will sack me."

The field workers continued to explain his need for treatment and that he would be cured in due course and Mosalla and his wife listened intelligently.

"I'll write a letter to the mine authorities asking them to keep your job for you," I promised them.

At that Mosalla agreed to return the next day to be admitted and to have a skin smear taken before leaving. We were relieved that he had taken the right decision and congratulated each other on our patience with him.

The next day Mosalla did not turn up. After a few days I sent a field worker to his home only to discover that he had gone back to the mine. Later we learned what had happened during those few days. He had visited a 'local doctor' who told him that his ancestors were not happy and this was the cause of his problems. He was to hire a car, go to the grave of one of his relatives and perform certain ceremonies. This whole process was very expensive but having done everything exactly as he was told, Mosalla was sure that he could safely return to the mine with complete faith that he would be cured.

What were we to do? If we did nothing Mosalla would eventually lose his job and while we delayed he was probably passing on the disease to other miners. I managed to get the address of the mine and wrote, telling the authorities that he needed treatment for three months and asking them to keep his job for his return.

I had talked with doctors who worked in the South African mines on several occasions and they always assured me that there were no cases of leprosy among the miners. I knew they were wrong. I firmly believed that the reason why we always had more female patients than male was because there were many undetected cases among migrant workers. I also realised that these doctors were not only ignorant about leprosy but that they were very scared of it. So it was not surprising that Mosalla was sent back to us as speedily as possible. He was admitted and his condition began to improve with multi-drug therapy. Not daring to keep him too long for fear that he would abscond, we allowed him to return to the mine with a supply of drugs which he promised faithfully to take as prescribed. It was a risky thing to do but at least he was no longer able to pass on the disease to other people.

Mosalla told me the name of the person I should write to at the mine.

"He will agree to my staying," he assured me, "He gets me to train his race horses when I am not working."

Sadly the letter did not convince the mine doctors that it was safe to reinstate Mosalla and he soon appeared at Bots'abelo again. I was very annoyed. How could they be so stupid? We had been kind enough to tell them that they had a man with an infectious type of leprosy and we had now told them that he was no longer infectious. More than that, if they did not take him back, all his friends would know that if they developed the disease they should hide the signs for as long as possible for fear of being dismissed like Mosalla.

I composed another letter and telephoned the mine. Eventually Mosalla was allowed to return. When he came for a check-up he told us that he had been promoted and was working in an office. He needed to continue with treatment for several years and we hoped he would be sufficiently reliable for the final outcome to be a success.

It was difficult enough to keep the outpatients on regular treatment even when they were working in Lesotho. Irregular treatment over several years caused resistance to the drugs. Matsie Pitso was admitted to Bots'abelo as a boy of thirteen in 1962. He spent six years as an inpatient, two years at home and another five years at Bots'abelo. In 1978 he was admitted again and was infectious. Because he was working as a tractor driver for the Department of Soil Conservation, he was not keen to remain an inpatient for long and we trusted him to attend an outpatient clinic near his home. When we checked the records at this clinic some months later we found that his treatment had been very irregular. Apparently he had moved to another work area further in the mountains. The only option was to go and find him. Molemo came with me.

We drove into the bleak mountains and after bumping many miles on rough tracks we came to a group of corrugated iron rondavels on a little hill. This was a Soil Conservation camp. Molemo made some gentle enquiries as we did not want people to know why we had come but, of course, they had guessed.

"Matsie has gone to Maseru with one of the tractors,"

someone told us. "Oh, we know he has leprosy – and his face and eyes look very bad these days…"

His work mates seemed glad that we were looking for him.

We watched out for Matsie as we drove back to Maseru. Sure enough we spotted him on a tractor on his way to the camp. We managed to stop him and he greeted us happily; by this time we knew each other rather well.

"Yes my eyes are troubling me – that's why I am wearing these dark glasses – but it's difficult to see…"

We were sure it was; it was getting dark and he had a long way to go.

"You could see my boss in Maseru and get him to keep my job for me while I stay in Bots'abelo," he agreed.

He was obviously resigned to the fact that he needed specialist care.

"What a pity," I said to Molemo. "He's a lovely chap, but he should have been cured years ago. Let's hope we can help him now."

"He wanted to provide for his family," Molemo said. "Perhaps we would feel the same way if we were in his position."

There were many patients whose conditions responded dramatically when they were fully co-operative. Majara was eight years old when a Dutch doctor brought him to Bots'abelo. He had a serious type of leprosy and was very miserable. We visited the home and explained about the necessary treatment. No one knew how the boy had contracted leprosy. It was probably passed on by someone who had stayed briefly at the home, for the family lived near to the South African border and often gave overnight accommodation to men on there way home from the mines. The parents agreed to leave Majara in our care. I took photographs of him both before and after treatment with four months in between and these showed such an amazing improvement that, with the parents' permission, we used them on our health education leaflets which were widely distributed throughout the country. In two years Majara was completely cured.

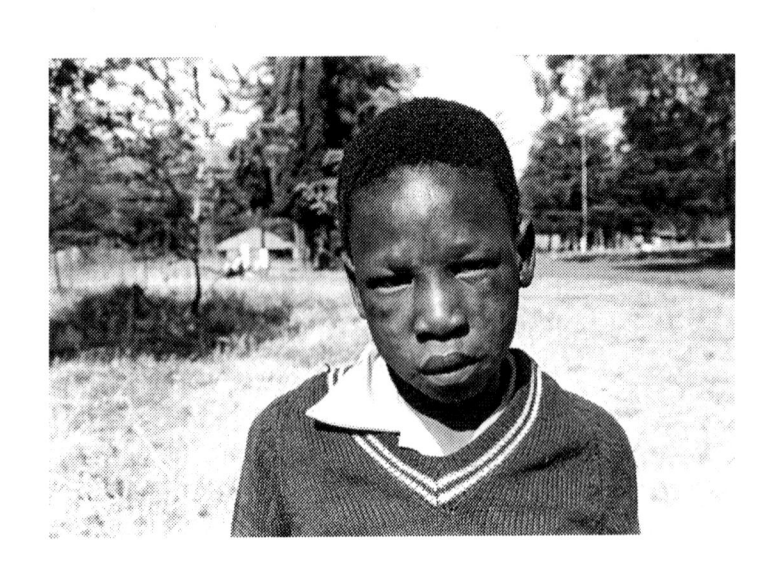

Above: Majara before treatment

Below: Majara after 4 months' treatment

Chapter 18
Just let me finish the job

"You've done a good job, and my Ministry is very grateful."

The Permanent Secretary beamed a polite smile. Alan Waudby and I were sitting in his office. It was nearing the end of 1985 and our contract was ending the following June. As we expected, it seemed that our work permits were not going to be renewed. Our services were no longer needed.

"You have trained quite a few people," the Permanent Secretary continued, "and we should now be able to carry on the good work."

"So we can get on and plan for the last six months," I said to Alan as soon as we had left the building.

Mary Stone had just arrived from England, sponsored by the Mission, to help me for a few months. Mary was a nurse and she had been at Kumi for twenty years, which included the time I had been there. As she was often away on safari in those days and she lived seven miles up the road, I never saw much of her, but I admired her work on a trial vaccination scheme for leprosy for which she was awarded an MBE. She had recently retired from similar research work in England, so she was free. On her way to Lesotho she spent some days at the ALERT centre in Addis Ababa to update her knowledge of leprosy, even though she was very experienced in all aspects of the disease.

I was delighted to have Mary. It was a great relief to draw on her expertise as well as her good humour and practical common sense. Our priority for the last few months was to be the training of selected nurses who managed clinics where leprosy patients were being treated. We planned five three-day courses with four nurses attending each time and they were accommodated in the Guest House with Mary organising the catering.

Do not unsaddle your horse

Unfortunately, despite careful planning, it was not always the nurses who actually had leprosy patients attending their clinics who applied to come, but we were surprisingly rewarded when a new patient turned up during one of the courses: she was from an area where there had not been any new cases for a long time and at the course was a nurse from her nearest clinic! We delighted in such simple encouragements that were clearly God-sent. The hospital and field-staff were able to do much of the teaching, thus setting a pattern that could be continued when the Mission left.

Relationships between Lesotho and South Africa had not been easy for several years. Lesotho was often accused of harbouring South Africans who had fled their country for political reasons, and sometimes helicopters were sent in at dawn with South African soldiers who rushed to certain houses and shot people who were suspects. Sometimes they killed the wrong people. Everyone resented such invasions even if they were not themselves directly affected by the brutality.

Early in 1986, because of increasingly strained relationships, the Lesotho border post into South Africa was closed. It had happened before, but this time it was more serious because no supplies were allowed into Lesotho. There was no petrol and food was scarce. It was a state of siege! To make matters worse we had long electricity cuts because the branches of a tall tree near our houses were being blown against the electricity wires and eventually they burned through. The weather was very hot and windy and we needed to keep our fridges going so that there was enough food for the course participants. Despite repeated requests the branches were never cut. The wires were looped together and in my absence one afternoon about thirty beautiful young trees well below the wires were hacked down. It was exasperating. I began to say to myself:

'Just let me finish the job and get home.'

At about this time there was a coup in Lesotho. The Prime Minister, Leabua Jonathan, was deposed and an army officer took charge of the country. Some fighting at the army barracks, just next door to the leprosy hospital, preceded the coup. A few of the patients sat around watching it through the fence.

"They are practising," Kokoza, one of the brighter patients told me confidently.

"It's a bit too noisy for a practice," I said doubtfully.

Sebolelo, who lived very near to the barracks, had all the news in the morning, telling me how many soldiers had been killed and then declaring triumphantly:

"Politics are now finished in Lesotho."

I wasn't sure if she knew what that meant and as I was certain that I didn't, I made no comment. At least the coup seemed to have cleared the air. King Moshoeshoe had been reinstated after a long period of excommunication and that was sure to be popular. The World Service of the BBC gave the most reliable reports of what was going on and it was a comfort to hear 'Lily Bolero' playing and 'This is London' followed by the news. Radio Lesotho and the South African radio reports were strikingly different, being biased in various ways.

Crossing the border into South Africa was never a speedy process but on one occasion I passed through surprisingly quickly. We were keen to get our patients home whenever possible. Thabo was a middle-aged man who had been an in-patient for many years. Although he had very poor eyesight and rather crippled hands, his leprosy was cured and we couldn't help him any further. He had also become a nuisance by frequently visiting homes in the locality and coming back to the hospital drunk. The problem was that his home was in South Africa and to get there he needed a passport, which he did not possess. The Government Social Workers were reluctant to help us, so I decided to tackle the challenge of getting Thabo home myself. It was one of my final jobs.

First I had to find his relatives. According to Thabo they were living on a farm some miles from the border town of Wepener. I spent a whole day in bleak, cold weather, hunting around the area. There were some very isolated farmsteads set in vast stretches of veldt but the few, shy Afrikaner people I managed to find were helpful and after carefully following their instructions I eventually found the family. Molemo, who was with me, explained our mission and it was reassuring to see how happy they were to hear that Thabo might be coming to share their very poor home. Thabo was happy too, but how were we to get him across the border?

I explained our problem to an Afrikaner official at some offices in Wepener. His reaction was interesting; I am sure he felt he needed to deal with such a fearful thing as leprosy as quickly as possible.

"No, you just tell me the day you are coming and I will instruct my people at the border to let you pass," he said.

So we provided Thabo with smart second hand clothes, made sure he was clean and tidy, settled him into the back of our vehicle and set off.

The border police knew all about us.

"We have our leprosy patient," I told them, "Would you like to see him?"

There was a quick and very negative response.

"No, no, you pass through," a powerful, blue-eyed officer ordered, and we were on our way without any of the routine inspection to which we were accustomed. It was laughable. Normally they would have checked inside the bonnet of the car and wheeled a large mirror under it, scrutinised the luggage and thoroughly checked the passengers. This time we could have carried anything through.

I had made a great effort to work myself out of my job so I now had four Health Assistants as leprosy field workers. They had all completed courses at Addis Ababa with good results. Ramatla Makong was a very sincere and capable man who worked methodically and cared a great deal for the patients. Mashesha Tshabalala was intelligent and quick. He was an excellent person but he needed someone to keep his feet on the ground, as it were. Being half Zulu and half Mosotho he seemed to have more initiative than many of his colleagues. Then there was Molemo Mokhothu. He had steadily worked his way through the Health Assistant training with good average results. He loved leprosy work and was always co-operative and loyal. Tsepo Manyeli was the last to join the team. He fitted in well and was a useful worker in the field.

Health staff in the hospitals and clinics realised that the men were experienced in leprosy control and increasingly they invited them to give talks, usually to Village Health Workers who were elected by the villagers and given training by their local clinic nurses. They were expected to give simple medical advice, recognise diseases like TB and leprosy, refer patients to the clinic or motivate patients who needed to take regular treatment. They received no salary but were allowed free medical treatment at the clinic for their whole family. It was a good system.

Ramatla and Mashesha had licences for driving motor vehicles and we had motor-cycles for Molemo and Tsepo, so they were all independent. The burden of maintaining the vehicles was considerable. I made it clear that if there was anything that did not work properly or any minor damage, I was to be told immediately. Most of the Government vehicles were used till they needed major repairs and I wanted to be sure this didn't happen with ours.

One day I heard someone mention that Mashesha was a very fast driver. I challenged him about it and he admitted it was true.

"That's not clever," I retorted. "Anyone can drive fast. All you have to do is to put you foot down hard on the accelerator. You can just stop that."

He accepted my fury and I hoped he would change his ways. When I left, these men would have to take responsibility for the vehicles in every way and use them reliably, but I was not too optimistic. There were so many pressures to use them for personal reasons especially if there were family problems.

Molemo had a nasty accident on his motor-bike. The first we knew of it was when we received a message from the hospital in Maseru. I rushed down and found him looking very shaken. He was waiting to have a broken wrist plastered. Apparently he had been knocked off the bike when a bus came round a corner on the wrong side of the road. He was lucky not to have been killed. He had seen the bus coming in the distance but was not experienced enough to wait for it in case it had not seen *him*.

It was early evening but I decided to go up the mountain road to rescue the bike and Tsepo and one of the guards went with me. After about an hour we came upon the wrecked bike which we heaved into the back of the truck together with some of the skin smear equipment that Molemo had been carrying, which was scattered around. The bike was a write off.

"He'll make a good driver now," one of the senior Health Assistants said to me later. "He will learn from that accident."

It took Molemo a week or two to come to terms with what had happened. He sat at home looking very miserable, nursing his bruises. He had been out for several days and the bag he had been carrying, containing his spare clothes, was lost. The police at Maseru seemed to know what had happened to the bag but when they delayed in getting it for us, I decided to go up the mountain road again and make enquiries at the police post near to where the accident had occurred. There I found some helpful people who thought the bag was still with the bus driver who had taken Molemo to Maseru.

"That bus will pass this way in fifteen minutes," they told me. "You could stop it and ask."

Sure enough, the driver had faithfully kept the bag and he was happy to hand it over. Everything was there. Molemo was encouraged to receive his carefully packed belongings.

"Will you ride a motor-bike again?" I asked him after a few weeks.

"Yes, 'Me," he replied without any hesitation.

I felt sure he had learned the hard way that you have to be

clever enough to avoid other people's mistakes.

Before my departure both Molemo and Tsepo learned to drive four wheeled vehicles. It was a struggle because the examiners asked such strange questions about the Highway Code which both men had carefully memorised. It seemed that everyone was failed many times. Perhaps the testers were looking for bribes.

Then one day Tsepo returned with a satisfied smile on his face.

"I was successful," he said.

"Now, Molemo," I said, "If Tsepo can do it, so can you!"

Molemo had not been quite so determined but at last he too managed to pass. It was a good achievement and a boost to his confidence.

While I was still around, Ramatla was keen to carry out a survey in a remote valley in the south east of the country. We had received several new patients from the area and he wanted to check all the households and also give intensive health education. He made very careful arrangements and all four men went on the two-week trip. It was a tough assignment. They had an eight-hour drive and then had to carry all their equipment and provisions to the Orange River which they crossed by boat. Then there was a two-mile walk to Tebellong Hospital where they spent the night before hiring horses and riding the next day to the valley.

Conditions were basic: the Chief gave them a house in which to stay but as in many mountain villages, latrines were non-existent, people using a communal *donga* or ditch. Molemo still had his arm in plaster when they set out, but on his return the plaster had gone.

"Who removed it?" I asked him.

"Dr Tshabalala," he said, grinning.

Ramatla's report of the survey was a credit to him. I hoped the senior members of the Ministry would read it and realise that Ramatla was well able to take over the leprosy control programme.

Apart from a nasty attack of measles I had kept reasonably fit during my time in Lesotho but now I was getting problems with my back. Sometimes I needed to run to the telephone in response to urgent cries of:

"'Me Ma Philipi, fono!"

There was only one external telephone and the buildings were far apart. As I ran I often found that my legs did not work properly and I was tripping over my feet. It was difficult to get comfortable at night because my back ached and my thighs got cramp. Mary offered to rub my back for me before I went to bed and this helped me to get to sleep.

"You'll be able to get it sorted out when you get home," she assured me and I also felt confident that medical care through the National Health Service would be preferable to any I would get in Lesotho or South Africa.

Because of the melanoma that had been removed from my ankle, I had regular checkups at a nearby mission hospital in case any more skin cancer developed. On my last visit several small lesions were found and a very inexperienced, young Dutch doctor decided to do three biopsies. He was nervous and I suspected he had done very little surgery before. He made unnecessarily large incisions on my thigh and shoulder and these were sore for several days. As I sat on the floor in my bedroom repainting my three tin trunks with my West Malling address and feeling sorry for myself, I hoped that the incisions would heal without any complications.

It was a comfort in those last few months to actually have an external telephone in my house. This was the only time I had such luxury during my twenty-one years in Africa and it was the result of many years of asking. It was even possible to talk to Alan Waudby in London! Rather easier to obtain was the radio link, which enabled us to contact all the clinics and hospitals in the country. The Mission provided the funds and Bud Isaacs of Mission Aviation Fellowship set it up, as he had done for many other health units. Harry patiently dug the hole for the tall mast and was justly congratulated on his work by

Bud, who said it was the neatest and deepest hole anyone had managed to gouge out in the rocky soil.

Although it was often necessary to try many times before someone was listening the other end, it was very useful to have the radio. I would sometimes hear other conversations while I was waiting for a pause so that I could send my message. One day I could hear my Swiss friend from Tebellong Hospital desperately trying to obtain some information about a patient of hers who had died in hospital in Maseru. Arrangements needed to be made for the body to be transported back to the home for burial. She was not getting the help she needed and gave up in frustration. I called her number over the radio and offered to go to the hospital and try to sort out the matter.

"You are an angel! You are an angel sent from the Lord!" Madeleine repeated with utter amazement.

It was exciting to be able to help but also slightly embarrassing because other people were sure to be listening in, including those who had not been very helpful.

Mary was asked to write an assessment of The Leprosy Mission's work during our time in Lesotho from 1976 to 1986.

"My hat! That's going to be a tough assignment!" Mary muttered, but she produced a report with great care and even covered the history of Bots'abelo from its beginnings in 1913. She concluded by highlighting the recent achievements and making recommendations.

One achievement, that was now very obvious, was the new buildings. The Ministry of Health had received much of the money from the Irish Government. Their representative in Lesotho had been interested in helping and the fact that I had been born in Dublin seemed to give him some added enthusiasm. The plans that I had drawn up for rooms to accommodate 36 short-term patients were completed with solar heating panels providing hot water when the sun shone, which it usually did. These buildings looked down on a newly planted orchard of peach, apricot and nectarine trees, Harry's vegetable garden and a lovely view of grassland and mountain side beyond. Much of the old Bots'abelo had been demolished but the old hospital block remained with some storerooms because the new hospital for 32 beds and some other buildings had not been started. However, the fitter patients had been moved to their new rooms. It was interesting that some of the women, who had been inpatients for a long time, did not want to move to such beautiful new quarters because they were told that they could not take their coal braziers or their chickens into the rooms at night. Electric fires were to be provided. One lady who had been at Bots'abelo for over 30 years decided to take herself home, having previously insisted that she had no relatives and nowhere to live.

The number of inpatients had dropped to 43 and the total number of patients throughout the country who were still on treatment was 403. The danger was that with only about 25 new patients reporting during each of the previous two years, the Ministry of Health would relax its efforts and concentrate on more pressing problems such as TB.

"They *must* keep up the momentum," Alan had said, but I wondered if they would.

I hoped that if all else failed, at least the teaching and health education would bear fruit. In the early years we had persuaded the person who set the papers for the final nursing exams to include a question about leprosy. This surprised the tutors and students so much that in future we were regularly asked to teach at the four training schools. We had taught at the National Teachers' Training College and at many schools. We had circulated thousands of booklets and pamphlets and given many radio talks. 240 health staff had attended one or other of two national seminars that we had organised. All this was of great value because in Lesotho there was always an unusually high number of infectious patients among the newly diagnosed cases. With the average incubation period of five years it was certain that if contacts were not properly checked then the numbers of new cases would eventually increase. The general public as well as the health staff would need their knowledge of leprosy in future years.

Time was running out. All I could do was to leave things in order and pack up my belongings. Anything that did not fit into the three tin trunks and a few parcels needed to be disposed of, so I had a sale in my garden. Sebolelo supervised this, keenly checking on anyone who looked as if they might cheat. She had already selected the things she wanted for herself and I had given her a kitchen cupboard which she had coveted. The sale was over very quickly and nothing remained.

It rained nearly all of my last day and the party that the four field workers had planned for me was somewhat delayed while Molemo struggled with a fire outside our office so that meat could be cooked. I was eventually summoned from my house for a late lunch but the feast was a solemn affair. The Superintendent sat in the central place with Mrs Senoko, the Matron at her side. They both wore rather pained expressions. The entire staff had assembled, and perhaps they had not been informed. In due course the speeches were made, first by Ramatla, followed by a flowery and carefully read dissertation by the schoolmaster. Then came the gifts, with everyone straining to see what each package contained. I felt humbled by the generosity. The field staff gave me a beautiful Basotho blanket and a wall clock in the shape of Lesotho. Another parcel contained a Basotho dress and having held it up for everyone to see, I was urged to put it on so that they could fully appreciate it. Retiring to another room, I struggled to oblige, only to find that the locally made dress had no side opening, so it was impossible to get into it.

"Never mind!" I reassured them, "It will be easy to put that right later on."

Gradually the party came to an end and I took my leave. Later Mashesha turned up at my house.

"We are really going to miss you," he said falteringly. "You know, when we set off on field work and you say, 'Take care', we know you really mean it."

He was almost in tears but before I could respond he made a request that was probably the real reason for his visit:

Do not unsaddle your horse

"'Me, could I take one of the vehicles to get home? It's got a bit late…"

"Have you been drinking?"

"No, 'Me."

I doubted his reply but he seemed fairly sober.

"All right," I agreed.

I spent the night with friends in Maseru and then headed for Johannesburg in one of the vehicles that was to be left with the South African Leprosy Mission. My three tin trunks had been sent off from Maseru by air, so I had just one suitcase and I felt relieved and strangely free. I was looking forward to an exciting holiday before leaving Africa. It was a time to relax and contemplate the future.

*The leprosy control team
left to right: Mashesha, myself, Tsepo,
Ramatla and Molemo (squatting)*

The new Bots'abelo buildings

Chapter 19
Homeward bound

"Where should I go before I leave Southern Africa?" I asked some American friends who seemed to have visited all the most exciting places.

I had already experienced so much beauty in the region. In the Cape I had marvelled at the views from the top of Table Mountain, absorbed the atmosphere of the vine growing areas and enjoyed the busy city of Cape Town, despite the confusion of travelling on trains that had separate compartments for Blacks, Whites and Coloureds. I had been many times to the Drakensberg Mountains, walking for miles and revelling in the grandiose scenery and the clear, clean air. Returning to Lesotho by remote roads provided further enjoyment: on one occasion I came upon thirty crested cranes dancing in a field. Within Lesotho I had explored valleys that led to big waterfalls, gazed at the beauty of pink cosmos flowers covering whole hillsides in April and delighted in the peach blossom in September, its pink contrasting so vividly with the straw-coloured landscape. I had driven with friends through the rough Ongeluksnek Pass on the way to the National Park at Sehlabathebe in the south-east, arriving in dense fog but being rewarded the next day with the sun shining down on incredible rock formations.

Further afield I had visited Swaziland and Zimbabwe where I had friends and I had travelled from the amazing Victoria Falls across northern Botswana to the Okavango Swamps. From the luxury of dug-out canoes, our party revelled in the wild life and the sheer beauty of sunsets from an island where we spent a night.

"So where should I go now?" I asked.

"Take a trip on Lake Malawi, there's a lake steamer, the Ilala, that takes a few passengers for six day cruises," came the suggestion.

So I made my plans.

After a couple of nights in a hotel in Lilongwe, I boarded a bus that was to take me to Monkey Bay on Lake Malawi. I enjoyed the scenery; it was so much like Eastern Uganda. The people on the bus were friendly and the driver assured me that he would get me safely to my destination. For a while I relaxed, feeling very much at home, but as the day wore on I became anxious. Dusk fell and soon it was dark and *still* we journeyed slowly on, stopping even more frequently to set people down or to pick up others who were relieved to be on their way home after a long, hot day.

"Is it far now to Monkey Bay?" I asked the driver.

"It is near," he replied," "But you must get off before Monkey Bay for your hotel."

After a while he triumphantly announced that I should alight. We seemed to be in the middle of the bush.

"You go that way," people told me, pointing into the darkness.

I must have looked rather doubtful about the safety of walking an unknown path and some of the passengers admitted that they were not sure if it was the right place. Soon it became evident that the hotel was a little further on. Once again I carried my two small bags onto the bus.

"This is the place," the driver said after another few miles.

Realising that I had no choice, I set out along a dusty road towards some distant lights, praying that I would not meet a lion; it seemed to be that sort of country.

A little way along the road a truck overtook me. The driver stopped and I gratefully accepted a lift to the hotel. Yes, they had my booking and after a welcome meal I thankfully tumbled into bed to get as much sleep as I could before the early start next day.

It seemed that everyone from miles around was heading for the Ilala. People were struggling with enormous loads of grain, baskets with chickens peering anxiously through the wicker-work and goats that had to be coaxed along, ropes fastened loosely around their necks. Other people had long lengths of sugar cane tied in huge bundles, baskets of citrus fruit and pawpaws, nets containing pineapples, sacks of cassava and peas and big hampers of fish.

The Ilala was a fine sight with the sun just rising over the lake. It was a steamer with three decks and was painted white. It was able to carry 460 passengers and 40 crew members. From the upper deck I watched all the activity as everything was loaded aboard. My cabin was small but very adequate and my excitement grew as I anticipated the days ahead.

A plaque on the upper deck stated that the Ilala had been made in Glasgow and I wondered how it had been transported from Scotland to this huge landlocked lake. Its main function was to ply back and forth across the water, to Mozambique on the east and then back to Malawi on the west, stopping two or three times a day to let off some of the passengers and to pick up others.

Most people were set on selling their goods at the lakeside villages. They were ferried precariously ashore in small boats, as there were no landing jetties. Usually the few first class passengers remained on board but we were able to land at several places including Likoma Island. It was good to be on firm ground and the place was very beautiful but quite poor. I had a quick look inside the clinic and it seemed to have only a few very basic supplies of drugs. Then there was the big cathedral that could have been picked up from some wealthy country and planted there. Two men were trying to repair the roof. The whole building was in a bad state.

'What a burden to leave for the people,' I thought. 'Really, missionaries have a lot to answer for.'

Meals on the Ilala were served for the first class passengers at the Captain's table and the full English breakfast was so adequate that I usually skipped lunch and ate bananas, tangerines and nuts that I could buy from people who came alongside us in small boats. The lunch and supper menus were always very similar with excellent chamba fish and often banana fritters.

I got to know the Captain a little. He had trained in the U.K. at Southampton, but he seemed to appreciate the beauty of his own country. Sometimes he was on the upper deck watching the few birds flying over the lake. Once a pelican landed on the deck, sitting close to a seagull for a while.

"It's lonely too," the Captain murmured.

I wondered if his remark was directed at me. Over the years I had become very independent and being alone did not bother me, but all of the other six passengers were in pairs.

What of the future though? I knew how much colleagues, friends and the mission staff had supported me and that was about to end. I would have to fend for myself when I reached home.

Chapter 20
Culture shock 1 – hospitalisation

"Goodbye, have a safe journey," the stewards said politely as they carried my bags off the Ilala.

The trip was over and after a couple of days I boarded a plane for Nairobi. Although I had a twelve hour wait in Kenya it seemed sensible to book my suitcase straight through to London so that I would not have to carry it and aggravate my back.

Time dragged at Nairobi airport. I ate a bread roll that I had saved from the flight from Malawi and some fruit and nuts. Later I bought tea and a sandwich. As usual I was able to sleep on the plane and it landed exactly on time at Heathrow.

"Welcome home!"

I hugged the friends who had come to meet me.

"Where's your luggage?" they asked.

"That's why you've had to wait so long," I said. "It hasn't arrived. I've given all the details to the enquiries desk, so hopefully it will come soon."

I was disappointed but not too worried, fully believing it would be traced. We were soon heading for West Malling, speeding out into the strangely familiar countryside with its lush green fields.

I was home! It was June 21st 1986. My tenant had left a few days before and I quickly settled into my cottage. The next day my three tin trunks arrived and I was happy to unpack the contents; but where was the suitcase? Every day I phoned the airport; the officials hoped it would be found at Nairobi and that it would come soon but I was beginning to doubt if I would ever see it again and I was very upset. The suitcase contained all my best winter and summer clothes – a full 20 kilos of precious things. In it were some of my most valuable transparencies – pictures of leprosy patients taken before and after treatment, different types of leprosy and various complications. These were irreplaceable.

The suitcase never arrived. I made a list of what was in it and guessed the value of each item, but I underestimated, so after a few weeks when I discovered the true cost of replacing everything, I revised the price list. The insurance company paid up but I was still very upset about the loss. It served to increase the sense of mourning I was beginning to feel – a deep sadness for all I had left behind in Africa in the way of friends, a worthwhile job and the many challenges and adventures.

After about a month I had a short debriefing at The Leprosy Mission's headquarters. People were very kind and appreciative but as I was resigning there was little to discuss after I had told them about the current state of leprosy control in Lesotho. They knew I needed to have my back problem investigated and assured me that they would continue to pay me until I was working again.

I had thought that it would be easy to get an appointment with a hospital consultant and was dismayed to find that there were waiting lists. I occupied myself by thoroughly cleaning the house and digging the garden. I picked blackberries from the hedgerows and made jelly. I felt that my needs were very few: 'All I need is a comfortable bed and armchair,' I told myself but all the time I was struggling to get used to the affluence in which I found myself. Of course I needed a car and a spin drier seemed necessary as well. Complicated decisions had to be made with every purchase because there was so much choice. Even if I only needed a packet of tea I was confronted with a dozen varieties from which to choose. It was very tiring and confusing.

My tenant had left behind an old black and white television set and I was particularly glad to be able to watch the documentary programmes that helped me to catch up on current affairs. I had never owned a television before so it was a luxury. Soon I yielded to suggestions that a small colour set would be more enjoyable, and a friend installed one for me.

Eventually the day for the hospital appointment arrived and after a brief examination, the orthopaedic consultant told me that I needed a myelogram and that it would be carried out at a different hospital to his. Another few weeks elapsed before I received the appointment by post and the letter implied that I was to be admitted.

"For how long?" I asked my doctor.

"Good question," was the reply, "I don't really know. They inject a dye into the spinal cord and take X-rays to see if there is any pressure on the nerves."

The hospital specialised in neurosurgery and although it was an old establishment it had a good reputation. I arrived there with a few belongings, including a half finished pullover that I was knitting, so that I would have something to do. I was allocated a bed and a nurse came to write down my details. I sat and knitted. Lunch arrived and the day wore on. There were no suitable chairs for patients with back problems and my bed sagged in the middle, so it was very uncomfortable. I insisted that pillows were placed under the mattress to make it level. This was eventually achieved but I was not popular because the ward was short of pillows.

My hopes were raised the next morning when some doctors came for a ward round, but they were not the ones I needed to see and they merely greeted me and passed on. By the afternoon I had finished knitting all the wool I had brought with me and was feeling exasperated and claustrophobic so I went to look for some nurses.

"Is anyone going to do anything for me?" I asked. "If not I might as well go home again and come back later."

It was an ungracious remark but my patience was running out. The nurses tried to calm me but it seemed that nothing was likely to happen that day.

"Well can I go for a walk then?" I asked.

Relieved to be able to satisfy this request, they agreed. Grabbing my handbag and a jacket I fled from the ward, tears streaming down my face. I negotiated some long passages and found my way to an exit door. Fresh air at last!

I didn't know the area well but I walked rapidly and found some shops where I bought some fruit. Then I walked swiftly in the other direction. There was a telephone box at a cross roads. I tried to phone some friends for a chat but I failed to get through – the telephone seemed to be out of action. Emerging from the box I noticed a signpost. In one direction it read, 'Sevenoaks 21 miles'. 'I could walk there and get home!' I thought in a crazy way. Why did I feel like this? Why did I hate that hospital ward so much? I looked at my watch. I would have to go back or they would wonder where I was. At least I had killed some time. Perhaps tomorrow they would do the myelogram.

I remembered how, years ago, I had spent a few days in a hospital in Kampala for some minor surgery. There was no running water but the nursing care was of a high standard and I passed the time in complete peace of mind. I suppose the difference was that I had been treated as a VIP because I was part of the medical profession. Here in England that didn't seem to count. I was expecting far too much.

The following morning I was taken to the radiography department for my myelogram. The procedure of injecting dye into the spinal cord was delicate and I was conscious that students were viewing every detail from a balcony and occasionally asking questions in suitably whispered tones. The X-rays were developed quickly for everyone to see. There were a few exclamations and the radiographer asked me whether I could still walk.

"Of course," I said.

"How far?"

"Oh, I suppose five or six miles."

"Courageous woman," he muttered. "Come and have a look at the X-rays."

I walked gingerly towards the plates that were pinned up on the wall.

"Here you can see the narrowing in the lower part of the spinal cord – the dye could hardly pass through when you were standing upright. Surgery should get that right."

So that was it! I was glad that the diagnosis was so clear. Even the next rather noisy night with disturbances in the ward did not bother me, and the following day some of the patients were well enough to play Scrabble, so the morning passed happily. Late in the afternoon when I noticed some doctors in the nurses' office I asked what was planned for me.

"Oh yes, you can go home," a young doctor informed me. "We can't do anything for you."

I was stunned. The staff were all very busy and unconcerned.

"You can use the telephone and ask your friends to come and collect you now," a nurse said, trying to be helpful.

"But haven't you seen the X-rays?" I was desperate. Surely they hadn't decided against the surgery!

The young doctor left the ward. I telephoned some friends, packed my belongings and sat near the office in a daze. Had my stay been a complete waste of time? ... But at least I was going home.

Just then the doctor returned.

"No," he said, "We can admit you at any time."

A nurse kindly explained that my problem was lumbar canal stenosis and that I would soon be given an appointment to see the surgeon.

"You'll be in the neurosurgical ward," she said. "It's a lovely ward and the surgeon is one of the best. He always goes to see his patients as soon as they come round from the anaesthetic."

I was under the impression that I would be admitted immediately after I had seen the surgeon, so when I kept the appointment with him some weeks later I took with me a carefully packed bag with all the things I might need for two weeks. The surgeon was West Indian, a quiet and polite gentleman. He agreed that a laminectomy was necessary to relieve the pressure on the spinal cord that was causing the cramp in my legs. The operation would take place as soon as he could fit it in but I certainly could not be admitted there and then. I would be notified in due course.

Autumn came and in a hopeful and positive mood I arrived at the hospital for my surgery. I was positioned near to the nurses' desk after the operation where I felt reasonably secure but as the days went by my bed was gradually moved further and further down the long ward. I had to lie flat and although after a few days I could turn myself over and also occupy myself with a little sewing and reading, I felt very vulnerable. The ward was noisy with disturbed patients some of whom had had strokes and were disorientated. Occasionally people were wandering around in confused states. The nurses were always changing and one or two were not very kind. There were no bells, so if the patients needed anything they had to shout.

The days were very long. One evening having struggled to wash and get into my nightclothes I felt completely exhausted. The night staff were working very slowly giving out sleeping tablets and other drugs and as they did so they were discussing their off-duty times and other personal matters as if the patients were of little concern. My back hurt and I longed for them to come to me soon.

"Could I have some painkillers, please?" I called out.

"We're on our way."

The casual conversation droned on as the nurses continued their round. By the time they reached me I was in tears, sweating profusely and feeling desolate, uncared for and very alone.

The nurses seemed scared. They gave me my tablets and disappeared. The pain gradually eased. Through my tears I suddenly noticed something across the darkened ward close to a light that was shining over the bed of a very sick patient. It was an object in the shape of a cross. It appeared to me as a special vision – a sign that it did not really matter how low I felt – Christ had done everything for me.

A doctor slipped into the ward and tiptoed to my bed.

"You had a problem?" he whispered, "Can I help?"

I was grateful.

"No," I said, "I'm all right now." And I was.

I looked across the ward again. The cross was still there but it was a stand for an intravenous drip.

The next day there was the usual ward round with the consultant, junior doctor and students.

"This is Mrs Phillips," the young lady doctor announced, making a guess at my age that was quite incorrect.

"I'm Miss, actually," I said.

Age did not concern me too much, especially as she had made me a lot younger than I was, but I hated being called 'Mrs'.

"Oh, we call everyone Mrs here," was the response, and the report on me continued. "She had a reaction last night, so she should rest today and not attempt any more walking."

The Indian physiotherapist who had been helping me to walk nodded gravely. Fortunately for me he decided to ignore the instruction. He arrived quietly a little later and took me to the stairs where I managed to go up and down without any problems.

To my great surprise my sister turned up one afternoon, travelling all the way from her home the other side of London.

"Oh, thank you for coming!" I said. "I never expected you to come such a long way!"

Two or three friends had come to see me every day but this was the most unexpected visit and the sweet peas she brought me from her garden, were the most treasured flowers that I received.

"You realise that if the operation had gone wrong, you would have been paralysed, don't you?" she said.

She always seemed to fear the worst, but it was good to know that she cared.

"Of course, but my legs work okay. I'll be fine."

I was discharged after the expected two weeks had passed.

How I appreciated the autumn sunshine as I walked slowly and carefully to a friend's waiting car! I felt frail but I was free from the ward that had tested my tolerance to its limits. Now I just needed to slowly rehabilitate myself and think about job applications.

Chapter 21
Culture shock 2 –
new fields of work

Four weeks after my discharge from hospital I was able to start driving again. My recovery was slow but steady and by this time I was able to walk two and a half miles. Over the next few weeks I gradually progressed to five miles. I enjoyed these walks, following local footpaths and taking photos of the glorious autumn colours, but the days were becoming occupied with more serious matters. I needed to find a job.

About this time I received an article from one of the former American pastors of the Maseru United Church who was back in the States. It was written by an Australian doctor who had been forced to leave her missionary work after seventeen years because of ill health. The article began:

'For many missionaries the hardest thing about overseas service is leaving it'.

I knew that was true and as I read on I found that I could identify with nearly everything the writer said. She had become depressed, discouraged, angry and resentful. She felt guilty that she was not using the gifts that God had given her and frustrated about her own negative emotions.

'Many returned missionaries,' the article continued, 'report taking years to adjust; quite a few never seem to succeed in overcoming their feelings of failure, uselessness, being forgotten by mission societies and generally being misunderstood by Christians. But because of their cross-cultural experience, they are potentially a rich resource.'

The writer went on to explain that the negative emotions, of which missionaries are so ashamed, are actually symptoms of legitimate grief: grief at the loss of what they had automatically enjoyed overseas: an important role or place in a team and prayer support and interest from people at home. Grief too at what they might have achieved in the way of professional promotion had they not gone overseas. She reasoned that the secret of healthy adjustment to the home situation was to see it as equal to God's calling to the overseas assignment.

I was very grateful that my understanding American friends had sent the article. It helped me to realise that my reactions were reasonable, but it was difficult to be enthusiastic about any of the available jobs. Occupational Therapists were in short supply, so it seemed as if I would be successful in any job application. I just needed to find one that interested me.

I took the plunge and applied for a job with Social Services. It involved visiting disabled people in their own homes and providing aids so that they could be as independent as possible. I was fairly confident because it was similar to the work I had done before I went to Africa, but of course that was twenty-one years ago. Things had changed.

It had been snowing hard and as a result I was unable to get my car out of its garage. A friend kindly came to my rescue and drove me in hers. The roads were very icy but I was glad to have been able to keep the appointment. It seemed I was the only applicant for the job.

The interview didn't go well.

"How would you set about visiting someone in their own home?" I was asked.

It seemed to be such an obvious question and I didn't know what they expected me to say. My mind flashed back to the many occasions when I had visited people in remote villages in Lesotho, where children were scared because they had never seen a white face before, and where I had always been so careful to enter homes with respect. I gave a simple answer and was relieved to be able to deal with the next question more easily:

"Who are you used to liaising with?"

I started with the Minister of Health for Lesotho, the Permanent Secretary, the Chief Health Inspector, the staff of 68 health units, the Mission staff in London.... I could see that

Do not unsaddle your horse

my reply was causing worry and unbelief. I had obviously said the wrong thing but at the time I couldn't understand why. It was much later that I realised that the people conducting the interview were probably scared that I would not keep within a specific job description. I might cause more problems than I was worth.

"Do you know that if you don't give a client what he wants, he may take you to court?"

I was aware that such difficulties did exist in England, although in Africa patients never blamed the medical staff if things went wrong. I nodded. Just what were they getting at?

The interview was soon over. They thought I was rather out of date, thanked me for coming and said I would be hearing from them in due course. A few days later I received a letter telling me that I had not been successful. It was no surprise but I felt misunderstood and greatly undervalued. I was also scared. I *had* to find a job and earn my living. The Mission would not go on paying me for ever. Who would employ me? I was still not sure if my back would allow me to work a full day or how I would manage if I was expected to lift patients.

I decided that at my next interview I must be very careful what I said. There was a vacancy at a hospital for mentally handicapped people that was due to close in less than a year, because of the policy of moving everyone out of large institutions and into the community. The authorities were finding it difficult to fill the post. I was fortunate because one of the administrators at the interview appreciated my previous experience and was very keen to offer me the job.

It was a relief to accept and to know that I was wanted. However, the four occupational therapy helpers who I was to supervise were demoralised, having watched all the most able patients leave the hospital over the previous months. The ones who remained were the most difficult to place in the community, either because they had behavioural problems or because they were severely physically handicapped. Having a new boss at this stage did not interest the four ladies very much. I had to work hard to give them a lead as well as work up some enthusiasm myself.

The patients were all very 'institutionalised' and part of our work was to familiarise them with the outside world. We took them on outings in the hospital mini-bus when the driver was free of other duties. I found this quite frightening and I often lay awake the night before we were due to go on one of these trips, wondering how we would cope. Our aim might be to take six patients and four staff to the coast, stop by the sea, get everyone out, walk a hundred yards, buy ice creams and walk back to the vehicle without any mishaps.

Some of our patients were tall, strong men. One would run in all directions and another delighted in letting his trousers drop to the ground so that he could enjoy people's reactions. We encouraged these active men to help push the patients who were in wheelchairs. This sometimes made them feel important and stopped them running in the road. We usually achieved our aim and felt hugely relieved when it was all over.

Was this a calling from God? I didn't feel it was. I wasn't making any use of the skills I had learned in Africa but perhaps it taught me something about patience and trust as well as giving me insight into one branch of the Health Service. When the hospital was almost due to close I was persuaded to move to another mentally handicapped institution where I had the task of supervising eight occupational therapy helpers. Once again the place was due to close as soon as the patients could be moved to smaller units.

The new job turned out to be an unwelcome challenge. The staff were not only discouraged by the deteriorating facilities but they resented having a new leader who did not know the patients. Most of them had considerable experience, having worked at the place for many years, but standards had fallen. I gained some respect because I never asked them to do anything I was not prepared to do myself, including cleaning dirty toilets and dealing with the most difficult patients, but sometimes the ladies were reluctant to comply with my requests, and I never managed to get smoking banned from the occupational therapy building.

About 60 patients had to be occupied at a time and there were a variety of activities including craft, dancing, gardening, cooking, housework, shopping in the nearby town and swimming. Once again the most difficult patients were the active ones with behavioural problems.

One very agile young man, who was unable to speak, had an incredible ability to undo screws. He was obsessional and fascinated with this skill and we tried our best to make his programme as interesting as possible to help him concentrate on something more useful and less dangerous. Everyone feared that Alan would undo electrical fittings, so all the screws in the establishment were changed for those needing a special jig. In angry frustration Alan took himself into the neighbouring gardens and started to dismantle people's greenhouses. We gave him old radios to unscrew but these held his interest for only a short time before he quietly disappeared again. He liked to hang around at the end of the afternoon sessions to make sure that a window was left ajar in the occupational therapy room, so that he could climb in later, collect screw drivers from the cupboard or undo screws with his finger nails. Often in the morning we found doors hanging by just one screw.

I made sure that I went with Alan when, for the first time, he joined the small group of patients who were going to the local swimming pool. I managed to keep him with me the whole time but even then I noticed him trying to undo a screw from a cubicle door.

'I'm getting too old for this sort of thing,' I told myself. I still felt frustrated. The job didn't use my skills and I wanted to work with normal people so that I could integrate myself with a general cross section of the public. My friends didn't understand my resentment; they thought I should find the work rewarding, but I determined to look around for other possible openings.

A local hospital was looking for an occupational therapist with experience with stroke patients. I called in one afternoon for an informal visit. The head occupational therapist clearly felt that I did not possess the necessary expertise.

"What a pity you stayed in Africa for so long so that you only know about leprosy," she said.

Her remark made me angry and upset.

"Well, I don't regret it," I responded.

What was God trying to say in all this? I could appreciate her reason for thinking I was unsuitable but it was all so unfair. Surely I could learn....

Some weeks later I found an advertisement for a job in a rehabilitation centre fairly near to home. I was reluctant to apply because being turned down was so discouraging, but in the end I decided to make just one more effort. I didn't expect to succeed for my confidence was now very low.

At the interview an orthopaedic consultant immediately put me at ease by commenting on my experience with leprosy patients.

"Of course I know about this disease," he remarked. "When I was in India we used to find the patients' fingers and toes lying around in the street."

Thinking he was making a joke or at least quizzing me, I laughed and said emphatically:

"Well that's nonsense!"

"Oh, of course I don't know what happens in Africa," he replied, "but it's true in India."

I was amazed. It seemed he was serious! Perhaps my bold reply had already spoilt my chance of being offered the job! I concentrated hard on giving the sort of answers that he might appreciate. It wasn't too difficult. He appeared to appreciate my rather unusual career and felt it would be advantageous to employ me. I started work in January 1989.

Do not unsaddle your horse

On my first day I felt like a child starting at a new school. My boss was a lady who had been in the same job for over thirty years. I needed a uniform and she had found some second hand dresses and a new green cardigan. When I was properly dressed she gently introduced me to various aspects of the work. I was to be responsible for the rehabilitation of disabled ex-service men and women who came for two weeks intensive treatment in the occupational therapy and physiotherapy departments. It was a scheme run by the British Legion. I was also to help with the treatment of local outpatients. Although I was rather out of my depth, the job was a definite improvement and the department was well equipped.

One of the first patients I was asked to treat was an intelligent young carpenter who had accidentally cut off the last centimetre of his index finger. The wound had healed and I was asked to mobilise the end joint in his finger, as it was stiff. I queried the referral because I was convinced that someone was playing a joke with me.

"Oh, we often get minor amputations to rehabilitate," I was told.

I still could hardly believe it. I thought of all the leprosy patients I had known who had lost fingers or who had no fingers at all and who never received more than the very basic advice and counselling. I just had to stop making these comparisons. This was a different world. I spent a long time working out activities and exercises for my patient and counselled him carefully during each of the ten sessions I had with him before we achieved an acceptable result.

Many of the ex-service men and women were stroke victims and others had long term problems resulting from head injuries. I studied books to update myself on these conditions and learned slowly as I worked with the patients. Most of them were vibrant characters and often the men came with their wives – women who had tirelessly helped and encouraged their partners over many years. I enjoyed getting to know them all.

There was just one frustrating problem: I had never worked under a head occupational therapist before and now that I was in my late 50s it was tiresome to be under very close supervision. My boss had very acute hearing and I was always conscious that she was listening in as I talked with the patients. Only once do I remember her overhearing something incorrectly: I was querying with a colleague some details about Huntington's Disease when she voiced some friendly advice from the depths of the office:

"Have a look in the AA book."

Despite the frustrations I was learning how to treat many different conditions, often working in conjunction with the physiotherapists, and after a few years I was gaining confidence. I attended as many courses on clinical work as I could, thinking that with my new skills I would be able to apply for a more senior job and boost my pension. Otherwise I would retire on a lower grade than I had reached in my 20s.

I was often offered the opportunity of attending courses on 'Management' but I never felt the need to participate in those. I presumed that if I was able to cover the whole of Lesotho, with its population of 1 million people, I would have no problem in organising a small department, but my lack of interest probably contributed to the fact that I never managed to be upgraded.

I applied for a head occupational therapist's job in a hospital nearer to London. The other applicants were smartly dressed young ladies. I was interviewed last and I knew without a doubt that I did not stand a chance; I had not acquired the right jargon. Trying not to be discouraged, I tried for the head post at the large hospital of which our rehabilitation centre was a part. By this time I was 59 years of age but I told the panel that if I were appointed I would give the job all my energy for the next two years, otherwise I would retire at sixty. I was the only applicant, but it seemed that there were already plans in people's minds to rearrange the existing staff so that a new appointment would be unnecessary.

Do not unsaddle your horse

God must have known that there was no need for me to work my way into a job that would have been largely administrative. It was better that I carried on with clinical work so that I met people, found out how they lived and what occupied their thoughts and got accustomed to the culture of my own country for a long as possible. As far as the increase in pension was concerned, I could manage without it. God continued to provide for everything I needed.

And so, at the age of sixty, I retired, happily looking forward to pursuing many interests in the years ahead.

Chapter 22
Continued links and friendships

Whenever I dream of Africa it is always of Uganda. One night I dreamt I was back at the Leprosy Centre: I was saying to someone, "I am always dreaming of coming back to help you and now I really am here." This was so real that when I woke up I was surprised to find that I was still in bed at my own home.

While I was in Lesotho I had kept in touch with various people in Uganda. Livingstone had occasionally sent letters. Although he usually found someone to do the writing for him, it was easy to imagine his feelings and his strong faith as I read what he had dictated. Idi Amin was overthrown in 1979 when Tanzanian troops invaded the country. The liberating soldiers reached Kumi on May 3rd and Livingstone sent me a picture he had made that illustrated the event. Later he described what had happened just before the liberation.

Livingstone's picture of Tanzanian soldiers liberating the Leprosy Centre – May 1979

Two Dutch doctors were taken to the centre's petrol pumps by thugs who were pointing guns at their backs. The staff and even some of the crippled patients all fled into the bush because people were so often killed. Livingstone could not run; he said:

"I remained in the workshop alone seeing through the window how the two would have faced their death. I prayed and said, 'These two are going to die innocently. May the Lord save their lives,' – but actually, to everyone's surprise, the two returned ...as a result the thugs seemed to fear the doctor (because he did not fear them); thus no human soul was lost in the centre." He concluded: "Jesus was the soldier that Almighty God sent to fight the thugs."

Apparently when the Tanzanian soldiers arrived they were opposed by the same thugs, many of whom were injured. One of the Dutch doctors calmly dealt with all the wounded. Livingstone recorded this with high praise. The admiration must have been mutual for when Livingstone died a few years later it was the same doctor who personally drove his body to his home in the mountains for burial.

In 1990 I paid a brief visit to Kumi. This was made possible because the Lesotho Government had invited me back for two months to help with combining the leprosy control with TB, which was a major health problem. The Leprosy Mission funded my trip and I took some unpaid leave. They also asked me to visit Kumi on my return trip and assess the situation there for them.

Over the previous year almost everyone in Teso had been forced to live in camps while soldiers rid the area of rebels, robbers and vandals. Because of the lack of proper food, medicines, sanitation and water, many people died. The Leprosy Centre was allowed to carry on its work but the staff were unable to travel to their own homes and many were completely destroyed. Visitors had been very few because of the insecurity, so I was given a royal welcome that started as soon as we entered the compound: 400 primary school children were gathered to greet me. It was fourteen years since had I left Kumi and none of them would have been born at that time! I was completely overwhelmed and quickly snatched a few photographs to record the scene before tears blinded my sight.

Max Acamun was one of the five orthopaedic technicians whom I had recruited and trained at Kumi. I had always known that he was the best, so I was glad when he eventually took charge of the workshop. He kept in touch with me and I helped him attend further training courses after I had left Uganda. Considering how much the people had suffered, I was amazed that all the workshop machines and equipment were still in good working order and shoes and artificial limbs were being produced as before, despite a restricted electricity supply (by generator) and shortages of materials. His department was a credit to him and I felt proud of his efforts as well as those of the other senior staff. I was able to report favourably on everything I was able to see in the allotted time.

But it was Winfred who I wanted to see most. She wrote to me once or twice after I left Uganda but then there was a long silence. For several years I heard nothing from her. I tried to find out where she was by writing to people who knew her and even to the Medical Superintendent at the hospital where she did her training. No one could give me any news and when I didn't receive a reply from the hospital I felt sure that she must have been killed in some sort of violence.

Then suddenly I received a letter from Winfred and it was as if miraculously she had been brought back to life again. Apparently she had mislaid my address. She had successfully qualified as a State Registered Nurse and was working at a Government Hospital about forty miles from Kumi. Stephen, her partner and the father of her children (she now had Susan as well as Sam) was teaching at Mukono, twenty miles from Kampala and she was hoping to be transferred there so that they could all live together.

I had always felt that God had given Winfred to me so that I could help her and I was genuinely happy that we could correspond again. Over the coming years I sent money for various projects including chickens but soon the need for school fees required assistance too. Government salaries were very low and as she and Stephen had no land, they had to buy food. Winfred was soon transferred to Mukono, where the family was provided with a school house because of Stephen's job.

I saw Winfred for just half a day during my visit to Uganda in 1990 but in 1996 I went again and spent Easter with the family at Mukono. Winfred's welcome was overwhelming. She gave me one enormous, long hug, then stood back to have a good look at me and express her great delight that I had come. There were now six children: Sam, Susan, Simon, John, Grace and little Michael who was only three years old. For a long time Winfred had not told me about Michael's birth; she had thought I would be angry that she had yet another child to educate – but there he was, a dear little chap, loved by everyone. After some initial fear he welcomed me as happily as everyone else.

Winfred provided me with a room that had a large bed and mattress.

"You've brought bed sheets?" she enquired.

Of course I hadn't. I knew I must be causing problems but she made light of everything and soon I was given some slightly damp sheets, a bowl of hot water in which to wash and a meal. John was sent to the shops on an errand. It was dark when he returned with a few coat hangers. These were for me but Winfred thought that it was best not to hang my clothes in the bedroom cupboard because it might contain rats.

None of this mattered to me. The welcome, the generosity, the richness of Ugandan hospitality – it was all so precious.

The next day Winfred took me to see the Government clinic that she managed and also her own drug shop that was a little further down the main street of Mukono Township. The shop had been her idea and I had helped to fund it. She kept it open till ten o'clock every night and over the years it had helped to boost their meagre income.

For a long time Winfred had been concerned that the family had no homestead of their own but, urged on by her wise old mother, she had managed to purchase some land in Teso District at a place called Kachumbala. Again I helped her with gifts of money. Often my friends would donate a little too and I would agonise as to how much I should send her because of the need to allow people the dignity of doing as much as they can by their own hard efforts.

After the Easter holidays Winfred and I travelled the 150 miles up-country by taxis to Kachumbala. There she proudly showed me her land and two neat little mud houses with thatched roofs and a little kitchen. She planned to build a 'permanent' house and already there were piles of sand, stones and bricks for this purpose. We sat in the shade of some mango trees admiring the site. It was a beautiful setting in the peace of the Teso bush. A local woman quietly prepared a meal for us and we were soon enjoying some tasty chicken and rice. This was Stephen's home area so his family were able to keep an eye on the new homestead, although Stephen himself seemed to have left Winfred to tackle the project alone.

While we were sitting in this pleasant setting, Winfred began to tell me of some of the hardships of the past years. While she was a student nurse at the big Government hospital in Kampala in 1977, a hijacked Israeli plane landed at Entebbe airport. One of the passengers was choking and needed medical attention and she was admitted to the private ward where Winfred worked. Winfred looked after her. One day some soldiers arrived and demanded to take the patient, presumably on orders from Idi Amin. Winfred told them that as a nurse she was not allowed to discharge a patient, but as she moved towards the telephone to call a doctor the soldiers put a gun to her back and dragged the lady from her bed and down the stairs. They took her to a forest and shot her.

"It was terrible," Winfred said. "They even left her false teeth behind."

Do not unsaddle your horse

I was amazed at the way she told me this. She did not appear to have been concerned for herself but only for the patient.

"She knew she was going to die," Winfred said. Then she added, "They wanted to post me to a different hospital after that, in case the soldiers returned for me, but because I was a student they couldn't. So they just put me on a different ward."

It was then that I realised why I hadn't been able to trace Winfred at that time. Obviously the hospital was trying to protect her.

Winfred told me of times when there was famine in Teso and many members of Stephen's family arrived at Mukono expecting accommodation and food. The family never respected Winfred, possibly because she had had leprosy. Certainly she and Stephen had never married, perhaps because she was not considered to be worth the bride price. She had tried to remain strong, determined to support the children and to resist the witchcraft that attracted many people when times were hard. One day when she was at Kachumbala she had seen a vision. There were three evil-looking people dressed in black and then Jesus appeared, quite clearly, with two other people.

"He was beckoning to me," she said. "There was such a brilliant light around him that I fell to the ground in a sort of trance. No one knew what was wrong with me and afterwards I felt it was so special that I have never told anyone except my mother."

The sun was still shining down relentlessly as we eventually stirred ourselves and moved to the roadside where we flagged down another overcrowded taxi, squeezing in with my big suitcase. Kumi was only 20 miles along the road. We hired another vehicle for the last five miles down the familiar rough road to the hospital, Winfred, as usual, bargaining hard for a reasonable price. A generous welcome awaited us. People knew I was coming to share some ideas with Max in the shoe workshop. Winfred left me there the following morning.

The work that I wanted to do with Max had developed over the previous two years. I had been involved with some techniques that Sheila Moore was anxious to introduce as part of her physiotherapy practice. (I had kept in touch with Sheila and Dundas after their year at Kumi in 1967, mainly because their eldest son, Jonathan, was my god-son). Sheila was finding that many of her patients with knee, hip and back problems also had poor foot alignment and that when the foot alignment was corrected with orthotic insoles in their shoes, the other problems were greatly reduced and sometimes completely eradicated. She was having to send her patients to a clinic some distance away for this orthotic service but suddenly one night she had a bright idea.

"How about you and I going on a course to learn about it," she challenged me. "It's called biomechanics. You've done so much with feet with leprosy patients – it should be second nature to you."

I was reluctant at first. It all sounded complicated and the course was expensive, but Sheila was bubbling with enthusiasm so I agreed.

After the course we made a slow and tentative start but before long we were getting encouraging results and I gained confidence. The work fascinated me because of my previous experience and I was now keen to see if my new knowledge would be helpful in preventing foot ulcers in leprosy patients.

Max was very quick to grasp the techniques and we used simple methods to assess a number of patients discovering that the problems of alignment were similar to those that I was commonly seeing at home. The difficulty was how to adapt tyre sandals to correct alignment. These floppy shoes did not fit securely enough and so we were not able to get much success when we modified the insoles.

"I just wish there could be funding for better shoe-making materials," I said to Max.

He agreed, but we both knew how the Centre struggled to keep within its budget and shoe-making was never going to be one of the top priorities. It was amazing that they were managing to make shoes at all. Talking with many of the staff who had remained at the Centre throughout the difficult years of terror made me respect their resilience. Everyone had endured hardships and atrocities and they had somehow survived and resurfaced with new hope and determination to at least maintain their former standards. After Idi Amin was overthrown his soldiers roamed the country killing and robbing people. The staff often slept under the patients' beds in the wards for safety and villagers moved into the staff houses thinking they would be safer than in their homes in the bush. Everyone said that it was only by God's mercy and protection that they were all kept safe at the Leprosy Centre. The frightening times had strengthened their faith and trust in a remarkable way.

Now the scourge of Aids was challenging everyone. About half the patients in the Centre were not suffering from leprosy. Some were being admitted for surgery but many had Aids related illnesses. Sometimes a patient would arrive in the last stages of Aids and die even before he could be placed in a bed. Relatives would probably have wheeled the sick person on a bicycle for many miles and now they would have the problem of taking a corpse all the way home for burial. The staff had to cope with such tragedies without becoming utterly depressed and frustrated.

The pastor at the Centre was responsible for arranging morning prayers which most of the staff attended before work every day. He asked me if I would lead and gave me the Bible passage on which to speak. It was James chapter 5 and verses 1 – 6. When I read the passage I wondered if he had selected the verses especially for me as a sort of trick, but apparently they were just the next references on a list. I agonised as to what to say, for the passage is a warning to rich people, failing to pay poor people correctly and living in luxury and self-indulgence. There was I, the rich person, and in comparison they were so poor in material things.

After much thought I began to see the passage in a different way. Spiritual poverty is so much worse than material poverty. When Jesus talked about treasure in a field he was talking about faith. Those who are truly rich in God's sight are those who cling to a living faith in Jesus their Saviour. There are many such people in Africa and to experience their friendship is humbling and refreshing. Their faith is radiant in the midst of material poverty and hardship.

I had no wish to become materially rich on my return home but my needs were met in a more wonderful way than I could ever have imagined when I set out for Africa all those years ago. In 1997 I moved into a newly converted house – a little larger and more pleasant than the cottage and with a small piece of land for a new garden. From time to time, in my role as a Reader in the local Church, I continue to share some of the lessons I learned in Africa: so many joys and sorrows, achievements and mistakes; but through it all God guided and provided.

My new house made me very happy and I longed that Winfred would soon be able to complete hers and experience the same joy and satisfaction. I sent her a larger gift than usual and although the family had many needs at the time, they agreed unanimously that it should all be used for the house.

"I can't hide my excitement," Winfred wrote.

She explained that she had been able to 'close' the house (which meant that all the outside doors and windows were fixed) and that it was now possible to sleep there.

"I wish you could come and see it," she said.

Of course I had to go.

"It will be a Millennium celebration," I wrote. "I'll come in May."

I spent time with the family at Mukono and with Winfred at the Kachumbala homestead. The house was well planned and more attractive than I had imagined. I was amazed at what she had achieved. Together we visited Kumi Leprosy Centre, now renamed Kumi Hospital as the number of leprosy patients has fallen so dramatically. A new Ugandan Medical Superintendent had made many improvements since my last visit and the work under his guidance was highly impressive. Everyone was busy serving the many sick people, some of whom travelled from as far away as Kampala, because of the hospital's good reputation. Max and his team were making hundreds of artificial limbs for victims of land mines and gun shot wounds. The workshop, being one of the best in the region, was being used for training courses for technicians from all over Africa.

I gave Winfred a small wooden cross that I had made out of yew wood. It was smooth and polished so that it felt special.

"It's the best gift of all," she exclaimed.

"It's not a magic charm," I warned.

"Oh, no," she replied, "I know that. But when I feel it in my pocket, it reminds me that God is with me all the time. That's what matters most."

'Immanuel, God with us.' What assurance and hope that promise can give if we know its truth. Indeed He was with me through all my days in Africa, wanting me to trust Him so that He could show me the way, even though I must have often taken wrong turnings.

What would have happened if I had never been to Africa? Would I have married and settled down, bringing up a family of my own? Would I have achieved a very senior position in my profession? Things might have been very different, but the richness of my memories of Africa is of more value and I have no regrets.

When I returned to England I wrote a hymn for a competition. It won no prizes but I can still echo its sentiments. Here is part of it:

O Father God, Your love to me is boundless.
Your mercy knows no ties of East or West;
Your faithfulness, Your promises of nearness,
Will go with me until I reach Your rest.
I thank You that Your wings have been my shelter
Against the storms and perils of this life.
In hours of darkness and in times of danger
Your strength can always lead us safely through the strife.